Adoption in Japan

The social stigma of adopting an unrelated child in Japan has meant that until recently many of these adoptions were conducted in secret. This changed in 1988 with the introduction of 'special adoption' that allowed legal and open arrangements for placing babies and young children with new families. *Adoption in Japan* looks at how agencies have responded to the challenge of placing children in special adoptions. Through interviews with parents and agency directors, it examines how parents are selected and matched with children, and compares the effectiveness of tacit bargaining and trial placements in helping to find homes for children in need.

Drawing on empirical source material gathered since the late 1980s, the book questions whether adoption agencies should be given the freedom to create their own policies or whether tighter regulation is needed through the introduction of a centralized policy. Currently the different approaches taken by agencies can vary greatly with some actively encouraging potential parents to go beyond traditional concerns with blood and family lineage, while others have created policies that emphasise Japan's long history of adoption and established cultural ethics. Hayes and Habu outline the controversy that can surround the process of adoption through a discussion of adoption 'contracts' with birth mothers and cases where undocumented migrants face the hard decision to place their baby for adoption in an anonymous bid to secure Japanese nationality for the child.

Adoption in Japan will make an important contribution to current literature as the first monograph published in English that fully compares the policies of child adoption agencies in Japan. It will be of interest to both academics and professionals working in the fields of Japanese studies, public policy, social work and sociology.

Peter Hayes is a Senior Lecturer in Politics at the University of Sunderland, UK.

Toshie Habu is a Visiting Research Fellow at Osaka University of Economics and Law, Japan.

Routledge Contemporary Japan Series

Adoption in Japan

Comparing policies for children in need

Peter Hayes and Toshie Habu

Routledge
Taylor & Francis Group

LONDON AND NEW YORK

First published 2006
by Routledge
2 Park Square, Milton Park,
Abingdon, Oxon OX14 4RN

Simultaneously published in the USA and Canada
by Routledge
270 Madison Ave, New York, NY 10016

Routledge is an imprint of the Taylor & Francis Group, an informa business

© 2006 Peter Hayes and Toshie Habu

Typeset in Times by Keyword Group Ltd
Printed and bound in Great Britain by Biddles Ltd, King's Lynn

British Library Cataloguing in Publication Data
A catalogue record for this book is available from the British Library

Library of Congress Cataloging in Publication Data
A catalog record for this book has been requested

ISBN10: 0-415-39181-4

ISBN13: 978-0-415-39181-8

To Nicholas Sho

Contents

Figures and tables

Figures

Tables

Preface

The authors have approached adoption in Japan from two different starting points. The first author has studied politics as an academic in the USA and UK, and after becoming involved in debates over adoption policies in these states has turned his attention to Japan in the hope of finding a positive alternative. The second author has an academic background studying the experiences of those who have faced discrimination in Japan. Her interest has been in understanding how some of the more negative aspects of Japanese culture may have adversely affected children in need of adoption.

One of these starting points might be felt to require some justification. Why should someone whose main focus has been on politics in the English-speaking world be interested in adoption in Japan, or indeed be concerned with adoption at all? In answer, politics is concerned with the workings of the state and one of the key functions of the state is, or ought to be, the protection of those who live within its borders (Karl Popper calls this the 'protectionist theory of the state'). Children in need of adoption are some of the most powerless and vulnerable members of society and are most in need of protection. The way in which the state organizes their protection, therefore, is critical to its purpose and is of essential political interest. Japan is of particular interest in this respect as it stands somewhat outside the political developments in adoption that have occurred in other advanced states.

In the late 1960s in the USA a vigorous campaign was launched in which it was claimed that adoption policy, far from being aimed at the protection of children in need, was in fact being used to oppress ethnic minorities by placing black and American Indian children in white families. This campaign has spread to other English-speaking countries; it has mutated and linked to issues of identity, class and power, and it has had far-reaching consequences for the way in which potential parents are selected and matched with children. If, as the first author believes, these policy developments have been ideologically motivated and have worked to the detriment of children in need, then it is helpful to gain a comparative sense of the policy alternatives in a state like Japan where this ideology has not taken root and where there is a quite different way of thinking about adoption. Different ways of dealing with adoption can also be found in continental Europe where the idea that the transethnic adoption of minorities is a tool of social oppression has had less influence. Here, however, there has been a second far reaching development, one that increases the comparative value of the Japanese case.

The protectionist theory of the state can move in two directions. The state can be seen as needing to do more to look after people by involving itself extensively in regulating society, or it can be seen as protecting people better by attempting to do less and by endeavouring to leave as much as possible to the workings of society. European policy towards adoption has broadly followed the first path. Thus, West European states took the leading role in developing the 1993 Hague Convention on adoption. While formally concerned only with regulating adoption between states, the Convention has had the effect of consolidating the power of central adoption authorities within the state. Japan is not a signatory to the Convention and has followed a policy that lies somewhere in between the diverging paths of extensive state involvement in adoptions and leaving society free to create its own solutions. The Japanese state provides a comprehensive and free adoption service, however, it has not, thus far, created a central professional body to govern the practice, but has taken a relatively *laissez faire* approach to the regulation of adoption.

A research background in the lives of Japanese women and minorities in Japan has given the second author a rather different way of approaching adoption. Her starting point has been a concern with inequality and discrimination in Japanese society and criticism of the state's ambiguous role in maintaining this state of affairs. At a constitutional level the Japanese state upholds equality and rejects discrimination. But rather than protecting the rights of the weakest members of society, the state has sometimes acted against them to maintain the structures of social, economic and legal inequality. Analysis of this problem leads fairly directly to the realization that alongside women and minorities, children in need may have been affected by prejudicial attitudes and policies. Unmarried mothers and mothers who are undocumented migrants are in a particularly difficult position as they are facing both societal discrimination and limited help, or no help at all, from the state. Pressure of circumstances leads some of these women to give up their children for adoption. Children in need of adoption have been stigmatised by notions of pure and impure or good and bad blood. This same blood ideology is used against Korean Japanese, against *burakumin,* against foreigners, and against those of an illegitimate or unknown parentage. The state stresses equality, and yet the household registers maintained by the state can be used to track down a person's blood lineage.

From these two beginnings, one optimistic of finding a successful adoption policy free from ideology and not overburdened by regulation and the other more pessimistic at the problems facing children in need of adoption, we have come together to explore how Japan's adoption system works in practice. We have focused on the development of a new form of adoption called special adoption that has been created specifically for children in need. We have looked at how state agencies and a variety of semi-autonomous and private agencies have responded to the dilemmas and challenges of placing children for adoption. We have considered international adoption, transethnic adoption, and the role of fostering and institutional care. We have paid particular attention to the way in which adoption agencies and prospective adopters interact with one another as parents are selected and matched with children. Our findings have not always agreed with either of our starting assumptions and neither have we always agreed with each other on the implications of what is happening in Japan. The book, therefore, can be read as part of a continuing and open-ended debate about what makes an optimum adoption policy.

Acknowledgements

After T.E. Lawrence had written the first draft of *The Seven Pillars of Wisdom* he lost it while changing trains at Reading Station in December 1919. The twenty-first century equivalent is to lose your manuscript when your computer crashes, and this happened to us in December 2004. After we had tried everything, and after the much vaunted technical support team of our computer manufacturer had told us that the only thing we could to do was to wipe the memory clean and start again, we turned to our friend Andre Batako. Andre has an extraordinary way with computers, he feels them and listens to them; he is more like a doctor than a technician, and somehow he managed to get the thing working again with our draft intact. So our first thanks go to Andre.

We have benefited from the input of several university colleagues. We learnt much from our discussions with Professor Katutugu Yoshida of the University of Hyôgo. We appreciate the thoughtful criticisms and comments made to us in a presentation to the political science faculty and graduate students at Karlstad University in Sweden, where we would particularly like to thank Dr Hans Lödén and Dr Kurt Raftegaard. In the UK we would like to thank Peter Selman at the University of Newcastle for his interest and encouragement. It was through Professor Selman that we met Makiko Komatsu of Mukogawa Women's University in Hyôgo. Professor Komatsu has very generously helped us through many discussions and has shared her own research into the area of adoption with us; we are very thankful to her.

For reasons of confidentiality we have not identified any of the adoptive parents who have helped us in our research (names in the text have been changed). We are, however, very grateful to them for agreeing to be interviewed and have felt honoured to have so many families share their stories with us. We are also highly indebted to all the agency directors, administrators, social workers and other individuals involved in adoption and foster care who have spoken to us. Again, to ensure confidentiality, we have made it a general rule not to identify the agencies and individuals with the exception of instances where there is already significant published information. In this respect, we can thank Ms Mieko Iwasaki of the Association for the Advancement of Family Care (Loving Hands) in Osaka and Mr Akira Hashimoto and Ms Hiroko Yonezawa of Loving Hands in Kobe. Ms Yonezawa was also very helpful in supplying us with the advert from the *Kobe Shinbun* that has been used to illustrate Chapter Three. We would also like to thank Ms Kazuko Yokota of the Motherly Network; Ms Keiko Terasaki of Japan International Social Service; Mr Izumi Ebisawa and Mr Atsumi Saoao of the National Foster Parents Association; Mr Hiroshi Otaguchi, of Aqua Yodoyabashi in Osaka, and Mrs Koko Kondo. We are grateful to Nishmoto San, Sugano San and Ishimura San for finding time to explain their work in child guidance centres. We would also like to thank the staff at the children's home we visited for providing us with a full account of their work there. And let us once again reiterate our thanks to all of the other anonymous interviewees for talking to us about sensitive family matters or for explaining the difficult decisions that they have to make in their work.

Institutional support for this research has come from the University of Sunderland and the Asian Research Institute at Osaka University of Economics and Law. The Japan Foundation (UK) has also been supportive in its award of a grant in 2001 to carry out research into the adoption of mixed-background children in Japan.

The Asian Research Institute has been an ideal research environment, providing both peaceful working facilities and a stimulating intellectual atmosphere. We would like to thank all those we have met at the Institute, where we have had many fruitful discussions, but there are three people in particular who receive our deepest thanks. Mr Sunyoon Hyun has been tremendously helpful and Mrs Myonok Lee and Mrs Honzya Paku have assisted us in countless ways, day in, day out. We are extremely grateful to them. We would like to also extend our thanks to Mrs Yoshimi Kajiya at the Institute of Legal Study, Osaka University of Economics and Law.

1 An overview of adoption in Japan

The Japanese concept of adoption (*yôshi*) is very broad. It establishes a new legal relationship but does not necessarily presume the beginnings of a new family life. Indeed, the scope of adoption in Japan is so wide that although the meaning of the word *yôshi* is rooted in the care of a growing child it denotes relationships between adults as well. The gap between adult and child has been narrowed to a fine distinction between younger and older individuals through the legal nicety that although the adoptee can be any age, the adopter must be older and an adult (Civil Code, Articles 792, 793). It does not matter how *much* older the adopter of an adult 'child' is, an age gap of one day is perfectly acceptable (Takenoshita 1997: 9). When adoptions take place between adults, this age requirement becomes meaningless; it is no more than a curious vestigial reminder of how such adoptions have evolved out of the placement of children. Sometimes, officials make a mistake – or turn a blind eye – and accept adoption applications from 'parents' who are younger than the 'child' (Nishioka 1991: 232–4).

Adult adoptions are generally arranged for family inheritance or business purposes. The reasons can often be quite cynical and include efforts to avoid rules on money lending regulations; to hide an affair, or as a form of tax evasion (Tamura 1996: 160; Bryant 1990). In 1988, for example, the government found that it was necessary to reform the tax law to stop families avoiding inheritance tax through multiple adoptions.[1] This worldly attitude to adoption is also found in the placement of minors in arrangements that may be more in the interests of the adults undertaking them than the children affected by them. Under the legitimising rubric of an 'adoption', children have been transferred into the care and control of adults outside their birth families for a variety of purposes. Before the Second World War the adoption of children could, in some instances, amount to little more than slavery, as it did when brothel owners adopted girls to work as prostitutes (Oppler 1976: 113, n. 3; Paulson 1984: 271, 275). On other occasions, an adoption was used to evade state duties. At times when there was a military call-up, the eldest son in a family was exempt from military service, so to avoid the army, the second son might be adopted by a family with no sons (Paulson, 1984: 278–9). Adoption has also been used to reconstruct a patriarchal family. Families with superfluous sons would pair them in a combined marriage and adoption to families with daughters. Prohibitions on incestuous marriage are limited to blood relationships so that one can wed an adoptive sibling; a daughter will marry a man who will either then be adopted by her parents or who has already been adopted by them, to become a *muko yôshi* (adopted husband), inheriting the family name and often the family business (Paulson, 1984: 165–75; Kurosu 1998). These marriage-adoptions are still made between adults, but in the past the adoption was sometimes initiated when the intended bridegroom was yet a child (Kurosu, 1998: 399). This appears to have been the case in the family of the novelist Junichiro Tanizaki:

> Grandfather doted on his daughters but cared nothing for his sons. As a result, he kept two of the three girls at home, adopting husbands into the family for them ... Of the boys, only the eldest was kept at home to become head of the main house; the younger three were all sent away to be raised elsewhere, or even adopted by and married into other families (Tanizaki 1991: 22).[2]

Today, all adoptions of minors in Japan are supposed to promote the best interests of the child (Ministry of Foreign Affairs 2001: 113, 143). According to official guidelines, adoption arrangements are directed towards child welfare by providing a caring home and legal stability to a child who is orphaned or who does not have a family (Jidôsôdansho 2005: Ch. 6 Sect. 4, 1 (1)). Nonetheless, parents continue to place children with relatives or other acquaintances for a variety of reasons. Sometimes the adoptive parents have no children of their own and no heir; sometimes there is work to be done on a farm, in a business, or around the house; sometimes an adoption facilitates tax avoidance. The majority of children placed for such reasons are boys (Paulson 1984: 165, 289). This reflects the business purposes behind many of these adoptions as well as the interest that adoptive parents often have in carrying on the family name through a male descendant.

Japanese adoptions, therefore, continue to be entered into for reasons that may be at odds with the western insistence that the welfare of the child is a cardinal principle in placements, at least insofar as loving parents are seen as the basis on which this welfare can be assured. In a Japanese adoption, the distinction between family life and the world of work and business can become blurred. As a result, in the eyes of those arranging the adoption, the positioning of the child in the social and economic sphere may count at least as heavily as his family environment. This can arguably provide a more complete picture of the welfare of the child as not just part of a family but also as part of society. However, it can also mean that the adoptive parents view the child with something less than full emotional commitment. In the western ideal, the parent and child in an adoptive family should have the same depth of relationship that they would have in a birth family. This imposes a duty on the adoptive parents to display – and make an honest effort to feel – the same love for an adopted child that they would to a child they had conceived themselves. The same ideal concept of adoption is implicit in official policy pronouncements by the Japanese state on the importance of family life for an adopted child. But in Japanese society there continues to be a vein of unsentimental pragmatism towards adoption arrangements. There is a fairly widespread view that it is ethically acceptable for parents to become adopters for worldly objectives, even if they do not intend, from the outset, to love the child as their own.

From ordinary adoption to special adoption

By no means all Japanese adoptions have been motivated by economic or other practical concerns. The various forms of adoption in Japan have included parents who undertake to create a new family with all that this involves in terms of emotional commitment. However, before 1988 the legal status that parents could achieve by openly declaring themselves as adopters fell short of the status of birth parents; a child gained new parents in an adoption, but did not entirely lose his old ones. This legal relationship is now identified as an 'ordinary adoption' (*futsû yôshi*). An ordinary adoption is an agreement between the natural and adoptive parents sanctioned by a family court. Ordinary adoptions can also be legally arranged within families without going to the court for permission if a child is adopted by grandparents or great grandparents or by a stepparent (Civil Code, 798). Both married couples and single people are eligible to be adopters.[3] Although the adoption creates a legal relationship between the child and the new family, the legal ties and responsibilities of the birth parents remain in place in the background. The child may, for example, still inherit property from birth parents and if the adoptive relationship is disrupted, the child will usually return to them. About 1,500 ordinary adoption cases are considered by the courts each year (Appendix 1: Table 8).

Ordinary adoption fits most easily into circumstances where the birth parents feel a continued sense of obligation towards an older child. It fits less comfortably where the birth parents, typically an unmarried mother and an absent father, do not wish to raise a newborn child and where adoptive parents are committed to making a full emotional adoption of the child. In these circumstances, the birth mother and adoptive parents have sometimes colluded to avoid having *de facto* adoptions legally acknowledged and validated. Instead, the adoptive parents have claimed that the child is theirs by birth.[4] The covert, private transfer of unwanted children at birth, or soon after birth, to new parents certainly occurred up until the 1970s in agreements made between single mothers and couples with fertility problems. By some accounts it continues today, despite the provision for full legal adoptions. One of our informants said that her own doctor made such arrangements (although she had adopted through an agency) and Kazuko Yokota, the director of the Motherly Network adoption agency has suggested that there are hundreds of secret adoptions each year (Jordan 1999).

Before Japan's family law was revised in the post-war occupation period, these unauthorized adoptions were finalized by the simple expedient of falsifying family registration records to identify the child as the natural offspring of the new parents. The deception could be directly arranged between the birth mother and an adoptive couple until 1948 when a new law required the signature of a doctor or midwife on the birth certificate (Nakamura 1994). An unknown number of health professionals were willing to provide their signatures and a few took on a more active mediating role. In 1973 Noboru Kikuta, an obstetrician who was regularly arranging unauthorized adoptions, placed an advertisement for adoptive parents in two local newspapers in Miyagi Prefecture in North East Japan. The national press took an interest and broke the silence that had previously surrounded such arrangements (Kikuta 1988: 63–104). Dr Kikuta was subsequently disbarred from medical practice. However, the public debate that was generated by his actions fed into a reformist agenda in child welfare provision, child protection and children's rights that began to emerge during this period, and which led, eventually, to a change in the law on adoption.

Reform in adoption was prompted by several problems. For Kikuta, a prime motivation was to promote policies that would reduce the number of abortions, particularly late abortions.[5] Amongst the public there was a growing awareness of the plight of unwanted children. This arose from a new, notorious method of infanticide with the discovery of dead, and occasionally still living, babies inside coin lockers. The number of such cases reached a highpoint in 1980 with 37 deaths representing 13% of the 287 known cases of infanticide (Kuono and Johnson 1995). Since the 1970s, there had also been a slowly increasing awareness of child abuse (Kuono and Johnson 1995: 29).[6] These factors helped to persuade the legislature to reform the law to create a new form of adoption that followed the western model in legally sanctioning the permanent and absolute transfer of the child from birth to adoptive parents (Ebisawa 1995: 145). The legislation establishing 'special adoption' (*tokubetsu yôshi*) was passed in 1987 and came into force in 1988. In the first year, over 3,000 applications were presented to the family courts. This represented a period of catch-up and in the following years, the numbers declined. The courts now deal with about 400–450 cases per year (Appendix 1: Table 1).

Special adoption rules

The idea that the members of an adoptive family can have bonds that are equal in strength to a birth family is fully reflected in the special adoption legislation, which transfers all the rights and duties of parenthood from the birth parents to the adoptive parents and severs all legal ties between the birth parent and child. However, those eligible to be involved in a special adoption are defined more narrowly than in the loose arrangements governing an ordinary adoption. (1) The adopters must be a married couple and must both adopt the child, unless one is the natural parent and the other the stepparent (Civil Code, Article 817, 3). (2) At least one of them must be over 25 and the other must be over 20 (Civil Code, Article 817, 4). (3) The child must be under six at the time of application, although foster parents may apply to adopt a child under the age of eight provided they have cared for him since he was under six (Civil Code, Article 817, 5). (4) The parents must have cared for the child for at least six months before applying to adopt him (Civil Code, Article 817, 8). This basic framework allows for a wide range of policies. The rules are concise and are mainly concerned with defining eligibility boundaries. They say nothing about selection criteria for parents beyond specifying that they should be a married couple above a certain age. They do not recommend how parents and children should be matched with each other, nor do they identify what factors are to be considered in determining where a child should be placed.

The official guidelines identify the purpose of adoption as providing a home for children who are orphaned or without a family. However, this purpose is implicitly extended in the special adoption rules. As well as being a way forward for children whose parents are dead, or unable to care for them, special adoption rules also provide a way of *protecting* children from their parents. The potential for special adoption to protect children from abuse within the family comes out in the limitations placed on the rights of natural parents over the child. Although it is stated in the Civil Code that the birth parents must consent to the adoption, this requirement is heavily qualified. Consent is not needed if the birth parents cannot express their will; if they have abused the child; abandoned the child, or if there are 'any other reasons' which harm the interests of the prospective adoptee (Civil Code, Article 817, 6). These exceptions allow judges considerable discretion in dispensing with consent, but so far, such dispensation has been little used. Traditional Japanese ethics stress the power of parents over their children rather than their duties towards them (Hendry 1981: 92). The Japan Federation of Bar Associations suggests that there is 'a deep-rooted notion that parents may exercise comprehensive control over their children' (JFBA 2003: 185). In this respect, family court decisions have generally been conservative in upholding the authority of birth parents and social workers have rarely forced the issue. This has meant that unless the parents cooperate, the function of special adoption as a way of protecting children from abuse within the family has remained latent.

Problems for single mothers

The unwillingness of the state authorities to forcibly remove children for the purpose of adoption means that few adopted children come from an abused and neglected background. They tend to come, instead, from single mothers who give up their child at birth or soon after birth (Appendix 1: Table 4, Table 7). The unmarried mothers who give up their child for adoption tend to be young, although in the experience of Mieko Iwasaki, the director of the Loving Hands adoption agency, teenage mothers are more likely than women in their early twenties to attempt to raise the child themselves – a tendency attributed to optimistic naivety of the teenagers towards the problems ahead (Iwasaki 1996).

A situation where most children available for adoption are babies born to single mothers is reminiscent of the situation in the UK and in other western states about forty years ago. It is also in contrast to the current position in the UK, as there has been a transition away from single mothers giving up their babies and an increased willingness to take children into care and free them for adoption if they have been abused and neglected. The divergence between Japan and the UK reflects the continuing strength of a conservative or paternalist ethos in Japan, one that is slow to challenge parental authority even where it is abusive but quick to condemn illegitimacy. This ethos makes the position facing single mothers in Japan very difficult and helps to explain why they may choose to relinquish their babies.

As illegitimate motherhood loses its stigma, as it becomes more common, and as the state steps in to provide support, so single mothers are less likely to relinquish their children for adoption.[7] However, these developments have been much less pronounced in Japan than in many other wealthy nations. The rate of children born outside marriage in Japan is low, according to official figures it is below 2%. (Naikakufu 2005: 55). In the UK the rate is about 40–43% (figures vary slightly) and in many other western states the figure is a third or more.[8] This striking difference can be overstated as it can be partly accounted for by western couples in long-term partnerships; were they Japanese, these couples would face a much stronger expectation that they ought to be married. Nonetheless, the low number of single mothers in Japan emphasizes how they remain outside the norm, and this may help to explain why a comparatively high proportion of children given up for adoption in Japan are babies. Thus, when Japan is compared with an advanced state with high rates of illegitimacy such as the UK there appears to be an inverse relationship between the proportion of children born to single mothers and the proportion of adopted children given up for adoption at or soon after birth (Appendix 1: Table 5).

In the 1970s, Kikuta would tell an expectant single mother that unless she had special job skills, she was placing herself and her child at a considerable economic disadvantage. It would be difficult to maintain work, she would only be able to claim limited welfare benefits and both mother and child could expect to suffer from social stigma (Kikuta 1988: 22–25). Thirty years later the situation is only slightly better. Single motherhood is more widely accepted than it was before, but is still regarded by more conservative members of society as a disgrace to the family name. Single mothers now have a formal political voice in the state after three pressure groups merged into an organization that has legal recognition (Akaishi 2003). Their influence, however, is small; job protection for single mothers has improved but remains limited and ineffectual with many confined to temporary employment. Welfare benefits are meagre.[9] Overall, single mothers live on about a third of the average household income (Kôseirôdôshô 2005).

Discrimination, low wages, unstable employment and inadequate welfare make the prospect of raising a child alone challenging enough under any conditions, and particularly daunting in Japan. This difficult combination of circumstances can be placed in a political context using the simple diagram shown in Figure 1.1. A nominal distinction can be drawn between a society that is prejudiced against illegitimate children and one that accepts them, while a state can provide either (a) limited or (b) extensive welfare benefits and job protection to single parents. This identifies four national circumstances, each related to distinct political outlooks. A conservative nation will be characterized by discriminatory attitudes in society and limited state welfare and job rights. A neo-liberal nation will be more socially accepting of illegitimacy, but will also have limited state welfare and job rights. A more social democratic nation is socially accepting and relatively generous in its welfare provision and job rights. The fourth category can be

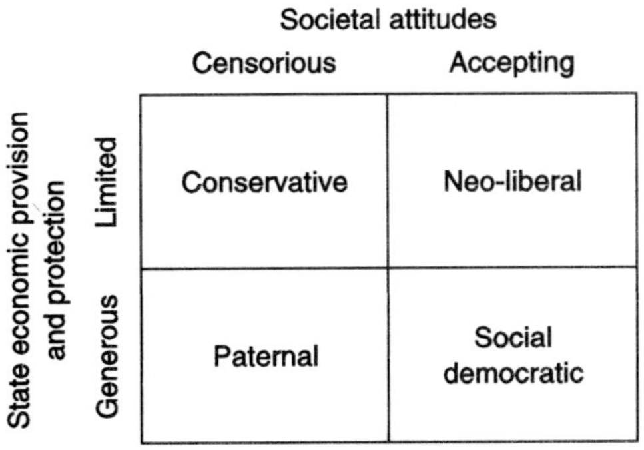

Societal attitudes

	Censorious	Accepting
Limited	Conservative	Neo-liberal
Generous	Paternal	Social democratic

(State economic provision and protection)

Figure 1.1 Single mothers and the political ethos

termed paternalism. Here there is societal condemnation of women who step outside patriarchal ethical codes, but at the same time a willingness by the state to make economic provision for the 'weaker' sex. It should be admitted at once that this classification does not capture the complexity of a society or of state policy. It is, nonetheless, a useful framework in two respects. First, it allows a broad comparison to be drawn between the situation in Japan and other states; second it helps us to consider the prospects for change over time by indicating possible alternatives to the *status quo*.

The traditionalistic ethos of many in Japan and the low ranking of single parents in state fiscal priorities suggests, at least initially, that single mothers face the most adverse of circumstances, a conservative polity. However, given that there has been some change in attitude in Japan over the last thirty years, can it be assumed that further reform is just a matter of time? The current difficulties facing Japan's single mothers are similar to those that confronted single mothers in other western states in the past, where things have now moved in a liberal or social democratic direction. It might be supposed, therefore, that Japan will also shift towards a more accommodating position. Modest social trends away from the nuclear family, including a divorce rate that has risen significantly over the last two decades of the twentieth century, might also be seen as heralding more generous attitudes towards single parents.[10]

In fact, such assumptions about the direction of change do not reflect current circumstances. The post-war expansion of social democracy in the West was accompanied by a sustained period of economic growth, but since the early 1990s, Japan has faced economic difficulties. In this uncertain economic climate, Japan's higher divorce rate has not, in fact, increased state generosity towards single parents but has rather been used to justify a cut in their welfare benefits ('State targets' 2002). The government defended this cut as a way of encouraging single mothers to take up training and has offered financial incentives to the employers who hire them (Fujiwara 2003).

These recent policy initiatives might be termed conservative, or neo-liberal, rather than social democratic. Therefore, if the nominal distinction between limited and extensive state welfare provision is taken as relative over time within a single state, then the late twentieth century in Japan was a period when single mothers experienced societal prejudice but were treated comparatively well by a paternalist state. From this position, Japan could now be said to be working its way towards neo-liberalism, that is, societal attitudes are softening but state policies are hardening.

Family, civil society and state

An analysis of the distribution of power between family, civil society and state in Japanese adoption helps us to understand how members of each sphere interact. It also allows us to compare the broad development of Japan's adoption policy against the statist dynamic that can be observed in Western Europe. Adoption always involves families, and, depending on the law (or the willingness of those involved to avoid the law), it is possible for the transfer of a child to be arranged wholly within the private sphere. However, adoptions can also be controlled and mediated by agencies operating in civil society and they can be arranged and regulated by state organizations.

The development of adoption services within western European states has tended to follow a single shifting orthodoxy in which decision making power becomes concentrated in successive institutions. The power to control an adoption has undergone a three-stage progression. In the first stage, adoption is undertaken as a private family matter between birth and adoptive parents. In the second stage, adoption becomes a process that involves the mediating institutions of civil society such as children's charities. In the third stage, adoption is regulated and administered by the state with decision making power over adoption policy placed in the hands of public officials and in quasi public organizations maintained by state funding. In Britain, for example, private adoptions are illegal. Parents who want to make their own arrangements without state oversight have sometimes avoided the rules by making inter-country adoptions, but there has been a concerted effort to prevent this (Hayes 2000). Independent and voluntary agencies have found it more difficult to operate since the 1976 Adoption Act privileged the role of local authority adoption agencies. The Adoption and Children Act 2002 has increased the difficulties for autonomous agencies by imposing additional duties upon all agencies whilst funding to undertake these duties has been given only to local authorities (Gayford 2004).

Since the beginning of the Meiji period, Japan has undergone a superficially similar statist dynamic. The first minimal regulation of private adoptions, the requirement to register them, was imposed in 1875 after the Meiji government established a comprehensive family register (Paulson 1984: 131). Autonomous agencies became active in mediating adoptions at the end of the Second World War, mainly as a response to the problem of war orphans at a time when state functions were paralysed. The role of these agencies has been supplemented by the state as post-war reconstruction increased state involvement in child welfare (Takahashi 2003: 98–9, Sakamoto 2002: 2). In 1947 all children in institutions became the subject of child welfare law and the following year the government set up a foster care system and started to give money to foster parents (Zenkoku Satooyakai 2001: 5). Prefectual child guidance centres were created after Child Welfare Law was introduced in January 1948 and 98 child guidance centres (CGCs) were opened and began to involve themselves in adoption (Sakamoto 2002: 3). However, this increasing involvement of civil society and then the state in adoption arrangements is best understood as a branching out of adoption possibilities. Instead of different modes of adoptions succeeding each other, with past institutions and practices being prohibited or marginalized as new forms are established, these new adoption practices have added to old ones, but have not necessarily replaced them. The involvement of autonomous organizations and then the state in adoption services has developed in parallel to the earlier private family adoptions so that they have provided additional rather than replacement routes to adoption. The Japanese state has undoubtedly increased its role in regulating and organizing adoptions. Its financial support also provides a strong inducement to adoptive parents – though not necessarily birth mothers – to apply to a state agency where adoption is free. The state has not, however, prohibited or crowded out other modes of adoption based around private family arrangements or autonomous adoption agencies in civil society.

Special adoptions created a new legal framework that required state child welfare agencies to have a greater degree of involvement in adoption; but they also gave semi-autonomous agencies and private agencies the chance to form, or to expand their activities beyond ordinary adoption. The state has been permissive in this respect. Agencies are meant to register, but it is possible to become involved in making adoptions without registering by making *de facto* arrangements and then seeking their *de jure* confirmation. The main check upon agency placements, whether public or private, are the courts that have to approve all adoptions. Parents who wish to adopt, therefore, have the opportunity either to go to their local child guidance centre (a state-run child welfare institution), seek out a state supported or private adoption agency or make their own arrangements. There are around 20 private agencies including semi-autonomous organizations; independent agencies; doctors associations; and religious groups with and without child care facilities (Yôshi 1999: 33–4). Private arrangements can be made through lawyers, individual doctors, independent social workers and other mediators.

Policy making without a profession

The diversity of routes to adoption in Japan is reflected in a diversity of opinion regarding adoption. Agencies can make radically different assumptions about what is ethical and unethical, practical and impractical. There is no one orthodoxy about the criteria used to select parents, methods of matching parents with children, or the time needed to gain a birth mother's informed consent.

The absence of an adoption orthodoxy in Japan is connected with the near lack of an adoption profession. If one shows sufficient initiative it is possible to go it alone and create an adoption agency. There are also a few lawyers and independent social workers who derive part of their income from adoption work. However, career opportunities for specializing in adoption as part of a larger organization are quite limited. With a few exceptions, child guidance centre staff who oversee adoption programmes are civil servants who are neither specialists in adoption nor even child welfare, but are rather rotated through different jobs and departments every few years (Sugioka 1993: 46). There are neither advanced educational expectations for adoption workers nor a structure to provide for them.[11] Semi-autonomous and private agencies tend to rely on paying the expenses of volunteers rather than hiring full time staff. There is no authoritative adoption organization controlling the process, not even an umbrella group bringing adoption mediators together, although there are fostering and adoption parenting groups and one scholarly association, the Society for Study of Adoption and Foster Placement of Children. With no central organization, and with no developed career structure, it is difficult to impose a standard idea of what constitutes best practice in adoption, or to claim that adoption mediation is a specialist field requiring its own expertise.

Japan may not have a controlling profession but neither does it have a static or parochial adoption system. Adoption mediators have considerable freedom to create and adapt policies as they think best, and the policies that they have developed are often influenced by practices in other parts of the world. In the semi-autonomous and private agencies, many directors and others with a sense of vocation about their work are informed and interested in the adoption practices in other states. Some have made extended visits abroad to gain comparative experience (Yonezawa 1993; Yôshi 1999; Shiseidô 1999). Further knowledge is gained when private agencies arrange international adoptions and child guidance centres deal with foreign children. In these cases it is often necessary to understand foreign adoption law and sometimes to liase with foreign adoption organizations. There is also comparative awareness of foreign foster care systems amongst those who wish to improve and expand foster care services (Shoji 2003; Yuzawa 2004).

The absence of an authoritative profession has arguably led to a situation where there is too little regulation of adoption. In 2005, the government commissioned the Society for Study of Adoption and Foster Placement of Children to investigate the activities of unregistered agencies and draw up guidelines ('Yôshiengumi' 2005). It also announced plans to recruit foster care specialists to the CGCs ('Government looking to boost adoption rate' 2005). It is possible, therefore, that Japan will start to undergo a change from the parallel development of state and societal adoption services, to one where a central organization begins to control and regulate adoption.

Tradition and modernity

There is an ambiguous relationship between the contemporary objectives of an adoption system that is directed towards helping a child in need through special adoption to unrelated parents, and the history of adoption and childcare in Japan. Japan falls within the orbit of Confucian influence and this may have encouraged the attitude that adoption should be confined to kin. The extent to which such attitudes can be attributed to Confucianism should not be overstated; the idea of keeping adoptions within the family is by no means confined to the East, and Confucianism itself is not a monolithic doctrine but an evolving and diverse set of ideas. Nonetheless, from the more rigid schools of Confucian thought, there is the notion that natural relationships should not be altered, and that the body of a child has a unique physical relationship with their birth family which makes it unnatural for them to be grafted onto another (McMullen 1975: 151–4). This idea is combined with Confucian reverence for family ancestry to end in the argument that adoption should be kept within the extended family. If Japan is compared to the West, therefore, Confucianism can be interpreted as constraining the possibilities of an adoption system that centres on the imperative to find homes for needy children whether or not the adopters are related to them. From this perspective, special adoption conflicts with the long term cultural influence of Confucianism in Japan.

If Japan is compared not with the West but rather with other nations in East Asia however, it can be seen that there has historically been a greater willingness to adopt or foster unrelated children in Japan than in the neighbouring states of China and Korea (Korusu 1998: 395; Peterson 1996; Lebra 1989: 185). Laws borrowed from China that date back to Japan's Taihô Code of 702 regulated adoption and attempted to limit it to relatives, but these restrictions tended to be eroded to allow for non-relative adoptions (Mass 1989: 9–11, 25, 72). The rules followed a series of pendulum swings as Confucian scholars argued on both sides over the propriety of non-relative adoptions (McMullen 1975; Peterson 1996: 195–6). Overall, the more rigid forms of Confucianism have not constrained non-relative adoption in Japan to nearly the same degree as elsewhere (Kaji 1999).

Where a traditional adoptive or fostering relationship in Japan was entered into between adults and an unrelated child, how many of these non-family arrangements approximated to the modern western ideal of adoption? In other words were traditional forms of fostering and adoption arranged in the hope that an affectionate and caring relationship would develop between parent and child? There are two broad responses to this question. One stresses (a) the economic rationale underlying adoption and other traditional childcare practices in Japan, and (b) the way that they were based in patriarchal and hierarchical relationships (Paulson 1984; Kurosu 1998). These forms of analysis tend to exclude or greatly downplay the idea that these adoptions involved love and emotional commitment. Even where the adoptee was destined to become the new head of the household, it has been argued that 'nurturance and intimacy were secondary or irrelevant to the mandate of positional succession, and often were completely absent from the adoptive relationship' (Lebra 1989: 203). The second approach to understanding traditional adoption and other childcare practices, stresses the benign outcomes for children involved. It does not deny that practical considerations might, for example, have impelled parents with several sons to have passed one on to a farming family who wanted an extra pair of hands, or in cases where farming prospects were poor that a farmer's son might have been passed on to a family that made its living from fishing. However, it goes on to argue that the children would have often benefited from such arrangements. Children who were passed to another family to work were clothed and fed and given a practical education in the skills they would need in adult life. In villages where there was a tradition of adopting children from poor families, the survival of these children was assured. Furthermore, a boy raised in another family might be presented with a plot of land on reaching adulthood and would sometimes inherit the position as head of the household (*ie*) or set up a new branch of the family (*bunke*). Adoptive parents and foster carers, therefore, acted in ways that were socially responsible, taking on the essential obligations of birth parents to preserve the life of the child as well as to train and to educate them and to give them a place in society (Kimura 2003: 23–7). From this more sympathetic perspective of traditional adoption practices it is a short step to suggest that relations between adoptive and foster parents and their children were informed not only by duty but also by affection.

Given the variety of practices in Japan, these differing interpretations might represent two sides of the same coin. It would be naïve to think that traditional forms of childcare were always entered into with the interests of the children at heart. But it would be overly cynical to think that the children did not benefit on some occasions and that there were not genuine ties of affection between a foster or adoptive parent and a child. The issue is complicated by the mixing of the private realm of the family and the social realm of work in Japan. Adoptions entered into for reasons that combine family and business objectives are one manifestation of this mixing. Another is the notion, developed in the Meiji period, that a business organization is itself a form of family (Goodman 2000: 20). The idea of the company as a family has been dismissed as an ideological obfuscation created by those at the top of the economic hierarchy, and it may be tempting to draw the same conclusion with regard to traditional adoptions entered into with business objectives in mind. However, cases of adopted children being given tangible economic benefits such as land, or even inheriting a family business, suggest that such generalizations are too sweeping. The overlap between family and business concerns, potentially at least, forms an integrated social ethos in which the aspirations of a powerless child can find a place.

The evidence, therefore, is mixed. Childcare practices in the past covered a range of *de facto* placements outside a child's family including adoption in the emotional sense, fostering, apprenticeship, servitude and slavery. In some cases these placements would be officially recorded as a *de jure* adoption, in other cases they were not, with the official or informal status of the placement bearing little relationship to whether the child was exploited or well cared for. Rather than a single homogeneous tradition, there were a variety of traditions, with some of them at least supporting a child's physical and emotional well-being.

Modernity has also had an ambiguous influence on the adoption of children in need in Japan. If modern attitudes correspond to liberal ethics, they will tend to be supportive of adoption. Children will be viewed on their own merits as individuals and their status and character will not be seen as being indelibly fixed in them from their biological parents. This may encourage adoptive parents to more readily consider children from a 'bad' background. However, other aspects of modernity are less conducive to the development of an effective adoption system for children in need. Modernity stresses abstract contractual relations. A contractual mentality is not the best way for parents to approach an adoption, as it may encourage them to calculate, rather impersonally, on the best child they can get, rather than responding with emotional warmth to children who are in need of adoption, but who – from a contractual perspective – fall short of the best 'bargain' available. The technological advances associated with modernity may also have a negative impact on adoption. The marriage age is increasing in Japan, as is the age of having a first child.[12] Given that fertility declines with age, childless couples who wish to adopt may be on the increase. Against this, the growing effectiveness of fertility treatment has a direct impact on reducing the number of childless couples seeking adoptive children. These advances may also have helped to create a climate of expectations in which the desirability of rearing a child with one's own genes is emphasized. The desire for one's own biological child is not wholly naturalistic as a greater awareness of genetic inheritance may lead to a greater significance being attached to it. The fertility treatment industry, therefore, may not only respond to a prior need, but also add to the feeling that having one's own child is of prime importance.

The assumption that there is a strong relationship between our genetic makeup and our individual character can be distinguished from the traditional concept of the importance of a child inheriting family blood. In the context of decisions over children, 'blood' is a somewhat wider, more inclusive concept than genes and not simply an old-fashioned synonym. Blood runs through a family as a collective unit rather than being unique to an individual. When a childless couple, with traditional beliefs about the significance of blood, make choices over infertility treatment as against adoption, they are also deciding whether to move inwards or outwards from the idea that their children must share their blood. If they concentrate exclusively on fertility treatment, they move inwards to a concern with their specific individual genes. If they consider adoption then they may broaden the idea of blood outwards beyond the extended family at least as far as other Japanese of 'good' blood.

Liberalism and conservatism

The end of the Second World War was a period of crisis and change for Japanese childcare. Thousands of orphans were crowding into newly formed institutions. At the same time, an occupying power was intent on liberalizing not only the Japanese constitution but also family relationships. From one perspective, the reform of family law including the law on adoption after the Second World War, and later the creation of special adoption can be seen as a natural evolution of earlier practices. From another perspective, these developments can appear as a radical departure from tradition and perhaps even as the imposition of a western mode of dealing with childcare.

In 1948, the Civil Code was revised to require the adoption of children under fifteen to be approved by the family court. The task that has been set for the courts since that time has been to prevent exploitative forms of adoption but to allow benign forms, that is, to allow only those placements that are in the best interests of the child. This can be understood not so much as an ending of tradition as a sifting of tradition to keep what is worth keeping. The family courts have used their gate-keeping role to winnow out 'adoptions' that are really no more than a cover for child exploitation. Special adoption represents a natural extension of this policy insofar as it allows for additional opportunities to make benign adoptions.

The change in the adoption law in 1948 was part of a broader effort to reconstruct social relations along more democratic lines by abolishing the *ie* system (Ochiai 1996: 181; Bryant 1990: 331). The *ie* system had divided Japanese society into households with the head of the *ie* having considerable authority. An *ie* was wider than a nuclear family as it might include adult children, members of an extended family, servants and unrelated but economically dependent families. Before 1948, an adoption into an *ie* had to be authorized by its head, even if he was not the adoptive parent. The new authority of the courts, therefore, was tied to the negation of the old authority structure of the *ie* (Oppler 1976: 111–120; Paulson 1984: 102–103). But although 'the *ie* system is gone ... the Japanese are still haunted by its ghost' (Kawanishi 2004: 27). The Civil Code, imposed after Japan's defeat in war, was an abrupt legal transition that did not necessarily result in the transformation of societal ethics or practices, and the development of a liberal ethos has been patchy (Habu 2000b: 45). There is a continuing tension in Japanese society – for example over sex-equality – between liberals who support the egalitarian and individualistic principles that formed the revised Civil Code and conservatives who retain more hierarchical or communitarian views.

The two forms of adoption now on offer in Japan can be interpreted as a manifestation of this duality of public opinion, as there is at least a mild affinity between special adoption and liberalism and ordinary adoption and conservatism. To understand these affinities, it is helpful to link each form of adoption to nature or nurture, and to individualism or collectivism. To these familiar dichotomies we can add a third distinction, one that identifies parental objectives in terms of either limited or open-ended time frames. Figure 1.2 summarizes the attitudes associated with each form of adoption.

In an ordinary adoption, the birth family of the child is often of critical importance in assessing the acceptability of the match. Ordinary adoptions are often arranged within an extended family, and where the child comes from outside the family their background is taken as a measure of whether or not the adoption should go ahead. In both cases, the children involved are assumed to inherit their nature from a bloodline that makes them as suitable candidates for adoption. Another way of expressing this belief is to say that in an ordinary adoption, the family ancestry of a child is taken as a collective unit that defines the character of the individual. The child's characteristics are assumed to come from their heritage rather than from expressing their individuality.

The purpose of the adoptive placement is also seen in collective terms. It is entered into for the good of the adoptive family (a) as a whole and (b) over time, in a way that betrays a continued preoccupation with the *ie*. A long view is taken

Ordinary adoption	Special adoption
Nature	Nurture
Collectivism	Individualism
Open-ended time-frame	Limited time-frame

Figure 1.2 Attitudes of adoptive parents

of the inheritance of the family name, the family business and the family line. The reasons for an ordinary adoption within an extended family, normally comes from pull factors not push factors; they are unlikely to involve an unmarried mother in difficult circumstances and may indeed be against the natural mother's wishes. Under the pre-war system, 'Household interests took priority over the bond between mother and child; therefore children belonged to the *ie* rather than to their mothers (Uno 1999: 23). The lingering conservative authority structure of the *ie* in some extended families can still put great pressure on mothers, married with several children, to give up a child in an ordinary adoption to a childless uncle and aunt.

Parents who enter into a special adoption do not have the same degree of assurance over the family background of a child that they would have in an ordinary adoption. In a typical special adoption, the child is unrelated to the adoptive parents and has a background that does not usually count in his favour. Often the child is illegitimate and the father unknown. If the origins of both the birth parents *are* known, they are likely to be considered dubious. Parents who are willing to adopt a child in these circumstances, to some degree at least, believe in their ability to nurture the child in a way that will result in a close and fulfilling family life regardless of the child's ancestry. In a special adoption, therefore, the child is more likely to be seen as an individual not bound by his or her past. In the mind of the parents, the focus of the adoption is also likely to be more tied to the immediate circumstances of the child and parents enjoying a family life rather than with the long term duration of the family line. However, the commitment is still life-long; a special adoption is created on the expectation of permanency and the parents can only annul it through an application to the family court.

When a childless couple announces an interest in adoption, these different attitudes sometimes come out in the deliberations of the extended family. A grandmother might act as a mediator, investigating the possibility of an ordinary adoption by suggesting to the parents of several grandchildren that one could be placed with an aunt and uncle (an appeal to the collective good of the whole family). These parents may counter with a compromise proposal: the childless couple should wait until one of their sons is grown up and *then* adopt him so that he can inherit the business and family name (the long durée). The childless couple insist that they want to raise a child and that inheritance is not an issue (time-limited objectives). They add that they have applied to be considered for a special adoption. The relatives express doubt about the bloodline of an unrelated child with a well-known phrase drawn from stockbreeding: 'We don't know where this horse's bones come from' (emphasis on nature).[13] The different views that emerge from this kind of debate indicate the split between conservative and liberal perspectives on adoption. An ordinary adoption stresses continuity; caution; concern with inheritance; the subordination of the individual to the collective, outlooks that indicate a conservative attitude of mind. Parents who enter into a special adoption take a more liberal approach. They are less concerned with heritage, lay greater stress on individuality, and focus on the present rather than having a long-term perspective linking past, present and future. Special adoptions repudiate the idea that ancestry is essential to defining the family unit and the place of a family in society. They are an affirmation that the bonds of love between parent and child do not depend on biological ties.

Conclusion

Until recently Japan did not draw a hard and fast distinction between the many different forms of adoption. The adoption of a child was not clearly separated from the adoption of an adult until 1948, and only since the coming into force of the special adoption law in 1988 has there been a concerted effort to make special provision for children in need of adoption. Other forms of adoption have been restricted by the courts but not abolished. Although all child adoptions are meant to promote the welfare of the child, this requirement has been interpreted quite broadly as children who could not be said to be in 'need' of adoption are still placed in ordinary adoptions. The underlying reasons concern business, inheritance and maintaining a family line. These forms of child adoption remain culturally embedded and legally tolerated in Japanese society.

The law and official guidance on special adoption is terse and allows for considerable discretion by the placing agency. This indicates that while the Japanese state has taken an active role in arranging special adoptions it has also been permissive in allowing adoption agencies in civil society to develop their own placement programmes. Independent agencies have not been shut out by the state and some have been created, or given a new lease of life, in response to the special adoption legislation. With no overarching adoption profession, the policies that have been developed vary considerably.

The initial phase of special adoption in Japan has been characterized by state involvement without state prescription. However, there may now be a transition towards more regulation and more centralization. This makes it an appropriate time to consider the story so far and to ask what might be gained and lost from such a step. In the chapters that follow, therefore, we look at a range of agencies in order to identify what their policies are, how successful they have been, and how they cope with the problems and ethical dilemmas that are intertwined with adoption.

2 Special adoption: A liberal policy in a conservative society

Regardless of their worldview and political orientation, most adults have feelings that will tend to be supportive of adoption or other measures to help children in need. Sympathy for a needy child is a natural impulse, and that such children deserve help is a universal moral imperative.[14] But whatever people's natural feelings and moral sense may tell them, their 'reason', or ideological leanings can push them in other directions. For example, there is sympathy for the plight of a needy child amongst people who favour neo-liberal welfare policies towards single mothers, policies that arguably contribute to the child's plight. Similarly, adopters often have to contend with political and social views that impinge on them in ways that are not necessarily either supportive or sympathetic. Furthermore, the adoptive parents themselves may hold ambivalent views in ways that may influence their choices about which children they adopt and whether or not to keep the adoption secret.

In Japan, special adoption has the greatest affinity with those who hold more liberal views. Liberals stress the human ability to break free from the past, whether this past refers to an oppressive state dominating society or to an individual child's family background. A liberal perspective, therefore, allows for optimism that an adoption will turn out for the best. More cautiously, conservatives stress continuity from one generation to the next, and are thus less sanguine about the likely success of a special adoption. From a western perspective this is slightly surprising; western conservatives tend to be strongly supportive of adoption, which is seen as being in accord with 'pro-family' principles. In Japan, however, the conservative defence of the family is tied to the retention of a system approximating to the old *ie* system, and the *ie* in turn is bound up with beliefs about the importance of ancestry and good bloodlines. From this perspective, the adoption of unknown children can be seen as weakening a family. These conservative views are not articulated in a way that creates opposition to adoption at a policy level; but they can create feelings of ambivalence or even slight hostility amongst relatives and friends of adopters.

The problems that such attitudes can cause should not be overstated; the testimony of parents who have pursued adoption in Japan indicates a general acceptance of adopted children amongst relatives, teachers and peers and a lack of discrimination. However, the feelings of adoptees looking back on their childhoods suggest that even seemingly trivial slights can be hurtful. In a typical minor incident, Takeshi's neighbour took his friends and him to a swimming pool. After the swim, they all bought juice, either with their own money if they had any or from the neighbour's purse if not. When Takeshi, who had no money, shouted out what he wanted, the neighbour ticked him off for demanding something for nothing and imputed that his rudeness was to be expected from an adopted child (Kateiyôgo 1999: 16). Adopted children also tend to want to conceal their status from their peers. Ayumi felt bitter that her classmates constantly reminded her that she was an adopted child. She was adopted when she was five years old. The neighbours must have realized this, but for a time she had managed to hide the fact at school. After her adopted mother and her teacher had a meeting, however, the teacher left his notebook on his desk and the children read it and discovered the secret (Kateiyôgo 1999: 17). With some justification, therefore, there is an undercurrent of anxiety amongst prospective parents about how other members of society will respond to an adopted child. This anxiety is sometimes manifested in attempts by adoptive parents to maintain secrecy, attempts which can complicate the otherwise smooth journey towards the legalization of an adoption.

Adoption through a Child Guidance Centre

The most frequent method of pursuing a special adoption in Japan is by applying to one's local state adoption agency. State adoptions are arranged through CGCs; these organizations deal with a range of child and family matters and are the approximate equivalent of a local authority social service department in the UK. Special adoption through a child guidance centre is straightforward, at least in theory. The process can be divided into three stages; couples are initially approved to foster a child with a view to adoption, the agency then places a child with them and if things go well, the family court will turn this foster placement into an adoption and the decision will be placed on the family register. In Tokyo, prospective parents are given a flow chart, adapted in Figure 2.1, which follows the process of a successful applicant couple up until placement. The steps are broadly similar in other areas.

As the flow chart indicates, a couple who wish to adopt a child first apply to the CGC to become registered foster parents. The child guidance centre conducts a home study and then passes its recommendation on the couple, first to the office of the governor for a rubber-stamp approval, and then to the Child Welfare Council which will almost certainly accept the advice of the CGC. An approved couple are then able to register as foster parents and attend an information meeting. In a parallel process, the couple's future child is identified as eligible for adoption by the CGC in consultation with the children's home or infant home that is caring for the child. In Tokyo there are then two meetings that consider a suitable match. The first is a monthly conference that includes representatives from the children's home, infant home and foster home centre. The second meeting takes place within the CGC where final matching decisions are taken. The would-be parents are then taken to the children's home or infant home to meet the child.

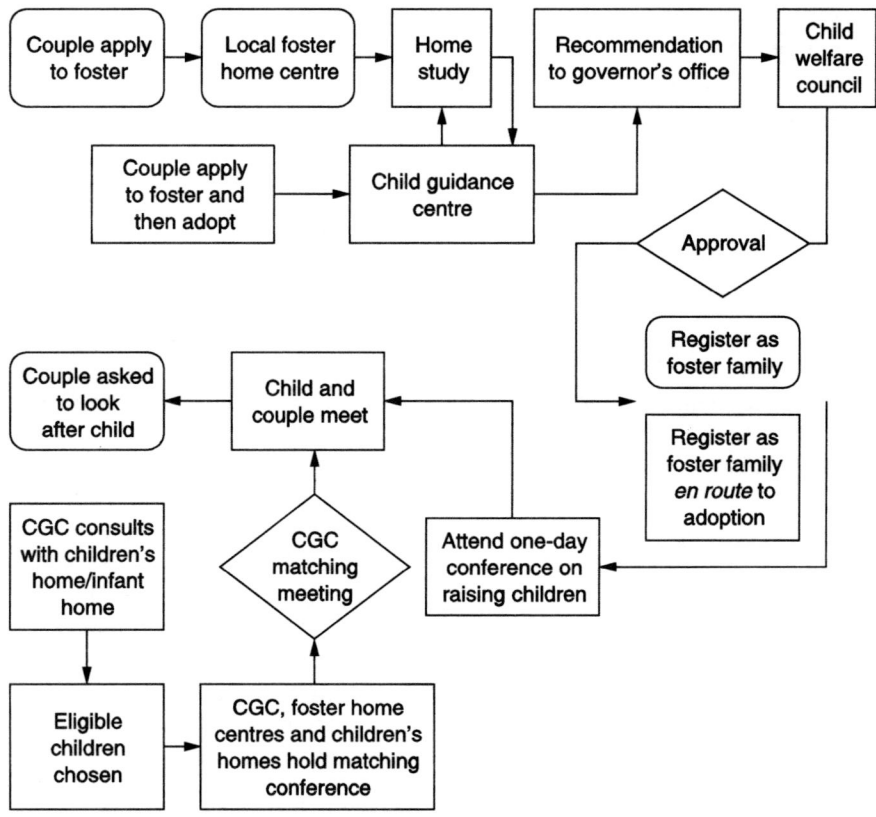

Figure 2.1 Applying to foster and adopt a child

If this meeting is successful, it will be arranged for the couple to look after the child after a process of familiarization. The final stage, not shown on the chart, is the parents' application to the courts to adopt the child they are fostering and to register the child as part of the family.

The flow chart gives the reassuring impression that the route to placement is orderly and uncomplicated. Parents who had adopted though a CGC told us that this was indeed their experience; their applications followed a fairly smooth and swift path from the time of applying for registration through to the time that they were matched with a child. The following case study of the pre-court stages of an adoption is, therefore, characteristic of many others in being reasonably straightforward.

From application to placement

A couple that we will call Mrs Tanaka and her husband, are urban dwellers in the vast metropolis that is centred on Osaka and which spreads from Kobe in the West to Kyoto in the East. Mrs Tanaka is Japanese; her husband is a foreign resident.

They are of middle income. When the couple were in their late thirties, and had no children, they decided that they wanted to adopt. They began the process by registering as parents who wished to foster with a view to adoption at their local child guidance centre.

The child guidance centre laid down three objective requirements for registration. The couple needed to show that they had enough income to live in modest comfort as a family. They needed to supply evidence that they were sufficiently healthy to be equal to the demands of raising a child. They also needed to submit a plan of their home and its environment, and in particular give evidence that the size of the home exceeded a minimum floor space, measured in *tatami* mats.[15] In Tokyo, for example, an acceptable apartment requires two rooms of at least 10 *tatami* mats (Tomita, 1998: 4). The couple were soon able to provide a suitable home plan as well as a satisfactory statement of income and medical certificates of good health.

Before being accepted onto the register, Mrs Tanaka and her husband also had an interview conducted by a social worker in their home. Once they had satisfied the more objective criteria of income, accommodation and health, the interview presented little obstacle to their registration. Although formally part of the assessment, it was used primarily as a means of gathering information for matching purposes. The social worker asked what kind of child the couple would like. What age? Which sex? What kind of background? What range of nationalities? The couple said that they wanted a healthy baby of either sex.

Three months after making initial contact with the CGC Mrs Tanaka and her husband were registered as parents who were suitable to foster a child with a view to adoption. They were invited to participate in a one-day adoption workshop. After this, they eagerly awaited news of an available baby.

The initial registration stage in applying to adopt a child was unproblematic for the couple. Neither the objective nor the subjective elements of the assessment were particularly onerous and the timescale from approaching the agency to becoming registered was reasonable. The smooth process thus far can be attributed to the attitudes and ways of behaving of those involved. (1) Tasks are completed speedily. The agency is prompt and responsive to the couple. The couple themselves act quickly to collect the necessary documents, and those supplying them also act with despatch. (2) There is a sense of proportion in the demands made of the couple. The tasks they are set are limited to compiling evidence on their health, income and home. (3) Objective criteria weigh much more heavily than subjective criteria in the assessment. The couple are assessed according to three fundamental measurable standards that apply to everyone. Decision making at this stage is based on universal rules laid down in advance. Once the objective criteria are met there is limited room for discretion by the social worker involved in the subjective side of the assessment. This creates a framework in which discussions with the social worker can be fact-finding rather than interrogative.

The registration experiences of Mrs Tanaka and her husband are typical. The three month time line from initial contact to registration is about average for child guidance centres. No parents complained to us of undue delays at this stage, although it can be noted that in many child guidance centres a committee that meets periodically to scrutinize and approve all applications can add delay. In Tokyo the child welfare council meets every two months for this purpose, but about 80% of CGCs hold a child welfare council only once or twice a year (Amino 2000). The requirements for evidence about the home, health and income of prospective parents are also typical, and were also generally found to be acceptable by applicants. However, in Tokyo, where it is not unusual for families to live in tiny apartments, *tatami* mat rules were sometimes criticized for setting too high a standard on the need for adequate space. The use of objective rules over the subjective views of the social worker in assessing applications is characteristic of CGC selection procedures. The parents we spoke to, however, did not necessarily describe their interviews as objective; some said that the social workers were highly opinionated, and one or two added that they had disagreed with them. However, even where the parents and social workers ended up positively disliking each other, this was not an obstacle to registration where the objective criteria had been met.

After Mrs Tanaka and her husband had registered to be foster parents they went away from home for two months and when, after a further two months, they had still heard nothing they phoned and asked what was going on. The CGC social worker responded 'Just because you've registered with us it doesn't mean that we will offer you a child. Go and try another agency.' The couple had indeed already approached the Loving Hands agency and applied, unsuccessfully, for an advertised child. However, a week or so after the phone call, the CGC offered a three-month-old boy to the couple.

Two case workers and an infant home nurse made an appointment to visit the house. Ostensibly this was to discuss the child, although when they arrived they were not all that informative about him. They had not brought any photographs with them, and when Mrs Tanaka asked 'Why does the baby need to be adopted?' she got only the vaguest response about how he was in an institution for economic reasons and no explanation for why he had been singled out for adoption. The caseworkers' real purpose was to invite the couple to come straight to the infant home to meet the baby. The couple accepted this invitation, went immediately by car to meet their prospective son, and found him to be very sweet.

After this initial meeting, the couple visited the baby boy frequently in the infant's home for the next six weeks before taking him home as his foster parents. Like all foster parents, Mrs Tanaka and her husband were paid quite generous fees and expenses by their prefecture as well as being given start-up costs, this money being based on nationally agreed rates for foster carers. A CGC social worker paid three monthly visits to the family to assess the placement. The parents were then told that the CGC would support their court application when they had completed a six month period as foster carers.

Several aspects of this next stage in the couple's progress toward being adoptive parents are typical. Being offered a baby is not unusual; many children made available for adoption in Japan are given up at birth by their mothers. Once Mrs Tanaka and her husband had said that they had no preference as to the sex of their child, it was predictable that they would be offered a boy: most adoptive parents ask for a girl, so boys are placed at every opportunity.[16] A three month old boy is younger than average as child guidance centres often look after children given up at birth for several months or a year in infant homes before offering them for adoption. The rationale for this delay is partly to give the birth mother time to reconsider her decision and partly because it allows the CGC to make health checks on the baby.

Arranging a meeting between the child and potential parents at an early stage, before the parents have made a commitment to adopt, appears to be an invariable practice amongst CGCs. The period of six weeks between visiting the child in an infant home and taking them home is about average. This transition is normally phased so that the parents look after the child overnight and then for a weekend before taking them home permanently.

Applying to the family court

For most parents, applying to the court to adopt the child they are fostering and then having the child's name recorded on the family register is a swift and straight-forward process, with successful applications generally resolved within months. This is confirmed by a survey in which Loving Hands asked legal adopters how long they waited from the time they submitted their initial application to the courts to the court's decision. Of the 101 parents who responded 14 said the decision was made in 2 months or less; 38 in 3–5 months; 36 in six months to a year; 12 in one to two years, and only one in over two years (Kateiyôgo 1995: 13). For a minority of parents, however, the court application can be a fraught process and the outcome uncertain. The difficulties that can occur at this stage vary considerably; sometimes there is an issue over the consent of the birth parents; sometimes there are other legal difficulties, particularly when an adoption has a foreign element; sometimes punctilious attitudes on the part of officials are unhelpful. But problems and worries for adoptive parents are also caused for an apparently trivial reason: the trepidation that parents feel toward having specific details of the adoption recorded in official documentation.

There are a number of reasons why an adoptive parent may be perturbed by official records of the adoption. They may be worried that address details will enable the child to contact the birth parents, or the birth parents contact the family. In the Loving Hands questionnaire, 52% of parents expressed concern that the written court decision included the home address of birth and adoptive parents. Some parents may want to avoid documentation of the adoption because of a wish to conceal it from the child. In the same questionnaire, 59% said that they thought it best to tell the child that they were adopted, but only 28% had actually done so (Kateiyôgo 1995: 28–9). Concerns about social attitudes can also play a part, as the adoption is being entered into in a society where conservative and naturalistic views about the inheritance of character are widespread. The parents themselves will probably hold these views to some degree, although those who complete a special adoption are more willing than most to believe that each individual has their own distinct identity and will respond positively to a loving upbringing. However, even if adoptive parents are at ease in their own minds when they consider the influence of a child's genetic inheritance, other members of society may still stigmatize a child placed in a special adoption as having 'bad' blood. Apprehension about societal discrimination, therefore, provides a further reason to try and limit information contained in official records of the adoption.

In accordance with CGC guidance and the Civil Code, Mrs Tanaka and her husband spent their six-month period as foster parents before making a court application to adopt the child (Civil Code Article 817, 8; Jidôsôdansyo 2005: Ch. 6, 3 (2); Ministry of Foreign Affairs 2001: 193). When this period expired, the couple applied to the family court, which sent a representative to visit them on two or three occasions. These visits satisfied the court that the placement was successful. But despite the support of the CGC for the adoption and the court's own corroboration that the placement was satisfactory, the couple's application to legalize the adoption was much more protracted than the initial placement. The courts had taken up the case nine months into the initial foster placement, a typical timeline (Kateiyôgo 1995: 6–7). From this point on, however, the case became unusually protracted. It took a further year and four months before Mrs Tanaka and her husband were finally allowed to adopt their son.

When a couple apply for a special adoption the questions that are usually posed by a family court concern why the parents want to adopt; their relations with the child and with each other; the attitude of relatives; the occupation, income and property of the couple, and the circumstances of the child (Kateiyôgo 1995: 11). In this case however, there were other problematic issues. The first problem with the adoption was the international marriage of the parents. Thus far, the fact that Mrs Tanaka's husband was a foreigner had not caused any difficulties. There was, for example, no suggestion that the couple would be notified only when a child of a similar ethnic mix to themselves was available. When the application came to court, however, the nationality of the father meant that the adoption was classified as an international one. In Japan an international adoption is defined very broadly. It includes not only circumstances in which a child living in one state is adopted by parents in another, but also domestic adoptions where either of the adoptive parents or the child is defined as a foreigner. This is true even if the child is born in Japan (to foreign parents), or if the adoptive parent is a long term resident. As a general rule (there are exceptions discussed in Ch. 7) international adoption can only go ahead if the court is satisfied that it is in accordance with both Japanese law and the law in the home state of the foreign national. A mixed or foreign couple do not actually have to go through the assessment process of the foreign state to satisfy this requirement, but they do have to show that there is nothing that would disbar the adoption in that state.

After a time-consuming investigation, the court eventually decided that the adoption was allowed under the law of the father's home state. However, before the adoption could go ahead, a second problem had to be resolved. This was the lack of explicit consent to the adoption by the birth mother. The child had been born to parents in the process of divorce. The mother had left the family home soon after her son's birth, and had not been in contact since. The father had given his consent to the adoption but the mother, because she had gone missing, had not.

There is a significant distinction in Japan between a parent that *abandons* a child and a parent that goes *missing*. A child's prospects for adoption or foster care as opposed to institutional care can often hang on this distinction, so that where a potential adoptive parent gains an interest in the child, the definition of what constitutes abandonment by a birth parent is liable to be contested. Roughly speaking, a 'missing' parent leaves the child in the care of other adults and then disappears without explanation, and an 'abandoning' parent leaves the child without care, for example, on the street. Parental rights over an abandoned child are vested with the director of the local CGC. Abandonment, therefore, means that the parent has forfeited their right to having any authority over the child. By contrast, if a parent is defined as missing, they retain parental rights and the courts are reluctant to assume that by their actions they have given implicit consent for adoption. It is possible, under the Civil Code (Article 817, 6), to dispense with parental consent if it harms the interests of the child (Nakayama and Kaneko: 1999). However, the courts tend to have a conservative bias in favour of formal parental authority and may be unwilling to take this step until several years have passed. Such problems affect a significant proportion of children in care. For example, about a third of the children that Loving Hands attempts to place are either abandoned or have missing parents. Twelve per cent are literally abandoned on the street or in a toilet; 7% are left in the care of other adults before the mother disappears, and 15% come from parents who leave their children at an institution before disappearing. These latter children are in a particularly difficult position because the parents are defined as 'missing', and the courts in Osaka are unwilling to allow children in institutional care to be adopted until they have spent more than three years without a single parental visit.

Let us return to the Tanaka case. To determine the wishes of the 'missing' mother, the family court sent letters to various possible addresses. All were returned with the message that no one of the mother's name lived there. Finally the court sent a letter that did not come back. The court interpreted this to mean that the mother lived at this address and had received the letter. By not replying to the letter, she indicated that she had given implicit consent for the adoption to go ahead. The judges relayed this good news to the couple and concluded by telling them that they could adopt the child. The judges said that they would set down a full written judgement describing the child's background and the reasons for their decision. Then, all that the parents needed to do to complete the adoption was to place a copy of the judgement with their family register. And there, one might think, the process ended. In fact it did not, as the requirement to file the full judgement with the family register, or *koseki,* greatly upset Mrs Tanaka, who appealed against the decision.

The koseki

A *koseki* is an official document held in a public registration office that records details of family members. It is a combination of a birth certificate, marriage certificate and a short family tree. This sounds innocuous, but these formal family records have encouraged the retention of attitudes towards the importance of heritage and ancestry even after the *ie* has been formally abandoned. For more traditionally minded citizens the lineage laid down in a *koseki*, both their own and other people's, is of great significance. In theory the *koseki* is a confidential document accessible only to the family members it records and those with a 'fair reason' to look at it (Yonekura 1998: 10–11). Somehow, however, others get to see it too.[17] Those who may be occasionally interested in looking at someone's *koseki* include employers making hiring decisions. They also include potential marriage partners, who maintain the tradition detailed by Tanizaki (1958) of making extensive investigations into their future spouse. Both employers and future marriage partners sometimes employ private detectives to undertake this task. Conversely, those who are in danger of being stigmatized, including members of the *buraku* community in Japan, may go to considerable lengths to hide the background revealed in their *koseki* by multiple shifts in residency (Hayashida 1976: 141, 193–4).

We can now begin to see why Mrs Tanaka objected to the full judgement being placed in the *koseki*. If a *koseki* reveals not only the fact that a child has been adopted but also describes the background to an adoption, this may create a disadvantage for the adoptee in both work and marriage. Furthermore, a child is allowed to look at their own *koseki* and so may learn sensitive details of their background, or in some cases discover for the first time that they have been adopted. For these reasons, Japanese adoptive parents generally want as few details as possible about an adoption placed with a *koseki*, and ideally no details at all.

Just as adoptive parents, like Mrs Tanaka, want few or no details of an adoption to appear on their *koseki*, so birth mothers would rather that the child's record did not appear on *their koseki*. A birth mother's understandable wish to keep private details of the birth is accentuated by the stigma bearing an illegitimate child. The child's record on the *koseki* may attach shame to the mother and reduce her marriage prospects. One of the advantages of the covert adoptions that special adoptions were meant to replace was that the child appeared to be the natural offspring of the adoptive parents and left no record on the birth mother's *koseki*. Thus, when special adoption was proposed, Kikuta wanted the law to take account of the interests and feelings of birth mothers as well as children and adoptive parents; he contended that the official *koseki* record should be similar to the false record in illicit arrangements. In particular, Kikuta argued that birth mothers who placed children in a special adoption should be allowed to keep the child's record off their *koseki* (Kikuta 1987). Kikuta, however, was overruled. The ostensible argument in favour of retaining the record of a child on the birth mother's *koseki* even after the child has been placed in a special adoption is to guard against the marriage of natural siblings (Hoshii 1987: 220; Yonekura 1998: 13; Goodman 2000: 151). It has also been suggested, however, that the underlying attraction of recording the illegitimate birth of a child on the natural mother's *koseki* is its function as a punitive moral sanction (Paulson 1984: 138–9).

In the face of this problem, various stratagems are used by birth mothers and adoptive parents to try and ensure that a *koseki* provides little or no information about the child's existence (the birth mother) or their adoption (the adoptive parents). The shame of a *koseki* record may help to explain the occasional actions of mothers who give birth in secret and abandon the child. Single mothers who decide to have their child legally adopted sometimes move away from their home prefecture before the birth, register the child in another prefecture and then move back and transfer a summary version of their *koseki* which omits the detailed background of the child's birth. This is expensive; a mother who gives birth in her home prefecture is subsidized, where if she travels elsewhere to have a baby she must meet the full cost of her hospital care. Adoptive parents also sometimes move house, or change their *honseki* (their original *koseki* registry) as a method of obscuring the *koseki* record (Kateiyôgo 1995: 14–15).

Mrs Tanaka and her husband were unusual in that they entered into a legal controversy to try and minimize the information on the *koseki*. They told the family court that they wanted a summary judgement only and that there was a precedent that gave them the right to insist upon this. They added that to get their way they were prepared to go all the way to the supreme court. This last action was not as dramatic as it sounded; the couple did indeed approach the supreme court by writing them a letter stating their case and asking for an authoritative opinion. While awaiting the reply, the local family court relented and said that it would supply a summary judgement. At the last minute the local *koseki* registration office, which had sided with the court's original decision, also acceded to Mrs Tanaka and said that it would accept a summary judgement. A few days later, the office of the supreme court replied to the letter: the question raised by the couple was an interesting one, it said, but they did not know the answer.[18]

While this dispute was taking place, there was a tight timescale (10 days) to place the judgement from the family court with the office of the *koseki*. If this transfer were not completed in time, the judgement would be invalidated and the parents would have to start again. On the final day, Mrs Tanaka took the papers to the registration office, which had at last agreed to take the summary judgement; her husband did not attend as he was away on business. An official scrutinized the documents and noticed a problem on one of the accompanying forms. The adoptive father had typed out his full name, including his middle name. But when he had signed, *he had left his middle name out.* This was unacceptable. And where was the husband?

'Don't worry,' said Mrs Tanaka. She took the form back from the official, went around the corner, signed her husband's middle name, and returned it. No problem.

Part of the rationale for special adoption is that it follows legal and open arrangements to replace covert and illicit transfers of children. Adoptive parents like Mrs Tanaka, however, while they want to act within the law also want to try and keep the adoptions as secret as possible. Mrs Tanaka held modern, liberal attitudes. She had, for example, forsaken the traditional *omiai* system of arranged marriage to wed a foreigner.[19] But when it came to the welfare of her son, she tempered liberalism with the pragmatic realization that adoption could lead to social discrimination from some of the more conservative members of society. This created a tension over the openness of the adoption. The more that an adoption becomes public knowledge, the greater the chance that not only the adoption itself but also the details of the child's background will become known to people who may then use this information to discriminate against the adoptee. Employers or potential marriage partners who illicitly read the information contained in an adoptee's *koseki*, exemplify such difficulties.

The terms of the debate over how open a special adoption should be, are confined largely to whether the adoption should be acknowledged and explained to the child, to friends and to neighbours. Being open about an adoption does not include continued contact with the birth parents. One of the purposes behind the creation of a special adoption was to provide for circumstances where there would be a complete break with the birth parents and this presumption still shapes special adoption practice. This can be contrasted with ordinary adoptions where birth parents and adoptive parents often know and deal directly with each other and where there are not the same imperatives to secrecy. Where a judge believes that there is no need to sever all contact with the birth parents, a special adoption application may be rejected. In one case a child whose natural parents were married was cared for by her uncle and aunt after her mother had died two days after giving birth and her father, who worked irregular hours, was unable to care for her. The uncle and aunt wanted a special adoption but the judge only allowed an ordinary adoption, reasoning that there was no need for the girl to cut her ties with the birth father (Tamura 1996: 202–4). In a second case, a child was conceived in an affair and given over for an adoption to a doctors association. However, the natural father, who earned quite a high income, then divorced and married the natural mother. The adoptive parents tried to turn the ordinary adoption into a special adoption as it would be easier to conceal on the *koseki*. The judge rejected the application, arguing that there was no need for the child to cut all ties with the birth parents who were married, well off, and who had never been abusive (Tamura 1996: 204–7). Nonetheless, there may occasionally be some indirect contact after special adoption. This has been advocated by Kirino (1998), is encouraged as a matter of policy by the Motherly Network and is arranged on a case-by-case basis by some CGCs and private agencies.

Custody disputes

In a straightforward legal adoption the birth parents agree to the placement. The main problem in the case of Mrs Tanaka was that the child's birth mother was missing, and this made the courts reluctant to assume that she had consented to the adoption or had forfeited her right to a say on the matter. There are also cases, however, when the birth mother may explicitly oppose an adoption. Child guidance centres rarely forcibly remove children from their natural parents for fostering and adoption, so that it is unusual to find birth parents fighting to regain custody from the outset of a placement.[20] Nonetheless, custody disputes sometimes occur where a birth mother changes her mind, or where an absent birth mother reappears after a child has been fostered but before they have been legally adopted.

If a birth mother who has been missing gets into contact with the courts and states that she is opposed to a special adoption, her objections are likely to be upheld and the foster parent's application turned down. However, even if an adoption application is rejected, there are three further ways in which the child can legally remain in the care of the foster parents. One method is through an ordinary adoption. A birth mother who opposes the complete severing of ties in a special adoption might be persuaded to agree to an ordinary adoption in its place. This option might seem little different from a special adoption insofar as the day-to-day care of the child will rest with the adoptive parents. However, an ordinary adoption keeps the ties of inheritance between birth parents and child. Thus, in a case in Niigita prefecture, the CGC entrusted a child who had spent two years in an institution to foster parents who hoped to turn the placement into a special adoption. The birth mother objected to the entrustment and adoption plans. Although the mother did not want to take daily care of the child, which was both financially and mentally difficult for her, she took the long view that she wanted the child to somehow stay a part of her family line. The dispute was resolved when the birth mother agreed to an ordinary adoption in which the child would inherit property from the birth mother and at least some of the original family connection was retained.

The two further options for the foster parents to be the legal carers for a child that they cannot adopt, are (a) for them to ensure that they continue to be entrusted with the child, or (b) to gain custody of the child. When a child guidance centre places a child with foster parents, it entrusts them with the child. The foster parents, however, do not gain rights through entrustment, which the CGC can withdraw at any time. If a birth mother objects to the entrustment, then the CGC has to decide whether to accept her objections, or whether to go to the courts to argue that she should lose her parental rights over the child. If the courts agree with the CGC, then the child can remain entrusted to the care of the foster parents. Custody gives foster carers parental power over a child, excluding only the management of the child's property. Conflicting legal judgements leave open the question of whether or not foster parents have the right to apply for custody to the family court. If the court agrees to hear the foster parents' application and approves it, the foster parents have the right to bring up a child even though the child is not adopted.

Custody and entrustment were issues in a case that was fought out in several courts in 1994–5. A baby girl was placed in an infant home by her mother and visited only very rarely. At the age of two the Osaka CGC entrusted the child to the care of parents in Yamagata prefecture, who fostered the child with a view to adoption. The birth mother had agreed to fostering in writing, but had only made a verbal agreement to have the child adopted. After the child was placed she briefly said she wanted the child back, but then disappeared. The foster parents wanted to apply to the court to adopt the child after six months but were told to wait by the CGC. Three years later the birth mother reappeared with a lawyer and demanded her daughter back. The CGC responded by changing the status of the foster parents from fostering with a view to adoption to temporary fostering. The CGC also arranged a meeting where the birth mother asked for and was told the address of the foster parents; she then contacted them saying that she was going to take the child. As the court would probably turn down an adoption application that was opposed by the birth mother, the foster parents applied instead for custody; the birth mother filed a counter lawsuit for the return of the child.

The family court argued that its prime purpose was to protect the child's interests. This purpose, according to the court, allowed it to include foster parents amongst those who were able to apply for custody rights. The CGC supported the petition of the foster parents on the grounds that as they had brought up the child for more than three years, they should continue to raise her. The court accepted that this solution was in the best interests of the child and awarded custody to the foster parents.

The birth mother appealed to the high court. The high court argued that it was not its role to take the welfare of the child into consideration, but only to uphold the integrity of the law in technical decisions. This led the court to interpret the law on custody more narrowly than the family court. The high court found that the family court had exceeded its authority in accepting the custody petition from the foster parents; only the birth parents of a child could file a lawsuit for custody. On this basis, the high court overturned the family court decision. The court did not, however, order that the child be immediately handed over to the birth mother as she had asked. It merely said, rather vaguely, that if there was a real problem, then the CGC could follow procedures to resolve it. It did not specify what these procedures were, nor identify what the CGC was permitted to do.

The foster parents appealed to the child guidance centre to support their application for a special adoption. The child guidance centre decided instead to cancel the entrustment of the child to the foster parents. Decision making hierarchies of state institutions in Japan are not always clear-cut and rely to some extent upon the norm of seeking consensus between institutions and an emphasis on seeing decisions as following from the logic of the situation. In this case, the CGC's cancellation was not directly ordered by the high court, but was a course of action taken on its own initiative. The stated reason was that the birth mother had never abused the child, and so there was no reason not to return her.

The foster parents, although still caring for the child, now had no right to her. The birth mother successfully filed a lawsuit for the return of the child in the local court. The foster parents, who from the time of the child's placement at the age of two had looked after her for four years and three months, were forced to give her up.[21]

Unavoidable problems

The process of special adoption through a child guidance centre is generally efficient, objective, and not unduly onerous for adoptive parents. But however rational the framework, the attempt to place children in need of adoption can still create a variety of problems. Adoption is not a mechanistic process; the beliefs, feelings and circumstances of adopters, birth parents, judges, child guidance centres and members of society can cause obstacles to the extent of bringing an adoption to a halt, or preventing it altogether.

Societal attitudes towards adoption are ambivalent. On the surface, the value of finding a home for a needy child is recognized. Beneath the surface, discriminatory attitudes towards anyone with 'bad blood' persist. The distinction between good and bad blood is tied via the notion of bloodlines to a bias towards natural families. These societal attitudes, although generally hidden, may have a dampening affect on a couple's decision to seek an adoption, and certainly cause anxiety to prospective adoptive parents like Mrs Tanaka and her husband. Prospective adoptive parents may themselves hold some of the same mixed feelings that are found in society, although they must have enough liberal optimism for the potential of a child to counter conservative caution, or they would not put themselves forward to adopt.

The courts are in a position of some ambiguity. In the post-war reform of the Japanese legal system, the courts were assigned to perform a liberal role in a conservative society by upholding individual rights. The instincts of judges, however, are generally rather conservative. If they are going to uphold individual rights, therefore, they tend to have a bias in favour of the natural family. The conservatism of the courts in upholding the authority of the natural family is suggested by their reluctance to authorize adoptions when parents are missing, by the ultimate success of the birth mother in reclaiming her child in the Yamagata foster parent case, and the low number of cases each year where birth parents have their custody rights legally revoked.[22] These mixed feelings towards adoption can create obstacles to placement and dilemmas for agencies that are doing their best to place as many children as they can. Perhaps the most serious problem is how to find a new family for a child in a category that is little sought after by prospective parents. The comparative difficulty of placing older children is as true for Japan as it is elsewhere. Furthermore, the widespread attitudes that place stress on blood and ancestry have contributed to highly restrictive views by many potential adoptive parents as to the type of child they are willing to adopt. The preference for girls over boys has also been noted and parents also attach considerable importance to a child's appearance and demeanour.

Agencies also face a series of dilemmas in how to relate to adoptive parents, to birth parents and to the courts. When adoptive parents approach an agency, how far should an agency be prepared to be supportive and responsive to their wishes, and how far should it insist that parents accept its own adoption philosophy? Should the agency, for example, encourage parents to be open about adoption rather than secretive, or to consider a wider range of children, and if so, how? An agency is faced with the question of whether it should ever attempt to forcibly remove a child from birth parents. It sometimes faces the question of how long it should wait before giving up on missing parents. Where the birth mother voluntarily relinquishes her child, there is always the possibility that she will later change her mind. What should be done then? The relationship between the agency and the courts also involves complex choices. Should the agency align itself with the conservative position that tends to be taken by the courts? Should it ever try to circumvent or force the hand of the courts? The following chapters look at how a variety of agencies deal with these issues. They begin with an examination of how Loving Hands tries to influence the way that prospective parents think about adoption.

3   Loving Hands

Kateiyôgo sokushin kyôkai, known in English as Loving Hands or the Association for the Advancement of Family Care, is a fostering and adoption agency established in the early 1960s in Osaka and Kobe. The agency office in Osaka is provided with the details of about 50 children per year by the Osaka CGC and the Kobe office deals with about 40 children a year from the Kobe CGC. Four local authorities, namely Kobe City, Hyôgo Prefecture, Osaka City and Osaka Prefecture contribute about 20% of its finance, with the rest coming from donations, membership fees and fundraising activities (Kateiyôgo 2004). The collaboration with the CGCs and service agreements with local authorities gives the agency a quasi-public status, part-way between a state-run child guidance centre and a private adoption agency. The quasi-official status of the voluntary organization is in keeping with other institutions in Japan that blur the boundaries between state and society (Neary 2003). These include volunteer welfare commissioners (*minsei i'in*) about 15,000 of whom have child welfare as their principal responsibility (Takahashi 2003: 104). In the area of adoption, however, the position of Loving Hands is unique.

Loving Hands' organizational philosophy has a distinctive emphasis on openness and on enabling potential parents to make decisions for themselves about which children to compete for. The agency shares information on the range of children available with prospective parents. It claims to tell would-be parents everything that is known about a child before the first meeting. It also advertises particular children in the public media. In its dealings with potential adopters, the agency stresses the need for them to reciprocate with openness on their part; it expects them to be candidly expressive about their feelings when they put themselves forward to be assessed. The agency also does its best to encourage adoptive parents not to keep the adoption a secret but to acknowledge the fact widely. These expectations do not always fit easily with the reserve or the desire for secrecy felt by some prospective parents, so the agency attempts to guide and encourage them to be open in stages as they go through the application process.

To make children known to prospective adopters, Loving Hands relies primarily on weekly advertisements in local papers. These advertising slots are not found elsewhere in Japan and reflect the way that Loving Hands has pursued an open policy to a greater degree than other agencies. Advertising has two purposes; to find a home for the child and to raise awareness of the opportunities for adoption amongst the public. The Osaka paper carries a photo of the child and brief details about the child, including age, and an account of character. This description is sometimes one that is frank to the extent of being off-putting with comments like 'if this girl had to fight for a toy she would not lose'. The children advertised for adoption are available singly, have no obvious special needs, and are young; their average age is about two years old.[23] When the Osaka branch has advertised all of the children on its books, it will readvertise an unplaced child in its weekly slot. The Kobe team also readvertises, but may also speculatively advertise a child in need but whom the agency considers very unlikely to be adopted, perhaps an older child, up to the age of 12, or one with special needs. Adverts for older children sometimes ask for couples who could undertake weekend fostering for a child once or twice a month. The Osaka agency almost invariably deals with special adoptions of children under six, although it occasionally attempts to place children up to the age of ten in ordinary adoptions.

Most couples who approach the agency have already obtained a certificate as foster carers. In Osaka, where many of the potential parents live, this certificate is awarded after an assessment by the Osaka Health Clinic. As in the case study in the last chapter, the assessment is based upon the objective criteria of income, home and health. In Osaka the criteria also include the length of the couple's marriage (single parents are not accepted).

When they apply to Loving Hands, the parents undergo more informal and subjective forms of assessment in group meetings and individual discussions. The discussions are aimed at ensuring that couples who apply are committed to adoption, for example, applicants are told that they must give up fertility treatment. In a series of three group meetings, the couples are observed and filmed by the staff, who are also attempting to assess their commitment to adoption. The staff are especially watchful to see whether there is a gap between the high level of commitment from the wife, and a more lukewarm or ambivalent attitude from the husband (it was only this way round). If the husband, for example, does not turn up to every meeting, this is interpreted as a negative sign. If it is thought that there is insufficient commitment by the couple, they are turned down. They are not ruled out altogether, however, but rather told to 'come again later', and they can, if they wish, start the process again.

Mainstream Japanese culture does not encourage individuals to be expressive about their feelings, added to which, the potential stigma of an adoption encourages secrecy. The Osaka agency counters this reserved culture and secrecy by requiring potential parents to be progressively more open in their feelings about adoption. The agency is also insistent that parents who go on to adopt a child should tell this fact to the child and to other adults (Iwasaki 2003). A meeting in Osaka shows this philosophy at work. Parents at the meeting are led into openness in three stages. (1) The first exercise, in which participants are split into twos to compile information about their partner, requires people to be open with a stranger, but only about relatively objective information. (2) The second step is a single-sex meeting in which men and women discuss their hopes and fears about adoption, opening up their feelings and emotions at this prospect. (3) The third step involves role-playing dialogues in front of the entire group in order to encourage a general openness after adoption. These exercises include telling the child that they have been adopted and being frank with neighbours and relatives; they are designed to stress the social benefits of being open about an adoption and to warn against the practical problems of trying to maintain secrecy.

A group meeting in Osaka

A large meeting room contains twenty-five prospective parents, ten men and fifteen women. Five women organizers are ranged around the room, one holding a video camera. This is the second gathering of a new group of prospective applicants to the Osaka branch of Loving Hands.

Ms Iwasaki, the head of the agency, introduces the meeting. 'This time *you* will have to do something. In the future you may be rivals, competing for the same child. But today you can be friends and work together'. The married couples in the circle of chairs need to be split up, she explains, and everyone thoroughly mixed. This is done through the first game in which people have to move seats if they fit a certain category.

'Move if you are over forty', Ms Iwasaki tells the group. This is a loaded instruction, as the agency attempts to find couples under that age. All but three people in the room move. The staff watch carefully.

'Move if you live with your parents'. This is another loaded question as there is a preference for adopters to have their own home. About seven people move. After a few more such questions, the seating pattern in the room has been reconfigured. The prospective parents are now told to form a couple with the person sitting next to them (one of the authors joins in to make up an even number). They are to interview their pair-partner and introduce them to the group. After a few minutes for the interview, everyone listens as, one by one, people introduce their neighbours. Most interviewers tell us the age of the person they have interviewed. This ranges from the low thirties to the low fifties, being typically in the mid-forties. Some describe the kind of child their interview-partner wants. Several people want a girl, but none explicitly want a boy. When the age of the child is mentioned, none say that they wish to adopt a child over three. Hobbies, interests and family circumstances are mentioned: several men are baseball fans, one plays the guitar and goes hiking. One woman uses the interview to explain the non-attendance of her husband: he is very busy with his accounts in this last month of the financial year. Some attendees have travelled a considerable distance to be at the meeting. Loving Hands does not limit applicants to residents of Osaka; people from all over Japan are eligible to apply to adopt children from the organization. One woman has slept overnight in her car. Another has travelled 300 miles by train from a remote region and is staying in a hotel.

The next stage divides the prospective parents into two groups, men and women. The women joke and laugh, apparently light-hearted. We listen to the men's group, where the conversation is serious and laden with concerns. Three of the men did not attend the previous week and want to find out about it. Last week, they are told, had been off-putting. The newly adopted child might have behavioural difficulties; regression to babyhood is common, so is intense jealousy; the child may even object to the wife talking to the husband. Parents will be tested by the child, and until you are trusted you must give in to their demands, for example, they will eat only a certain kind of pudding at meal times and nothing else. One man asks: 'Were any good things said last week?'

No one could think of any.

At the end of the session the men and women draw up a list of their expectations and their worries. The women have a list of ten expectations and four worries. The men strike the opposite balance, their list contains only four expectations, but ten worries.

Women's expectations

Pass on interests to the next generation

Open up the future

Parents will mature with a child

Child will be 'lubricating oil' with a mother-in-law – and stimulate conversation

It will be fun to bring up a child

Children allow you to go to fairs, and hiking as a family

See the face of a sleeping child

Have conversations with other mothers

The child will inherit the parents' way of thinking and values

A child gives life meaning.

Women's worries

The reaction of the neighbours

Telling the child that they are adopted

The physical abilities of the child

The mental abilities of the child

Men's expectations

Playing catch, if the child is a boy

The process of raising a child is interesting

Having conversations with the child

Go to places that one could not go without children

Men's worries

The reactions of the neighbours

Telling the child they are adopted.

Can the child get used to us?

The complete 180 degree change of life

Bullying at school

Truancy

The child may look for their natural parents and become distanced from their adoptive parents

Too old for a child

Lack of stamina for a child

A child who is not a birth child may make the workload of caring for them feel too much.

It is notable that the two areas that both prospective fathers and mothers identified as subjects of concern were relations with neighbours, and explaining the adoption to the child. Both of these concerns are tackled in the next activity at the meeting, role-playing about 'telling'.

Training courses in adoption in Japan tend to focus as much or more on how to deal with society as how to deal with the child. At this meeting, societal reactions are treated in the first of two role-playing games. The games are intended to reinforce the message that neighbours, relatives and the child must all be informed about an adoption. First, an agency volunteer, acting as a neighbour, persistently asks 'where is this child from?' The parents in the role-play are evasive; they are very reluctant to say that the child is adopted. Finally they tell her.

Parents: This is our child. Please don't ask for any details. We have decided to adopt. Please be caring toward this child, too.

Neighbour: Will the child be yours if the natural parents say they want it back?

Parents: We'll tell you another time.

Afterwards, the father says that he dislikes the attitude of the persistent neighbour, but he wants to tell the truth rather than to lie. The agency volunteer responds that the kind of neighbour she was playing was one who, once she realized that something was being hidden from her, would relentlessly want to find out more.

The next role playing game continues on a similar theme by looking at the reaction of relations. One couple act as vociferously hostile relatives to a second couple who have a birth child and who are thinking of adopting a second child.

Relative: You've got one. One's enough. There'll be no blood relationship.

Mother: I'm consulting you. I haven't decided yet.

Relative: Can you love that child?

Relative: You already *have* a child, it would be difficult to treat a birth child and an adopted child equally.

Relative: Two may be better than one, but you may discriminate. Once the child finds out they're adopted, you might rethink. If you have another birth child you might regret what you've done.

Mother:	Blood relations don't matter. We will pour the same love into both of them, even if the children are different.
Relative:	Could you put up with bad behaviour by a non-blood relation? And what about the money it will cost you?
Mother:	I can put up with less money. I want time to play with the child. I was an only child and had no connection with brothers and sisters. One child and two children are not the same.
Relative:	Where's the child from? You don't know!
Father:	It doesn't really matter. The child will become a member of the family. Thinking about worries won't do anything to help. Maybe we will get pregnant again, but still…
Mother:	The real parents want the child to be adopted.
Relative:	School and statistics say, 'A crime's child becomes a criminal'.

Everyone laughs at this last statement. Afterwards, the couple who played the hostile relatives explain that they were simply repeating exactly what they were told by *their* relatives.

The child becomes the focus of the third role-playing game, telling a teenager. Here too, the social responses to adoption are incorporated into the game, this time in the context of school. A young agency volunteer assumes the role of a fourteen-year-old discovering for the first time that she is adopted.

Teenager:	Where is my *boshi techô* [medical record]?[24]
Mother:	I must tell you the truth. I could not get pregnant. I haven't told you, but we decided to bring you up.
Teenager:	So I have other parents? You have not said so for fourteen years.
Mother:	We thought it better not to tell.
Teenager:	I feel strange. Did my real parents abandon me? Why? I have no baby photos. Why? What will I do about show-and-tell at school, about being a baby?
Mother:	We though you would be happier not knowing.
Teenager:	My friend always shows me lots of photos. I feel a bit betrayed. Father, say something. Have you met the parents? I want to meet my parents, to find out why I was abandoned. They might be younger than you, and look similar to me.
Mother:	You could see them, but we have brought you up as our real child.
Teenager:	I understand, but did I say that I *wanted* to be your child?
Mother:	We really liked you to choose you.
Teenager:	Were there others?
Mother:	Yes, but you were the best.
Teenager:	You thought I was sweet?
Father:	I will tell the teacher.
Mother:	We will borrow relatives' photos [of their baby and pass them off as you to your schoolmates].
Teenager:	I am shocked. Can I ask more?

The game serves as a warning not to keep the adoption secret. In the following discussion the agency workers emphasize that it is impossible to conceal an adoption, and that parents should tell children before they become teenagers and begin to question the gaps in the records of their early life.[25] This leads to the next role playing game: starting to explain adoption to a young child. In this game Ms Iwasaki, the agency head, pretends to be an adopted child of four.

Child: [cries] Am I your child?
Mother: When you were little, you had another mother. My tummy was hurting. Your real mother passed away. My tummy can't get bigger.
Child: Who are my parents?
Mother: Dead.
Child: Where did you find me?
Mother: Osaka. Ask your father when you're older.
Child: Where am I from?
Father: I was in bed that day and can't remember.
Child: Tell me the truth.
Father: When you're older we'll explain.
Child: Why adopt me?
Father: You were sweet.
Child: How? Where was I?
Father: Osaka.
Child: The zoo? I remember, I think, were there lots of children there? I sometimes dream of lots of other children. Are there lots of people without mothers? Why me?
Mother: We were happy.
Child: How happy?
Mother: After you came, the house felt very bright.
Child: What dress did I wear?
Mother: Jeans. We picked you up by car.
Child: What about the sweet bit?

Afterwards, Ms Iwasaki explains that children might want to be reassured about how sweet they are. In a society where great emphasis is placed upon having a cute (*kawaii*) child, this may be a sensitive topic.

With the role playing over, there is a further presentation by the agency head. She stresses that adopted children are apt to be demanding, particularly of the mother. Some children, she adds, come out from the futon bedding and pretend that they have been born from the mother. The meeting then closes with final comments from the would-be parents. Many express concerns about the difficulties of adoption, and some are disheartened. In particular, women who have attended alone say that they will need to discuss things further with their husbands. They have ascertained correctly that unless their husbands attend the meetings too, their chances of being offered a child are small. Other parents continue to express optimism, although only one explains why he has been positively encouraged by the meeting: a man who after the shared discussion with other men feels more confident that he could cope with an adoption.

There were several breaks during the meeting, and during the first of these periods, the prospective parents had been told, rather casually, that they were free to go over to the corner of the room where there were photos of twenty one children. All were either babies or toddlers at the time of the photo. All appeared healthy. Some had mild squints, others were indubitably cute in appearance. The attendees were told that none of the children had been adopted for two years (this was actually a slight exaggeration) and that if they were interested in any of them, then they should say so.

In conversation with Ms Iwasaki after the meeting we asked whether she anticipated that the prospective parents would enquire after many of the children shown in the photos. She said no. In any event, she added, most of the attendees at the meeting were too old. The agency strove to ensure that there was no more than a forty-year age gap between parents and children. Older parents who stayed with the agency might, if they had strong support from relatives, be offered a child of about six.

Advertising and matching

When Loving Hands places a weekly advert in the paper for a child, prospective parents who are already approved as foster parents and probably already registered with the agency will make contact to express an interest. Those who are deemed suitable potential adopters are invited in for a discussion. Body language as well as the declared feelings of the parents are closely scrutinized at this meeting. When the couple attend in the office, they are given a portfolio of photographs of the child to look through. The agency staff watch for parents who give an excited, delighted response, taking up the photographs with *loving hands*, passing them eagerly back and forth between one another. These parents, it is hoped, will be loving parents. The open display of emotion is a crucial step in the matching process.

Placement of the child follows the pattern in the case study of Mrs Tanaka and her husband. The initial placement is made on a fostering basis. After the minimum period of six months the parents can apply to the family court to become adoptive parents. In the interim period, the agency conducts a home study and makes a recommendation to the child guidance centre. Strong recommendations are always accepted by the child guidance centre, weak 'recommendations' may lead to the child being taken from the parents and returned to an institution before being advertised again.

The Kobe Branch of Loving Hands is a largely autonomous agency and follows policies that differ from Osaka in some respects. It uses a weekly advertising slot in the local newspaper, *Kobe Shinbun*, and a ten-minute radio broadcast to make children known to prospective parents. (The Osaka branch uses a newspaper but not the radio.) It then makes an initial assessment of the expressions of interest

あなたの愛の手を

1859回

せいやちゃん　　8歳男児

小学校の体操服姿で現れたせいやちゃん。緊張からか少し落ち着かない様子だが、笑うとほっぺにできるえくぼがなんともかわいらしい。

三年生。「何の科目が好き?」「ん…、体育」。「すごく照れ屋さんなんですよ」と担当職員。授業参観に職員が行ったときは、うれしい半面、恥ずかしさで机の下に頭を隠してしまったそう。

マイペースで、興味があることにじっくりと取り組む。最近夢中なのが、職員からもらったクワガタ。虫かごをじっと眺めたり、昆虫図鑑に見入ったりしている。

身長一三〇㌢、体重二七㌔。生後十カ月のころに施設へ預けられた。休日に家へ帰っていく友人を見ると、時折、職員に「オレもどこかに帰りたい」ともらしている。月に一、二回家庭に迎えてくれる週末里親を求めている。

【寄託】橘千草（三千円）▽ポポニの仲間達（二千円）▽中山（三千円）▽谷義信（一万円）▽H一同（五千円）▽たぶち（一万円）＝敬称略

申し込み　月～金曜の午前九時から午後五時まで、下記の電話番号で受け付け。里親には養育・教育費の一部が公費で支給されます。ラジオ関西は毎週日曜日の午前六時から「里親さがしの時間」を放送しています。

せいやちゃんの作品

・・・・・事務局から

先日、滋賀県で開催された近畿地区里親研修会に参加してきました。私が参加した分科会では、成人した里子や養子もコメンテーターとして参加し、思春期のかかわりや真実告知について意見が交わされました。

その中で、里子が「家族とは何か」と問われたときに、「血はつながっていなくても、安心できる場所、ホッとできる場所」と答えたことが印象的でした。参加者は里子や養子からの生の声に耳を傾け、その思いに共感していました。

（M）

家庭養護促進協会
〒650-0016　神戸市中央区橘通３－４－１
神戸市総合福祉センター２階
☎078・341・5046　http://www5f.biglobe.ne.jp/~ainote

Figure 3.1 A picture by the child illustrates an advertisement for foster parents

Source: *Kobe Shinbun* 21 June 2004.

The advertisement describes Seiya, an eight-year-old boy with cheeks that dimple when he smiles. He enjoys PE, is shy, is interested in stag beetles and reads an insect encyclopedia.

received and rules out all but one or two. Some couples will be rejected on grounds that may also rule them out for other children, such as ones who are considered too old. Other couples who are rejected for the child they apply for, may be asked whether they are interested in any other children. For example, one couple who were turned down in their application for a three-month-old baby girl, adopted a 9-month-old baby boy that they were offered (Kateiyôgo 2005: 55).

Applicants who are provisionally matched with a child are given a home study to evaluate their suitability as adopters. The majority of applicants pass the home study assessment, although a significant minority are rejected. Reasons for rejecting parents appear to be based on experience and intuition. Couples may be turned down if it is felt that there is a bad relationship between them, or that they are liable to be abusive, or that they show a lack of love. Prospective parents do not need to be married to adopt through the Kobe agency in an ordinary adoption, although single parents are placed at the bottom of the list for a child. The agency only accepts parental applicants from Hyôgo, the prefecture that incorporates Kobe. This restriction is attributed partly to the exigencies of the local financing of the organization, partly out of concern at the varying standards required to be registered as foster parents in other prefectures, and partly to area-pride in looking after one's own.

Kobe asks a journalist to write the copy for the child. The description gives no mention of why the child has to be adopted or fostered, rather it concentrates on how they are growing up and tries to make them sound as attractive as possible. Younger children have their photographs included. However, once the child goes to school, classmates may notice the image and stigmatize the child. The agency does not, therefore, show the child's photo in the paper, but rather illustrates the advert with a picture that the child has created. Loving Hand's philosophy of openness does not extend to a child's peers and this method of advertising, which does not compromise confidentiality, may be advantageous for a less photogenic child. The picture allows would-be parents to imagine something of the child's personality in a way that is arguably more revealing than a photograph. Impressed by a picture drawn by a child with Down's syndrome, one couple decided to apply to become foster parents (Kateiyôgo 2001: 92).

Popular and unpopular children

All children without parents to care for them are in equal need of a loving family. However, they are not equally adoptable. Some categories of children, such as healthy babies, are popular with parents, while others, for example older or disabled children, are much less appealing. Japanese adoptive parents have marked preferences with respect to the age, sex and appearance of a child; they prefer younger children to older children, they prefer girls to boys, and they prefer children to look sweet. In Ms Iwasaki's experience of advertising children in Osaka, a good picture of a little girl would always bring in the highest number of responses. By contrast, a child who did not photograph so well, even a very young child, was not guaranteed to elicit a response.

The Kobe agency receives about 300 applications over the course of the year for the 40 or so children that it advertises. Over 250 of these applicants will come from adults already approved as foster carers. The experience in Kobe bears out the Agency Head's observations in Osaka; applications are skewed, with girls under three being the most popular category, and older boys sometimes eliciting no response. The bias in applications helps to explain why, despite an apparent excess of parents, only about half of the children that are advertised each year are placed.

Potential parents not only discriminate in favour of younger children, sweet-looking children and girls, but also draw a marked distinction between an acceptable and an unacceptable family background. They are willing to adopt children of teenage mothers, single mothers and the children of affairs, but generally do not want children born to parents who have mental health problems, or who are drug addicts. This distinction between an acceptable and unacceptable background has some rationale on health grounds. Illegitimacy, which is acceptable, carries a social stigma but does not carry health risks, whilst mental health and drug taking raise concerns either about a child's genetic inheritance or about the lasting effects of narcotics transmitted in the womb.

The shared preferences of adoptive parents create a hierarchy of categories of children. Some excite intense competition, while others elicit no response.

The child who has evoked the greatest response to a Loving Hands advertisement in Osaka was a three-year-old girl whose parents had died in a car crash. From the perspective of adoptive parents, the little girl's tragic background was ideal, and one hundred and fifty couples were interested in adopting her. The problem for placing such a child, one who embodies all the right qualities, is of being spoilt for choice in making a match. But what of children who are less attractive to potential parents? A fundamental problem is how to place children who, at least at the outset, are less appealing because they fall short of parents' preconceptions of an ideal child. Loving Hands, like all adoption agencies that venture beyond the placement of healthy babies, is faced with this difficulty.

One notable response to the problem of the hard-to-place child, is the attempt by the Kobe branch of Loving Hands to get parents to assess the child as an individual rather than as part of a category. A child's sex, appearance and background are categories based on their biological and family heritage rather than characteristics that reflect how the child has developed as an individual. If parents can go beyond these general qualities to appreciate the individual qualities of a child, this offers one way around the problem of the initial negative categorization of a child. The weekly adoption advertisement in Kobe aims to help potential parents view the available children as unique individuals rather than as more or less desirable categories. The advertisement's stress on the development and personality of the child, and its silence about the child's background is designed to lead parents to think of the child as an individual. Picturing works of art by children rather than their photo also substitutes an individual trait: a child's creativity, for an inherited category, the child's appearance, which is liable to be viewed in terms of its 'cuteness'.

Loving Hands in Osaka highlighted hard-to-place children in its corner display of their photos at the group meeting. But as Ms Iwasaki told us, this display was unlikely to evoke a response. We were surprised by this – and are still puzzled by it – as the children included sweet looking girls. However, one set of potential parents shared their feelings over the display with us, alerting us to at least some of the difficulties involved in placing these children.

Decision making by prospective parents

A month after the meeting for prospective parents in Osaka we spoke to one of the couples that had been there. They had found the organization over the Internet and had registered with them after the father had attended what he described as a rather cold interview with off-putting questions. The couple assumed that this interview was an initial weeding-out technique used by the agency. They had been told that because of their age they were unable to adopt a child under five. However, they had just sent in an application for a three-year-old girl advertised in the paper and were waiting to hear about the result.

We asked about the children whose photos had been displayed in the corner of the room during the group meeting; why had they not applied for them? The mother explained:

> There were so many parents there, we thought that it might be very competitive, because the children were displayed for everyone to see. And then we are quite old to be parents and those children were very young, so we thought we might be rejected.

This reasoning, we pointed out, was rather odd. The children were displayed to all the couples at the meeting, but a child in a newspaper has a much larger audience so that the competition to adopt them is potentially greater. Further, the photos were obviously out of date as the children had been said to be available for adoption for at least two years, but some of the images were of babies. It was possible, therefore, that they might not have been considered too old for at least some of the children. The couple looked at each other and laughed.

> As a matter of fact, the child we are applying for *had* been advertised in the meeting. She was one of the children in the photos, but we did not apply for her at that time. We felt that the children in the corner must have had something very wrong in their backgrounds to be left-over after two years. If we had asked about only *one* child, then we would have felt obliged to follow through with our enquiry and apply to adopt them. But then we felt that we could not go pointing to each one asking 'What's wrong with that one?'

There are at least three ways of interpreting the couple's reasoning. (1) Taking a decision to ask about a child in a break from a public meeting is very different from applying for a child in private. This may be either because potential parents do not wish to take such a momentous decision in hurried public circumstances, or that the group dynamics are not conducive to parents coming forward. Afterwards, perhaps, the opportunity is seen to have passed. (2) A child who is part of a group display of hard-to-place children is stigmatized, where the same child advertised on their own loses that stigma. (3) A parent finds it difficult to calculate which child to ask for when faced with a photographic display. The series of photos on the wall implicitly invites potential parents to choose a child through comparison with others. This comparison, however, is based on limited information, as all that the photos reveal are the children's sex and appearance. The only further information that the couple knows is that there must be *something* about the child that makes them less desirable to other parents. If it is not their looks, then it is, presumably, something in their background.

What might potential parents deduce in these circumstances? We can roughly characterize their framework of assumptions by drawing a nominal distinction between children who are perceived as cute and children who are not, and children of a relatively good background, as against those of a 'bad' background. Because there is a photo but no description, it might appear that the only way in which the children can be divided is between those who are 'cute' and those who are not. However, if a 'cute' child is unadopted after two years, there is probably something 'bad' about their background that has prevented it. If – a safe assumption – potential parents have cute children of good background as their first choice, then this may explain the lack of response. There is a further difficulty with regard to comparing less photogenic children. A child who does not look cute may not have been adopted purely for that reason. They may, therefore, have a relatively good background. But as there is no information on this, it may be that the unfortunate child has a 'bad' background too.

Another parent at the meeting, Ms Yamada, succeeded in getting one of the children in the corner display placed with her about nine months later. She had married her partner expressly for the purpose of becoming eligible to adopt a child; after the adoption was concluded she and her husband divorced, although they continued to live together. Ms Yamada had an inauspicious start in her dealings with the agency. In her initial individual meeting she had objected to the demand that she cease fertility treatment: 'This should be my decision, I do not want to be told'. She had questioned the age rules – the couple were in their early forties. She had complained at the demand that she stop work to care for the child, which she thought was both unreasonable and sexist. Then she had come to the second group meeting without her husband, and so both of them had to attend all three group sessions again.

At the meeting Ms Yamada quickly gained strong feelings for a three-year-old girl whose photo appeared in the corner display. She had not, she said, set out to adopt a girl rather than a boy, but her eyes were attracted to girls. She and her husband enquired after the child and were shown a dossier including photos and an article that described the girl as lively. This information was enough for Ms Yamada and her partner to fall in love with the girl. They were also encouraged by her liveliness as they anticipated that this would make her less appealing to other parents who would thus be less competitive. Loving Hands would not share any further information with them on the grounds that they were not yet registered as foster parents; they had just missed one of the approval meetings and had to wait three months until the next. On almost the same day that they were approved, the child was readvertised. The couple applied immediately, but were told that there were problems about the 'missing' status of the mother. Six months later they met the girl for about 15 to 20 minutes at the institution where she lived. They continued to visit her there as often as they could, before taking their daughter home to foster and then successfully applying to adopt her. They also managed to ensure that the *koseki* record of the adoption was impossible to trace, possibly with the mild connivance of the courts and *koseki* office. The adoption decision was sent to the record office for the child's old institutional address rather than to the office for her new home address. A *koseki* official then phoned Ms Yamada to ask if she would like the adoption record transferred to the office that covered the family's home address, so that it could appear with their *koseki*. Ms Yamada simply replied 'No'.

As we have seen in the previous chapter, the child guidance centres typically select a child for the parents first, and then invite the potential parents to choose whether or not they would like to adopt the child. Loving Hands reverses this order. It allows the parents to select first by choosing a child that they would like to adopt from the weekly advertisements, only then does the agency select a couple from amongst the applicants. There may be good reasons for doing things this way round. The Yamadas' experience of quickly gaining strong feelings for their prospective daughter even though they had never met her in the flesh is reflected in the accounts of other adoptive parents (Mostyn 1993: 87–8). It is possible that these initial impressions and snap judgements may have some lasting positive impact on the relationship between parents and child, so that where prospective parents are able to act on their instincts by applying for a child on the basis of a photo and brief description, this may increase the chance of a successful match. Against this possible advantage, the problem of allowing applicants a choice amongst a number of children is that it encourages a skewed application process; parents, aiming to maximize their preferences, compete for a small number of highly desirable children, whilst others are left unrequested. It has been seen how in the Osaka branch of Loving Hands, the three-year-old girl with a good and sympathetic background had 150 applications, whereas other children had not been adopted after two years. Such a system inevitably produces numerous prospective parents disappointed at rejection and some of them may be discouraged from applying for other children.

An open approach

Loving Hands encourages openness in all aspects of its adoption process. Parents are encouraged to be open to each other in the training sessions. They are taught how to be open about an adoption. The expectation of the agency is that would-be parents can leave behind traditionalistic ideas about adoption as something to be kept hidden, and do their bit to challenge these attitudes in society. The agency's approach to the children in need of adoption is also one of openness. The children who are available are advertised in the press and all hard-to-place children are advertised together in the training sessions for prospective parents.

This open philosophy has some affinity with the modern western impetus in Japan dating back to the US occupation. From a modern liberal perspective, the democratic workings of organizations are seen as being facilitated by openness, which allows people to make informed choices and to engage in free competition. These virtues are usually associated with issues such as freedom of information and tendering for contracts, but the same principles are at work in the Loving Hands adoption policy of providing details on a range of children and in having an open application process for advertised children. The emphasis on articulating and showing feelings in Loving Hands is also associated with broader western cultural values. Openness in personal and social relationships is particularly associated with the culture of the USA, where it is linked to being demonstrative through expressing feelings and sharing with others what are generally considered private or family matters in Japan (Barnlund 1975). Openness is also linked, indirectly, to individualism in allowing for the assertion of one's rights and one's own distinct personality.

The approach of the agency is reasonably successful. However, not every child who is offered to Loving Hands by the CGCs is placed. The policy it has chosen is also potentially problematic for parents who prefer a more discreet approach to adoption. The open philosophy is somewhat at odds with the traditional Japanese cultural emphasis on reserve, social duty and the masking of individual feelings. There are also potential conflicts of interest between an agency and parents; if an adoption agency is too forthcoming about the backgrounds of the children in its care, then this may make their placement more difficult. This means that a policy of openness is not necessarily an advantage in helping as many needy children as possible.

In the next chapter, we look at an agency that has taken a different approach. This agency is less concerned with creating an adoption policy that encourages openness and choice, and more concerned to make the most of established elements of Japanese culture that are supportive of adoption. In fact, the methods developed by this agency have been designed, quite deliberately, *not* to provide potential adoptive parents with information about available children and *not* to give them a choice in whom they adopt.

4   The Motherly Network

The Motherly Network, a private agency based in Tokyo, operates by allocating children to parents, rather than having the parents apply for a specific child. This system has initial similarities to child guidance centre policies. However, parents who apply through a CGC can turn down a child without prejudice and ask for another. By contrast, the Motherly Network attempts to preclude choice by potential parents, making them commit in advance to adopt a child about whom they know nothing.

The Motherly Network, arranges adoptions with expectant mothers, mothers of new born babies and occasionally with mothers of older children. Many of the expectant mothers are teenagers and still at school. In such cases, it may well be the teenager's own mother who makes the initial approach, perhaps after discovering her daughter's pregnancy when it is too late to arrange an abortion, which has a legal limit of under 22 weeks (Ashino 2001). The mother-to-be is able to discuss her feelings about having the baby with the Network's director and founder Kazuko Yokota. These discussions raise adoption as a possibility, although it is not promoted as a better alternative than keeping the baby. If the expectant mother says that she wants to keep the baby, Ms Yokota offers advice on nurseries and other sources of support. If the expectant mother says that she wishes to have her child adopted, new parents are selected by a committee from a dossier of potential parents held by the organization. The choice of adoptive parents is made in a way that allows the wishes of the birth mother to be respected, as she is able to suggest the type of parents that she wants for her child. She might, for example, stipulate that the couple should be childless because of concerns over favouritism.

After the baby has been born, it is passed on to its new parents within days. However, over the next three months the birth mother can change her mind. The Motherly Network argues that although the birth mother may have clear reasons to choose to have the child adopted while she is pregnant, she might still develop feelings for the child after it has been born. To respect these feelings the birth mother needs these three months to reflect on her feelings over the adoption. In one or two cases the birth mothers have changed their mind and the child has been returned. For other birth mothers, there is the prospect of maintaining some degree of contact with the child through the Network. Typically this contact is indirect, with Ms Yokota acting as a mediator and passing on questions about the progress of the child from the birth mother.

In the Motherly Network the birth mother is seen as having a need or even a right to know about the progress of her child through these reports. This approach is uncommon in Japan as the more usual attitude is to stress confidentiality on both sides. For example, an independent mediator described being phoned by birth mothers clearly hoping, although they might not say so, to hear news of the child they had given up. Unless they explicitly pressed her, she said that she would not respond. From the other side, an infant home director has described turning down several requests from grown-up adopted children to help them find their birth mothers on the grounds that the mother has her own life to lead ('Zoku akachan attusen' 2005). Questioned about unusually high levels of contact in a survey distributed by the Network, adoptive parents professed to support the semi-open ethos. They did not, however, support direct communication between adoptive children and the birth parents through means such as phone calls or visits on special occasions (Kirino 1998: 135–7).

The Motherly Network is approached by many more potential adoptive parents than birth mothers. The Network collects objective information from applicants, and assesses whether they fulfil its requirements. This information includes a floor plan of the home. However, the Network does not have rigid *tatami* mat rules. This can be an advantage to would-be parents in crowded Tokyo, some of whom approach the agency after being rejected by their local CGC for this reason. The Motherly Network does, however, require the wife to be at home full-time to look after an adopted child. Ms Yokota commented 'We don't send children for adoption to put them in a full time nursery'.

In contrast to their efforts to respect the wishes and feelings of the birth mother, the Motherly Network excludes potential adoptive parents from any decision making input in matching and in planning for the adoption. Although it investigates the attitude of the parents towards different types of children, the agency does not allow the would-be adopters to make prior stipulations about the type of baby they want and does not discuss with them the background of babies that it may choose for them. As one couple who had adopted through the agency put it, 'Ms Yokota never asked us anything about our hopes for the child, although she would pose us questions such as: "If you get a mixed-race child, what are you going to do?"' If would-be parents attempt to make their preferences known, saying perhaps that they want a girl, a boy, or a healthy baby, the organization refuses to register them. The Motherly Network has a waiting list of parents who want to join the organization. With the demand from parents greater than the supply of children to the Network, Ms Yokota can safely disqualify applicants who want to specify the type of child they receive without losing the chance of making a placement. In one respect, however, prospective parents *are* specifying the kind of child they want. Simply by registering with the Motherly Network the parents indicate that they want a baby – a most sought after category amongst adopters.

Once parents are registered they are kept in the dark about plans that are being made, until, without any warning, they receive a call telling them of a rendezvous from where they can go to meet their child. Even at this stage adoptive parents are not told the sex or given any other information about the child; they have to wait to meet the child chosen for them.

> Out of the blue she phoned up and said 'You will pick up a child the day after tomorrow'. It was a weekday, and my husband had to suddenly take three days off. She told us to come to a certain train station. We met here there, went to a nearby hospital and she gave us our baby girl, though I thought she was a boy; she didn't have much hair. We had no nappies.

Newborn babies in Japan stay in hospital, as a matter of course, for about a week (Fetters 1997). The adoptive parents typically get to see the baby in hospital when it is a few days old and soon ready to be discharged. The child enters into the care of the adoptive parents as soon as they are introduced to it. They may also meet the birth mother, who sometimes physically passes the child to them. However, Ms Yokota is authorized by the birth mother to act as the guardian of the child. She will visit the new parents in the hospital and subsequently at home, and if – as has happened at least twice – she considers that the adoptive parents do not bond with the child, then she will remove the child from them.

A four point philosophy

The Motherly Network is not unusual in announcing to parents at short notice that a child is available, nor in placing newborn babies. However, the Network does more than reflect common practices in Japan, as it has a distinct philosophy based around four ideas. The first idea is to allow for 'baby power' on the birth mother, in other words, to allow for a change in the birth mother's feelings about keeping the child. The second idea is that a feeling of 'gratitude for unseen things' should be created between the birth mother and adoptive parents. The third idea is that the adoptive parents commit themselves unconditionally in advance to the child selected for them, rather than approaching the agency with a wish list. The fourth idea is to keep the child out of institutional care, even including a transitional institution.

Baby power

However much a mother may have been determined to have her baby adopted before its birth, she may feel drawn to the child after it is born. 'Baby power' refers to this pull felt by the mother. The Motherly Network contends that it is important to recognize that the feelings of the mother can change in this way after she has given birth. The Motherly Network does not, therefore, attempt to hold a birth mother to her earlier decision to adopt but allows her, for three months, to reclaim the child. The pull of baby power also helps to explain why the Network enables birth mothers to maintain indirect contact with the child after it has been adopted.

Gratitude for unseen things

'Gratitude for unseen things' is an attitude that creates mutual feelings of goodwill between the birth mother and adoptive parents. Although the adoptive parents do not know and may or may not meet the birth mother, they are encouraged to realize that if it were not for her they would not have their baby, and accordingly to feel very grateful. This attitude by the adoptive parents also helps the birth mother to have positive feelings towards passing on the baby. The mother knows that she is providing a gift for which the adoptive parents are very grateful, so she knows too that the child will be cherished. She is better able to realize the joy that she has brought and to feel grateful in turn to the adopters for giving the child a loving upbringing. The Motherly Network describes a birth mother passing a child on to new parents as acting with love for the child. The gratitude owed to the birth mother, helps to affirm and recognize this act of love.

Unconditional commitment

The idea of the parents committing themselves in advance to the child follows the naturalistic situation of a couple awaiting the birth of a child without having a choice as to what the child will be like. The contrary idea of an agency searching around for a certain category of child on behalf of adoptive parents goes against the concept of gratitude for unseen things. The child is a gift of the birth mother and cannot be demanded by the parents, who have no connection to or claim over him or her. A child freely given should be freely accepted without qualifications. The Motherly Network also supports the formula (a familiar slogan in the UK) that adoption provides a service for needy children not childless couples. The insistence that parents commit themselves to the unconditional acceptance, in advance, to whichever child is given to them, is seen as consistent with this asymmetric concept of the proper purpose of an adoption agency.

Avoiding institutions

The Motherly Network attempts to circumvent the infant homes and orphanages that provide institutional care for children in need of adoption. It is common ground amongst many adoption agencies that institutional care should be avoided, first because care within a family is intrinsically better and second to minimize placement moves. However, institutional care also runs counter to the distinct adoption philosophy of the Motherly Network for reasons that go beyond these two objections. CGCs partly justify placing babies in an infant home before an adoption is arranged on the grounds of making health investigations. It is argued that it is best for any health problems with the babies to be detected before they are offered to a new family. These checks, however, also allow adoptive parents to impose conditions about the state of health of the baby they will adopt, violating the Motherly Network's principle that parents should accept children unconditionally.

The Motherly Network is also opposed to transitional institutional care because it inhibits the establishment of good feelings between the birth mother and adoptive parents. There is, perhaps, a psychological difference between passing on a baby and giving up a baby. When a baby is passed from the birth mother to the adoptive parents, gratitude for unseen things is able to come into play, creating positive feelings on each side. Where a baby is given up and then adopted, each stage in the process is compartmentalized. The mother deals with a mediating institution that does not want or feel grateful for a child in the way that adoptive parents do. The parents deal with the agency after the mother has already relinquished the child. This breaks the direct connection between birth mother and adoptive parents and weakens feelings of gratitude.

Antithetical policies

The Motherly Network's mode of operation bears some similarity with adoptions organized privately with doctors. In both cases the adoption is often arranged, provisionally at least, before the baby is born, through liaison with the mother-to-be and the identification of adopters. The Network, however, reverses the commitment required of each party. When a private doctor makes an adoption arrangement, there is likely to be an expectation placed on the birth mother that she has committed herself in advance to relinquishing her baby, so that when she gives birth, her decision is already fixed. The adoptive parents are unlikely to be placed under the same expectation of prior commitment, although they may well be fully informed about the circumstances of the birth mother. In the Motherly Network, by contrast, the birth mother is not put under pressure to commit to an adoption before the baby is born, but the adoptive parents *are* required to commit to adopting the child before they are taken to see them, and before they learn any information about the child's sex, health or background.

The sudden introduction of the baby to its new parents bears some resemblance to the practice of CGC social workers, who sometimes call on prospective parents virtually without notice and take them to see a child. Parents who adopt through the CGC, however, are taken to see a child without any commitment required of them to take that child; it is a meeting to explore the possibility of adoption, the first step in a gradual process of familiarization. If and when the parents take the child home with them, this will not be until some weeks later and will first consist of only a short overnight visit. By contrast, parents who adopt through the Motherly Network have promised in advance to accept whichever child may be offered to them, and are expected to immediately commence full-time care for the child.

The Motherly Network was established in 1991. Ms Yokota could have created an organization similar to Loving Hands, but decided that an independent agency was the best way to pursue her distinct philosophy, particularly as Loving Hands placed babies and children who first went to institutions. This philosophy was formed, antithetically, out of Ms Yokota's experience and ultimate repudiation of the practices of a doctors' association that functioned as an international adoption agency. The Motherly Network was formed as an alternative way forward for adoption in Japan. The principles on which it operates, including respecting the feelings of birth mothers, allowing for 'baby power', requiring unconditional acceptance of children by adoptive parents and using gratitude for unseen things as its model for the transfer of a child, can all be seen as reacting against the principles of the international agency.

Ms Yokota had worked as a volunteer for the international adoption agency until 1988, a period when the only framework for domestic adoption was either through an ordinary adoption or an illicit agreement between a birth mother, doctor and adoptive couple. Given the limited opportunities for a full domestic adoption, international adoption appeared to Ms Yokota to be a good alternative for children. Nonetheless, she began to question elements of her work with the international agency. Ms Yokota's task was to fly with children born in Japan to a rendezvous at the airport in Hawaii, where she would hand them to their new adoptive parents. Ms Yokota keenly felt her absence of control over the process; her ability to protect the child was very limited as she had no choice but to hand the child over regardless of her views of the parents. She was also concerned that adoption overseas imposed an absolute break between the birth mother and the child, despite any wishes the mother might have for continued contact. The Motherly Network tackles both of these problems. Adoptive parents are not guaranteed a child in advance; Ms Yokota holds guardianship. The exclusive focus on adoption to Japanese couples makes continued contact a much more practical proposition than in an overseas adoption, and the Network is designed to allow for indirect contact between the birth mother and adopted child.

Ms Yokota was also unhappy at the lack of control that birth mothers had over the fate of their children. Sometimes she believed that birth mothers were – and are – coerced by private agencies into give up their children by being pressed to sign 'contracts' while they were still in hospital. A doctor, working in conjunction with the agency might, for example, pressurize a new mother to sign a statement of consent to adoption by claiming that she had to before being allowed to leave the hospital. These 'contracts' do not, in fact, have any legal force in Japan, but birth mothers are unlikely to appreciate this.

One occasion, when a birth mother was possibly prevented from changing her mind, was particularly troubling. A geisha, who had borne a child by her lover not her 'sponsor', gave the child up for adoption. Ms Yokota was handed the girl by the agency director at Narita airport so that she could escort her to new parents in the USA. She was about to leave when the birth mother unexpectedly appeared and asked:

'Can I see my child once more?'
The director replied, 'Yes, but at a distance'.
'Why', Ms Yokota thought, 'should a mother not be allowed near her child?'

The geisha, feeling the pull of 'baby power', may have been poised to have a last minute change of heart – this prospect is implicit in the director's refusal to allow her to touch the child. In this situation the birth mother finds that it is too late to make decisions over the child. She has no rights, or at least the agency has constructed the situation to make it appear that she has no rights by denying her the chance to get close to her child. The feelings of a birth mother for a child after it has been born are not allowed to interfere with the process of transferring the child to new parents. Ms Yokota saw this policy as wrong. Respecting the wishes of birth mothers and recognizing the pull of baby power has been built into the philosophy of the Motherly Network. This counters other pressures that militate against birth mothers changing their minds, including the wishes of adoptive parents, financial problems, and organizational imperatives to have a smooth running process.

Contracts vs gratitude

The final problem with the international agency concerned the attitudes sometimes displayed by adoptive parents. Again, a particular incident stood out, this time in the airport in Hawaii, when it seemed that a child was treated like a batch of goods. Ms Yokota handed over a girl to a couple who then examined the child naked. After this examination, the couple said, 'Yes. She's OK'.

In the eyes of Ms Yokota, this incident encapsulated much of what was wrong with the international agency. The parents examining the child, made her feel that she was engaged in a business transaction, the last stage in a contractual exchange. Gratitude for unseen things within the Motherly Network is an alternative approach that is quite different from a contract. Contractual relationships are modelled on the assumption that people are legitimately selfish, and make agreements to their mutual advantage. There is no need to feel gratitude toward someone with whom one strikes a bargain. The gratitude for the very existence of the child may also be absent from a contractual exchange. The child exists only because he or she has been cradled in the womb by the birth mother. However, although this is indisputable, it is not acknowledged in the contractual relationship. The only way in which the birth mother is seen as relating to the child is as someone who, initially at least, has *ownership* of the child. The examination of the child that so shocked Ms Yokota follows from this notion of contract: the value of the child depends upon her physical condition; this is part of the bargain. The unconditional acceptance of a child by adoptive parents, the principle insisted upon by the Motherly Network, emphasizes that the child is not part of a contractual exchange and that nothing is owing to the adoptive parents.

It has been suggested that people with liberal attitudes are more accepting of adoptions than conservatives, at least with respect to publicly acknowledged adoptions. However, the experiences of Ms Yokota and the activities of the Motherly Network suggest that liberalism is no panacea for the problems inherent in adoption, and that more conservative attitudes can, on occasion, be helpful. Members of a conservative and traditionalistic society have a strong sense of collective identity so that the ethics and expectations of the social group to which an individual belongs guide his actions. In a more individualistic society these social expectations are weaker, and are replaced to some extent by explicit constraining agreements, that is, contracts. A belief in individualism may help people to view others on their merits, but it is also, potentially, something that breaks down social solidarity. If inherited ties between people are to be discounted, then there needs to be some alternative method of forming social relationships. The method of choice in a liberal modern society is to relate to each other through contracts. Liberal individualism *per se* does not necessarily equate to selfishness (Popper 1966: 100–102). However, once one relates to others through contracts, a climate of expectations is created in which individuals are presumed to act in pursuit of their own interests; a contract makes it plain that in doing something for someone else, you intend to get something back.

The relationships established in the international agency were based around contracts. Mothers gave an irrevocable commitment, and were, apparently, some-times pressured into signing a consent form. Adoptive parents were seen as entitled to make demands concerning the child in a way that suggested that they were entering into a market agreement. This contractual way of arranging an adoption is closely related to the liberal stress on individualism. The Motherly Network was formed in reaction against this contractual approach. Instead of a contract, the relationship between birth mother and adoptive parents is modelled around gratitude for unseen things. This attitude has an affinity with a particular aspect of Japanese culture, the respectful relationship towards (unseen) ancestors and so resonates with the strong sense of loyalty and ties to one's heritage and family background that might otherwise lead one to oppose the adoption of an unknown child. The principles of the Motherly Network suggest that an adop-tion policy can be created that engages sympathetically with ideas rooted in tradition to encourage positive feelings between the birth mother and adoptive parents.

What are we to make of the conflict between the principles on which the Motherly Network was founded, and the principles apparently operating in the international agency? Consider, first, the couple who conducted the immediate examination of the girl at the airport, with their acceptance of the child being con-ditional upon her physical condition. At the level of an emotional gut-reaction, this examination may well be felt to be shocking, but when one considers the underlying rationale of the couple, it is not obvious *why* it is shocking. In logic, there seems to be little to distinguish the actions of the couple at the airport from the actions of another couple who specify in advance that they want a healthy child. If it is reasonable to make this advance specification, then examining the child might be unseemly and distrustful, but not, in reason, shocking. One could even defend the couple by pointing out that it was best to examine the child immediately, before they became attached to her and before the passage of time made the adoption more difficult to undo, had they later found anything that they felt to be wrong with her. In short, if it is not unreasonable to ask for a healthy child it appears not unreasonable to examine a child to check that the child is healthy. However, what is unusual about the parents' action in examining the child, is exactly its cold reasoning. Adoptive parents sometimes describe immediate feelings of love on first seeing the child (Sumner and Noguchi 2001). Where the parents' feelings for a new child grow more gradually, there is still an immediate awareness of the child as an individual. By examining the child, the couple at the airport did not display feelings of love or even awareness of the child's humanity. The couple continued to treat the child as an abstract category, rather than as an individual. They wanted to confirm that she fell into the category of healthy children. Part of what makes us human is that we are unique rather than interchangeable, but the child at the airport was treated as a generic entity that had to confirm to certain standards. This may help explain why Ms Yokota felt that she was delivering a batch of goods and this is what makes the story shocking.

Logic vs feelings

The Motherly Network has set itself against contracts by refusing to deal with potential adoptive parents who try to stipulate conditions. But this is not an inevitable consequence of avoiding a contractual relationship. It can be agreed that it is admirable for adoptive parents to enter into an adoption with an attitude of unconditional acceptance in advance of seeing a child, or even hearing a description of the child. It can also be agreed that given the high demand amongst would-be adopters to be registered with the Motherly Network it is reasonable for the agency to insist upon this attitude. It is less clear whether imposing a requirement of unconditional acceptance in advance upon adopters is helpful as a more general principle for other adoption agencies. The Motherly Network deals primarily with newborn babies, where the disparity between supply and demand allows it to apply stringent conditions to parents without risking its 100% adoption rate. These circumstances are not applicable to an agency that deals with older children and children with known disabilities. Where agencies are trying to place a wide range of children, it may be more promising to allow parents to meet a child before committing to him or her, to enable them to relate to the child as an individual. This approach affirms the child's individuality by saying, in effect, that the child may not be from a 'perfect' category, but is unique as an individual. By getting to know the child as an individual it is possible that parents can develop tender feelings for the child that replace their reasons for wanting a child who conforms to an abstract category.

The feelings of an adoptive couple confronted with the reality of an individual child, can work to overcome reservations that prior logic might have given them about accepting a certain type of child. It is possible that a similar response can act on a birth mother, and that feelings transcending logic might be another way of describing the effect of 'baby power' on birth mothers who decide to relinquish the child when pregnant, but change their minds after seeing the baby.

To consider some of the complications involved in a birth mother keeping a child when logic tells her to have it adopted, we can return to the case of the geisha denied the chance to hold her child before it was flown abroad. In these circumstances, Ms Yokota's disquiet at the airport was surely justified. If the birth mother is going to change her mind and keep a child, then it is better to do so before the baby has been introduced to its adoptive parents. At this stage there is a clear asymmetry between feelings of the birth mother for her own child, and the adoptive parents who, however much they may be eagerly awaiting their new baby, cannot have the same feelings for a child they have not yet seen. It would seem clear, therefore, that the transfer of the child should have been stopped while the birth mother reassessed her wishes.

This conclusion is hardly very controversial; the idea that a child should not be adopted unless all the options for maintaining the birth family together have been thoroughly explored is a near-universal orthodoxy, and the airport incident violated this principle. However, nothing in adoption is simple and an ethical case can be made for the alternative position that the agency director was correct in pushing ahead with the adoption and keeping the mother at a distance. These arguments, we think, are insufficient to counter the right of a mother to change her mind before the baby has been handed over. However, they should not be disregarded as they gain weight after a handover, when a birth mother wants to reclaim a child from a loving adoptive family.

The first argument that an agency might make for ignoring a change in the birth mother's feelings is to note that the plight of the mother has not changed, even if her feelings have. An expectant mother who decides to have her baby adopted may have made this decision because of the situational logic that confronts her and more or less forces her to do so. The mother's situation may include a lack of support or hostility by other family members and a precarious economic position, circumstances that combine to make it extremely difficult if not impossible for her to envisage being able to cope with raising a child. If the agency has investigated and corroborated the mother's straitened circumstances before the birth, then it is arguably the job of an agency to maintain that objective judgement against the mother's changed feelings after the birth. From this perspective, it is the purpose of the agency, once it has taken responsibility for the child, to maintain the judgement that adoption is the best course, a decision already reached with the mother. The job of the agency is to ensure that 'baby power' does not get in the way of the rational decision to adopt. Thus, one independent adoption mediator told us:

> When the child is born, I get the birth mother to tell the doctor, 'I do not want to see the child'. It is better, from the beginning, to feed the baby formula milk and not to breastfeed; then anyone can look after the child and the birth mother has no memories.

The second argument for not allowing the mother a change of heart is based on an uncompromising interpretation of the principle that the agency should advance the welfare of the child. In pursuit of this duty an agency should ensure that the child is placed in the best home. If the adoptive family can provide a better home for the child than the birth mother, then it is best for the child to be adopted, regardless of the changed feelings of the birth mother. In the next chapter we examine an adoption agency that holds to these principles.

5   A Christian adoption agency

The overarching adoption rules in Japan set down broad principles but are comparatively light on specifics. There is no authoritative adoption organization enforcing its code of practice, adoption has been low on the political agenda, and the activities of groups in civil society are lightly regulated. These conditions have given determined individuals the scope to create agencies with adoption policies that reflect their particular beliefs. Ms Yokota's formation of the Motherly Network and Ms Iwasaki's role as director of Loving Hands in Osaka both show how an organization can be strongly influenced by a charismatic, strongly motivated individual. In this chapter it is seen how a Christian adoption agency also bears the stamp of its founder. In contrast to Loving Hands and the Motherly Network, who have raised awareness of adoption by operating very publicly, the Christian agency works discreetly; it does not arrange public meetings and only has limited published material. The principles that inform the policy of the agency also differ considerably from the organizations considered thus far. In fact, the director's approach to adoption is more or less the opposite of Ms Yokota's, although like the Motherly Network, the agency she leads deals mainly with babies.

A Christian missionary organization, led by US residents in Japan, extended its activities to adoption in 1991 and now places a child about once a month. The agency engages in adoption for humanitarian reasons and in pursuit of its proselytising mission. All the children that it cares for are placed with Christian families. Japanese adherents of Christianity are the adoptive parents most favoured by the agency. However, Christianity is followed by only a tiny minority of the Japanese population and this limits the pool of domestic adopters. For children who cannot be placed with Japanese Christians, the organisation turns, in descending order of priority, to foreign Christians who are long-term residents in Japan, to temporary residents such as Christian members of the US armed services stationed in Japan, and finally to Christians in the USA. According to the director, where a child is sent directly to parents who are abroad this is normally because they have special needs.

In attempting to prioritise placements with Japanese Christians the organization is faced not only with low numbers but also with restrictive prior preferences; some prospective parents will even specify the blood group the child should have. Sometimes the agency places children who do not fulfil the prior stipulations of Japanese adoptive parents on a trial basis. According to the director, a child placed on trial had never been returned. As she put it: 'Before [meeting a child] parents have lots of requirements. Afterwards they have any child, blue, green…'. Like other adoption agencies, the organization has found a strong prior preference for girls amongst Japanese adoptive parents, but, as things have turned out, about two-thirds of the children it has placed have been boys. This statistical anomaly is interpreted as God's will. The boys, because of their sex, are seen as potential future leaders who will either grow up in or return to Japan and convert their compatriots to Christianity.[26]

Aside from Christian beliefs, the organization imposes few formal requirements on adopters and these are related to its experience of what a family court will expect of parents. Like the court, it asks about the educational plans of the parents for their children. It looks for couples with a combined age of under 100, as this will be acceptable to the court. It considers the jobs of the applicants and rejects families on low incomes, as according to the director this too can be problematic with the courts. But although formal requirements are limited, the organization conducts fairly extensive home study interviews in deciding whether or not to accept prospective parents. The would-be parents are interviewed separately and then together, and any children in the family are interviewed too. Particular care has been taken in these interviews after a troubling experience in which a placement did not go well and the adoption application was rejected by the family court. The home study conducted by the agency is followed by a second home study undertaken by an independent licensed social worker who is paid by the applicant couple for this service. A social worker of Japanese background and a resident of Japan, but with advanced qualifications in social work gained in the USA, often conducts these home studies. He conducts a series of interviews, sometimes by telephone, with the couple, any children, their neighbours, referees and for those in the US military their supervisors. On this basis he prepares a report that covers a wide range of topics in some detail.[27] Despite the detail of his report, this is a formalistic step (the couples are always approved) but it is one that is legally necessary, as the organization is not registered as a welfare organization.

The adoption activities of the organization are permitted, as it is a licensed ministry with a right to help people in distress. However, its move into adoption has neither been encouraged by government officials nor supported by the established childcare providers in Japan. The agency has not, for example, been able to link up with infant homes to find family placements for the children in their care. The agency has also had rather fraught dealings with family court judges who must authorize every adoption, and who have objected to some of its decisions and procedures. There may be a chicken and egg element to the agency's lack of integration into the broader childcare system as had it been allowed, say, to place children from infant homes, it might have adapted itself more readily to Japan's procedural norms. However, now that the agency has developed its policies autonomously, there appear to be at least three reasons for the continuing friction with the courts. First, the agency enters into a 'contractual' relationship with birth mothers – although these agreements have no legal standing. Second, the agency appears to have arranged at least one international adoption in a way that avoided the oversight of the Japanese courts, and third, it uses what might be regarded as disingenuous methods to help foreign children in need of adoption to become Japanese citizens. One of us discussed these three aspects of the agency's work with the director, and the account that follows is based upon this conversation.

'Contracts' with birth mothers

The adoption agency's dealings with birth mothers typically begin while they are still pregnant. Expectant mothers learn of the agency from a variety of sources, including doctors, another missionary organization, a helpline and word of mouth. As with the Motherly Network, the organization may also be contacted by the parents of pregnant teenagers. These parents are often insistent that the baby will be adopted, and as the director pointed out, if the birth mother is under 20, it is the grandparents and not the mother who are the legal guardians of the baby.

Once the organization has been contacted, the mothers-to-be are given a decision sheet, asking about the support they might get from the father or family members, this allows the mother to think through the different options for the child, and come to a considered judgement on her best course of action. Whether or not the birth mothers decide to have the child adopted, they are also offered the opportunity, usually declined, of a home stay with a member of the organization during their confinement.

If the expectant mother agrees to an adoption, she is told that the organization wants this decision to be final. Once the birth mothers have confirmed that they definitely wish to have the child adopted, then prior arrangements are completed, as far as possible, before the birth, including information on family history and on the course of the pregnancy. This emphasis on sorting out as much documentation as possible before the birth appears to be based partly on grounds of efficiency, partly on making the separation less painful for the birth mothers, but also on the reasoning that the more steps in the process that can be completed before the birth, the less opportunity that there is for the mother to back out of the adoption after the birth because her feelings have changed. In the words of the director, 'although these women are giving up their babies, they have hearts'.

Shortly after the baby has been born, the birth mother makes two formal written agreements with the agency. These agreements are usually made thirty-six to seventy-two hours after birth, based on the timescale of the minimum acceptable periods in various states of the USA where the adoptions of some of the children will be completed.[28] The mother signs a statement that reads:

> I want my child to be placed in an adoptive family and I give [the agency] the right to do this, and to take care of the child until then.

She also writes an affidavit, in her own handwriting, one that begins with the declaration:

> I will never do anything to stop the adoption …

The contracts used by the agency are similar to the release forms used by lawyers who arrange private adoptions. Lawyers, like doctors, will arrange for a handover very soon after birth. A birth mother will be given a release form to sign by the lawyer perhaps only two days after the birth. The lawyer will also seek to get a release form from the father, if known, and from grandparents if the mother is under 20. Although the statements have no legal force, such documents make it appear that the mother has signed away her rights to the child. The lawyer will then apply to the family court to get the placement authorized and the court will assign a social worker to assess it. During this process the mother (or grandparents) remains the legal guardian of the child unless the court reassigns guardianship. If an adoption order is made by the court, the mother has a short period in which to appeal.

Adoption into the USA

Intercountry adoptions are arranged by the Christian organization in conjunction with a second Christian adoption agency in the USA. The US agency selects parents for the child and the organization in Japan then has a courier fly with the child to a US airport. The new parents meet the child at the airport, where the courier hands over the documentation to the US agency's lawyers. In order to travel to the USA, however, the organization needs to obtain a Japanese passport for the child and then a visa from the US embassy in Japan.

Although the birth mother has apparently signed away all rights to the child shortly after its birth, she (or the grandparents) actually retains guardianship rights in Japanese law. In *this* capacity, the birth mother signs another form, one that authorizes the director to obtain a passport for the child on the mother's behalf. In other words, the agency is able to obtain a passport for the child on the authority of the birth mother as the child's legal guardian. Obtaining a passport in this way has resolved an obstacle that had faced the organization's director in making international placements. The director had previously attempted to obtain guardianship over a boy destined for adoption in the USA by applying to the courts. Had her application for guardianship been accepted, she would have gained the right to apply for a passport for the child so that he could travel to be placed in the USA. The court, however, refused guardianship and, as things turned out, the director ended up adopting the child herself.

To obtain a visa, the agency presents the US embassy with the baby's passport, alongside the affidavit of the mother. The organization also presents the evidence that it has collected to show that there is no one else to care for the child. US law requires that an international adoption must be of a child who has been abandoned by both of its parents (Bartholet 1993: 147). The affidavit makes it clear that the child has been abandoned by its mother and, if the father is unknown, the embassy will normally issue a visa.

The final steps in the agency's process of international adoption are a little difficult to follow. It appears that where the parents are already living in the USA, the child will travel there with a courier and will then be legally adopted in the

USA rather than in Japan. Where the parents are US citizens resident in Japan, the child will be adopted in Japan. However, there may occasionally be an element of forum shopping in securing legal recognition for the adoption:

> In one case the birth mother changed her mind with us. She had originally said, specifically, that she wanted the child adopted in America. She came back, after over a year, and said she wanted the child back. I said:
>
> 'I'm sorry, but it's too late'.
>
> So she went to the family court, who stopped the adoption. So we said
>
> 'OK'.
>
> And had the child sent abroad and concluded the adoption. A child can immigrate, for purposes of adoption, *legally.*

The agency's ability to prevent the birth mother reclaiming her child was aided by the limited powers of the family court. The director observed to us that there are several children in Japan who have had their adoptions stopped by the courts after objections from the birth mother, but who remain with their *de facto* adoptive parents. She added that although a family court can stop an adoption, it does not have the power to order that the child be returned. This can only be done through a civil court, and it is expensive to pursue such a case.

Adoption as a *fait accompli*

The case of the child adopted against the wishes of the birth mother, despite the decision of the family court, highlights the way in which the agency prioritises adoption carried out in accordance with its own principles over the requirements of a legal adoption. Rather than structuring its mode of operation around the legal rules, the agency has, as far as possible, created an independent set of procedures. This is seen, for example, in the two-stage home study. One stage, the assessment of the qualified social worker can be relied upon to be supportive of the parents; this is the report later presented to the courts. It is the study conducted by the agency itself, however, which has the decisive weight in whether to accept or reject the prospective parents.

The adoptions arranged by the agency are carried out autonomously in accordance with its own standards, safeguards and processes. It then draws upon the law selectively to maintain these procedures. The agency uses the *de facto* power that it has as the actual guardian of the child to make an adoption a *fait accompli*, with the expectation that *de jure* recognition will be gained in one way or another. It operates within a legal framework because it is necessary, but does not regard legal requirements as particularly helpful. The agency views the law on adoption analytically rather than as a whole; there is a keen awareness of how aspects of the law taken in isolation can be used to further adoptions that are not in keeping with the overall spirit of adoption law in Japan. The agency is also aware of different practices between the family courts. Trial and error has given the agency a working knowledge of the ways in which the law and procedures are interpreted in different prefectures. In one case, for example, a judge assumed guardianship of a child himself. In another, court officials persuaded a grandmother not to have the child adopted. In such cases, where the court is seen as having acted unfavourably, the agency attempts to avoid it in the future.

The determination of the agency to follow its own rules is evident in the case of the birth mother who tried to get her baby back. The agency's 'contracts' with birth mothers, are not enforceable in Japanese law, but in this case the contract was maintained in spite of Japanese law. Passports were obtained by the agency by recognizing that the mother had guardianship over the child, but the passport was then used to take the child abroad and so avoid the mother's assertion of these same guardianship rights. Similarly, the legal right of the child to emigrate from Japan for purposes of adoption was used, in this case, to forward an adoption that had been stopped in Japan by the family court.

Creating Japanese citizens

The way in which particular aspects of the law in Japan can be exploited to go against broader policies is evident in another controversial activity undertaken by the organization: turning foreign-born adoptees into Japanese citizens. About twice a year a mother approaches the director, hands over a child for adoption and then leaves without revealing her name and address. These mothers fall into two categories. First, there are Japanese single mothers who are either trying to hide the birth altogether or avoid having it recorded on their *koseki*, but without going to the extreme of abandoning the child to chance. Second, there are foreign single mothers, perhaps Filipino, Thai or Chinese, who are undocumented migrants.

The precarious position of undocumented migrants leads some women to conclude that their child is best served by being given up for adoption without revealing their identity, and the agency provides them with this opportunity. A mother who is an undocumented migrant may be unwilling to bring herself to the attention of the authorities by registering the birth of a child because she fears deportation. Furthermore, if the child is defined as not Japanese, then even if the mother gives the child up for adoption in Japan, its prospects are blighted by its lack of citizenship. If the birth parents of a child are unknown, however, then that child has the opportunity to acquire Japanese citizenship. This follows a 1993 court case in which Christian missionaries from the USA adopted the child of an unknown birth mother and successfully argued that he should be defined as a Japanese national. The position of such children subsequently improved, although the Ministry of Justice has attempted to undermine the 1993 decision by contending that the child's appearance is also significant. Thus, if a doctor opines that the child does not look Japanese, the court may still refuse to grant citizenship (Tomita 1998: 5).

Once the agency succeeds in registering a child as a Japanese citizen, an adoption placement is straightforward. In fact, as the director explained, adoption is made simpler than usual 'because there is no birth mother to talk to'. The director acquires citizenship for a child by limiting her discussion with the mother. She commented that if a woman who comes to her with a baby is determined to remain anonymous, then there is nothing that she can do about it. 'I do not know where the mothers are from; I cannot tell by looking, and some speak very good Japanese'. She does, however, get the women to write a note that says why they are giving up the child (although not presumably one that says 'because I am foreign…'). Armed with this information, she approaches the city hall, informs them that she is caring for the child, and requests citizenship. If the case is deemed to be a simple one, then the city authorities grant citizenship in about a month. More complex cases are slower and are passed up the administrative ladder. When the director started to receive children from anonymous mothers she gained quite extensive written information about the birth from them, until an official pointed out to her that the less information she provided the less information that they were duty-bound to follow up.

Autonomy and ethics

Loving Hands and the Motherly Network, for all their differences of approach, both fit comfortably alongside the CGCs in the legal framework and official statements of intent for special adoption in Japan. By contrast, the Christian agency has established its own set of norms, ones that are most comparable with private adoption arrangements made with doctors or lawyers. As the special adoption regime was partly designed to allow CGCs and other adoption agencies to replace these private arrangements rather than partially replicate them, this sets the organization apart from the agencies we have considered so far. In some respects, the Christian agency's activities also present a challenge to the broad consensus that the other agencies share. Its use of contracts with birth mothers; its arrangement of a contested adoption; its exclusive reliance on Christian adoptive parents in a way that increases international placements, and its method of acquiring Japanese nationality for foreign children, not only raise moral and practical considerations in their own right, but also raise issues about how far an agency can reasonably step outside the official expectations that are placed upon it.

Contracts

The signing of the contract by a birth mother 36–72 hours after the birth returns us to the question of whether vulnerable women are put under undue pressure to sign away their children while they are still in hospital. As with most aspects of adoption there are things to be said on both sides of this issue. The case for an adoption contract entered into by the mother can be defended in several ways:

1   A formal written agreement by the mother to have her child adopted, entered into soon after birth, is like any other contract. It provides a fair method of regulating relations between adults in a way that recognizes their rationality, independence and responsibility for their own actions.

2   The time period, calculated since the birth, might appear short. However, the birth mother has had the opportunity to explore and come to terms with the option of adoption ever since she learnt she was pregnant. This period of reflection is furthered by the discussion and advice given to the expectant mother after she has contacted the agency.

3   By saying that she wants her child to be adopted, a birth mother sets in train a series of arrangements made by the adoption agency that places an obligation upon her to keep to her decision. The agency will, at the very least, cover her hospital fees and medical expenses. The agency will also make matching decisions, begin to make legal preparations and organize a handover. The mother's written agreement to have the child adopted confirms the bargain that she has already entered into.

4   The pressure for the birth mother to agree to have her child adopted does not come from the adoption agency but is the result of pressure of circumstances, such as the single status of the mother, her limited means of support and negative family attitudes towards the child. More time will not relieve this pressure.

5   The same pressure of circumstances indicates that the child will be better off in a new home. Anything that increases this prospect, including a contract, promotes the welfare of the child.

6   A quick adoption placement is better for the child; the contract speeds the process.

7   A clean break is better for the mother; the contract helps to make this break.

These arguments have some force, but are outweighed by counter arguments about the particular vulnerability of the birth mother in the period shortly after birth. The advantages attributed to all contracts may be reasonable when the contracting parties are in a rough position of equality. The birth mother, however, is in a very unequal position when compared to the agency. She may be extremely tired soon after birth and this may adversely affect her decision-making ability. Her status as a patient may make her feel in a state of psychological dependency and so apt to agree with the demands of any authority figure. She may be young and naïve. She may be unaware of her legal rights. Indeed, the advantage of the contract depends, in part upon the mother subsequently believing that she has waived her legal rights.

It is reasonable to point out that a mother has a period of decision making during her pregnancy as well as after the birth, so that she is not being asked to sign a contract out of the blue. However, the time before the birth cannot simply be aggregated to the time after the birth; each period is qualitatively different. To use the terms of the Motherly Network, an apparently firm decision made by an expectant mother does not take 'baby power' into account. To put it another way, there is a difference between thinking about a future child as an abstract category, and being confronted with an actual, individual child.

The success of the trial placements made by the Christian agency with previously picky Japanese parents suggests that *before* they have seen a child, adoptive parents may be highly rational and calculating about the type of child they do, and do not want. *After* they have been introduced to a child the same adoptive parents may be much more accepting of the child as it is. An analogous transition may sometimes affect birth mothers. The period before the birth is one where rational calculations may have a greater weight for an expectant mother. After the birth, a mother's emotional attachment to the child may become much more intense. To a limited extent, by leaving the contract until after the birth (which is useful in the US courts) the agency is allowing for the effect of this transition. We learned indirectly that other Christian agencies arranging domestic adoptions in Japan had the mother sign a contract *before* the birth. However, the speed with which the contract is entered into after the birth seems designed, in part, to nip in the bud any attachment of the mother for the child.

In the days after birth, the mother may be in a vulnerable position physically, psychologically and in terms of her limited understanding of her rights. Furthermore, she may also be indebted to the agency for her hospital bills. If she has made efforts to conceal the birth this is liable to have pushed up the costs. A mother who gives birth in her home prefecture has some of her costs met by the local authority, however, some women travel outside their prefecture to give birth as a stratagem to avoid having the child on their *koseki*. Other women again may have concealed their pregnancy from their parents, who might otherwise have helped; or from the company they worked for, preventing them from claiming on company insurance. Before the birth, the opportunity to get hospital costs paid for may have appeared as a bonus to what was, in any event, a rational decision to have a child adopted. With the agency offering to meet costs, the expectant mother is absolved from having to make any other advance financial arrangements, and is given a greater opportunity to keep her pregnancy secret. If the mother's feelings change after the birth, then the pressures upon her increase, as she faces the immediate problem of how to pay for her hospital bills. This is in addition to the long-term pressure of circumstances she would face in trying to raise a child.

The notion of a child being objectively better off with adoptive parents is problematic if it is used to overrule the wishes of the mother, as this denies a birth mother her rights. The calculation of the best outcome for the child, to the exclusion of the feelings of the birth mother, is also too narrowly conceived. The agency can be reasonably confident that the adoptive couple selected for the child will love that child. Nonetheless, focusing exclusively on the child in working out what is best is unreasonable if a mother's feelings change, as it discounts the intrinsic value of these feelings for the child.

For these reasons, we concur with Ms Yokota's argument that the mother should not be given a contract to sign shortly after the birth as she needs a longer time to know her mind. The child can be removed from the birth mother, at her request, without a contract being entered into, and a clean break can still be made in this sense. However, removing the child should not entail signing documents that are presented to the mother as an irrevocable commitment to have the child adopted. Further, the financing of the birth should not be used to add pressure to the mother. Money paid to the hospital by the agency should be *unconditional*. If the mother decides to keep her baby, the agency will just have to absorb the cost. In a sense, this would extend a practice already followed by the Christian agency in offering a home stay to all expectant mothers, whether or not they wish to have their child adopted.

These objections to contracts made in hospital make it difficult to assess the case in which a mother tried to reclaim her child over a year after giving him up for adoption. Taking the facts as laid down by the director, it is agreed that it is too late for a birth mother who has consented to adoption and had her baby placed for over a year to change her mind. The question, therefore, appears to be one of how far one can reasonably go in legal manoeuvring to keep the child with its adoptive family. However, there is a difficulty in accepting without question that the birth mother had in fact given her consent to the adoption. If usual agency procedures were followed she would have signed a contract 36–72 hours after birth, at the time the baby was removed from her. This contract cannot be considered evidence of consent because of the disadvantaged position of the mother.

Christian placements abroad

The Christian agency takes the orthodox view that domestic adoptions are preferable to intercountry adoptions. Their hierarchy of adoptive parents with Japanese couples at the top, and the director's stress on the way that direct overseas adoptions were undertaken mainly to help children with special needs, indicate this preference. However, the agency views placing the children with Christian families as a higher priority than ensuring domestic adoption and this has increased the number of international placements. From a secular perspective, the stipulation that the child should be raised by a Christian couple may be reasonable as a way of respecting the wishes of birth parents (or the child if they are old enough to have a view). Whether an agency should be able to make the same stipulation is more questionable. On the one hand, there is no evidence that Christians have better adoption outcomes than other categories of parents. The many successful adoptions in Japan itself provide evidence to confute such a theory. There are few court applications to dissolve special adoptions and this is suggestive of a high success rate in a country where few are Christian (Appendix 1: Table 1). On the other hand, when considering the policies of an agency, one must take into account not only evidence but also what inspires the agency to act on a child's behalf. There is at least some relationship between (a) the amount of leeway an agency has to pursue its own values in adoption placements and (b) its enthusiasm for the task, or indeed its willingness to operate at all. In this case it can be asked: what if the agency's policy of placing exclusively with Christians was disallowed? Would the agency shift to develop more domestic placements with non-Christian Japanese parents, or would it simply fold up? If the agency is helping more children in need to get placed, and if Christian placements are vital to the continuation of its work, then child welfare considerations would seem to justify placements with Christians abroad.

Foreign birth mothers

The issue of anonymous mothers whose children may or may not be eligible to acquire Japanese citizenship presents two ethical dilemmas that, potentially at least, may be faced by all adoption agencies and not just the Christian agency. The first dilemma concerns the relationship between the agency and the state in determining the status of the child. Here there is a conflict between the authority of the state to act in what it claims is the public interest, and the agency's commitment to the welfare of the child. Japan has a policy of restricting Japanese citizenship to children of at least one Japanese parent, even if children of foreign parents are born on Japanese soil. If this rule leaves some children in legal limbo, then the attitude appears to be: so be it (Otani 2001; Okuda 2003). By obtaining only very limited information about the child of a (possibly) undocumented migrant, an agency is able to avoid this outcome by gaining citizenship for the child. Citizenship confers obvious tangible benefits on the child, including, for example, the right to be educated and to travel. By acquiring citizenship for the child, therefore, the agency is promoting the child's welfare. If the agency insisted on carrying out a more thorough investigation to determine the nationality of the child's parents, then the child might well lose the chance to gain citizenship rights. In modifying its procedures with an eye to citizenship requirements, an agency's willingness to act autonomously in accordance with its own principles, and to regard the law opportunistically is of benefit to the child.

A second dilemma raised by such cases concerns the relationship between an agency and a birth mother. If the child is to acquire citizenship, the law, in effect, requires the contact between the agency and the mother to be limited to a brief, anonymous meeting. However, once it is conceded that there is an ethical case for an agency to be deliberately obtuse in failing to determine the nationality of the birth mother, it is hard to see why the agency should not go further and enter into a confidential relationship with a birth mother in order to involve her in decisions over the child. The mother's helpless position, her inability to have any legal say without jeopardizing the nationality of the child, add to the moral duty of the agency to give the mother the opportunity to be involved in decision making about the child's future.

A different approach to adoption

The practices of the Christian agency do not easily fit into the adoption framework developed by the Japanese state. The agency's understanding of welfare includes the desirability of a Christian upbringing in an adoptive family, even if this requires an international adoption. It includes a belief that the birth mother should make a final decision to have a child adopted before the birth and confirm this in writing shortly after the birth. It also includes the belief that children of possibly foreign mothers should be helped to acquire Japanese citizenship. In some circumstances, notably in being able to acquire citizenship for children of undocumented migrants, the willingness of the agency to test to the limit the rules laid down by the state is both to the child's advantage and in accordance with the wishes of the birth mother. In other cases, the agency's pursuit of the welfare of the child can be seen as rather narrowly focused, as it may not always give birth mothers sufficient opportunity to assess their feelings about adoption. In working only with Christian adopters the agency is excluding large numbers of Japanese parents who could give a child a home.

When the Christian agency is compared with the CGCs, Loving Hands and the Motherly Network, one may get the impression that it has an anomalous approach out of keeping with the ethics of adoption that have been developed since special adoptions were introduced. In fact, the attitude and procedures of the agency help to cast light on methods of adoption that are also used by other adoption agencies and mediators, including other Christian child welfare organizations in Japan. The opportunities for birth mothers to conceal their identity by placing babies through the agency has a similarity with the informal arrangements for adoption made through doctors. The use of birth mother 'contracts' by doctors and by lawyers bears some similarity to the practices of the agency, and there are several agencies involved in intercountry adoptions. The fact that the organisation has not registered as an adoption agency is also not unusual. A 2004 newspaper investigation found that at least 12 organisations were arranging adoptions without registering, with seven of them making placements abroad ('Yôshiengumi' 2005).

Others involved in making international placements from Japan to the US may also try and work around national rules, if not those of Japan then those of the USA. This can be seen in the advice that is sometimes given to birth mothers and other members of the birth family. To be eligible for intercountry adoption into the USA via the recognized routes for unrelated children, the child must be orphaned in the sense of being abandoned by both parents, or have only one parent who is unable to care for the child and have no other family members able to care for them either (Bartholet 1993: 147). This rule can make it more difficult to obtain a visa, and sometimes leads to the coaching of birth mothers when they prepare statements for the embassy as to why they are giving up a child. Birth mothers might, for example, be warned that if they write 'I had a fiancé...' this will only lead to the demand that he be brought into the process. In one case, the grandparents of a very young mother were advised to divorce, the father keeping the sons, the grandmother keeping the mother as a *single* grandparent and so in a position of great hardship. After the visa had been issued and the child adopted, the grandparents remarried.

Seen in this wider context, the practices of the Christian agency are not especially anomalous, rather in considering the work of the agency we have stepped across three fault lines. There is a divide between agencies that have attempted to use special adoption to create a distinct alternative to the secret adoptions between a birth mother and an adoptive couple and agencies that have modelled their policies quite closely on these secret adoptions. There is a divide between agencies that use a contract model as against those that do not. There are also differences in approach between agencies that pursue intercountry adoptions against those that concentrate on domestic adoptions. Agencies that concentrate on intercountry and other international placements are considered in Chapter Seven. But first Chapter Six explores the arrangements for the domestic adoption of newborn children by an association of doctors. Like the Christian agency, the association uses contracts in its dealings with birth mothers. In other respects its practices, while wholly legal, correspond quite closely to the informal arrangements that came to light in the Kikuta case.

6   The doctors' association

Some doctors are involved in making direct arrangements for special adoption of babies. They generally operate in a low-key way with the job of mediating placements being only a part of the work that they do. Only a small minority of doctors are involved; a questionnaire that gained responses from 453 gynaecologist-obstetricians who were members of the Obstetrician Association in Osaka found just 31 (6%) who affirmed that they personally assisted in adoptions. When asked to comment on the activities of a doctors' association making adoptions, a slightly higher figure of 45 (10%) said that this was a natural extension of an obstetrician's work (Iwasaki 2000: 7).

Doctors who arrange adoptions are not involved in seeking out potential parents and do not have the high public profile of Loving Hands or the Motherly Network. There is, however, some published material available. An obstetrician based in Saitama Prefecture has described helping children to be adopted (Kawakami 2000). One association, the Okayama Baby Rescue Unit, reported that between 1992 and 2004, a total of 267 women with an unwanted pregnancy consulted the organization alongside 420 couples who wanted to adopt children. These two groups were brought together and 262 special adoptions were arranged of which 242 were permitted by the courts, four were rejected and 16 were still in progress. Although not registered as an adoption agency, the organization is recognized as a non-profit welfare business audited by the municipal government and under a duty to report to the prefecture (Nihon sanfujinka ishikai Okayama-shibu 2005). A second organization, the Agency to Rescue Children is run by an obstetrician based in Chiba prefecture (Iwase, no date).

This chapter provides a three-part discussion of a doctors' association that operates as an adoption agency. First, the workings of the organisation are described, including the range of birth mothers, the factors considered in the assessment of adoptive parents, the matching process and the costs involved. As will be seen, the association's mode of operation is characterized by its simplicity and bears comparison to the past practice of some doctors in arranging discreet adoptions. Second, the experiences and the choices made by a couple who adopted through the association are reported. Third, the chapter considers the ethical and practical issues that are raised by the activities of the association.

A simple adoption system

The method of matching children and parents is straightforward. Throughout Japan, members of the association pass on the names of patients who are expectant mothers and who want to have their children adopted to an administrator, who works as a volunteer on an expense basis. They may also pass on the names of patients who wish to become adoptive parents. Other would-be adoptive couples hear of the association by word of mouth, and sometimes names are passed on by another agency, by an independent social worker, or by a volunteer. When potential adoptive parents contact the association, a meeting is arranged with its chairman who vets all applicants. Couples whom the chairman considers acceptable are consulted by the administrator over possible matches. When the parents agree to a match, they travel to the maternity hospital within days of the baby being born and take the child home with them. The formal legal adoption follows at a pace dictated by the family courts.

The administrator estimated that about 30% of the mothers were teenagers who had become pregnant while still at high school. Another 10% were married couples unable to cope financially with raising another child. The remaining 60% were mainly single mothers who were either 20 or younger, or who had had an affair with a married man. He characterized birth mothers in general as women who had missed the time limit for obtaining an abortion after their pregnancy had entered the 22nd week.[29] Once an expectant mother has indicated her wish to have her child adopted, the association begins to consider possible parents. Soon after the child is born, the birth mother is asked to sign a consent form relinquishing the child. The timing of this consent is dictated by circumstances; it is as soon as the administrator is able to visit the mother in the post-natal ward of the hospital. This may be on the day of birth and will always be within ten days. Before the administrator travels to visit a birth mother she is required to name her baby; the consent form signed by the mother always specifies the baby's name.

The number of children available for adoption through the association is greater than the number of eligible parents. This might seem odd as babies are highly sought after by adopters. However, it can be noted first that the agency does not advertise and second that there is a high rejection rate of potential parents. The selection procedure is unusually brief. Parents are chosen after a single meeting with the chairman. At the time of our discussion, the agency had a list of ten couples that it considered viable adoptive parents out of fifty couples who had recently applied.

The criteria for selecting adoptive parents, aside from the atmosphere of the meeting with the chairman, include the approval of relatives; sufficient finances – with a minimum threshold of about 5 million yen per annum annual income – and an acceptable level of education. The latter requirements suggest that there is a selection bias toward middle-class and wealthier applicants. Like many Japanese adoption agencies, the doctors' association requires that potential parents who are taking fertility treatment should stop.[30] Much more idiosyncratic is the agency's peculiar age rule, one that favours older couples. Other Japanese adoption agencies take 40 or thereabouts as the upper age limit for parents to adopt a baby, however, the doctors association has the opposite rule, stipulating that 40 is the *lower* age limit. The rule is justified on the grounds that younger parents might have their own children. There is an internal logic of a sort to this age rule, as it is congruent with the stipulations against fertility treatment. Couples who come to the organization have often tried fertility treatment without success in their later 30s. Older couples are also more likely to be better off under Japan's seniority rewards system in which salaries are tied to the length of employment. The upper limit for adoption through the doctors' association is 50 for salaried couples. This cut-off is imposed because it will be financially difficult to raise a child after retirement. Self-employed couples are not ruled out above the age of 50.

Adoptive parents are advised that they may need between 800,000 and 1 million yen to adopt a child. The costs include:

1 The expenses of the administrator, for example, travel involving an overnight stay would cost about 100,000 yen.
2 Hospital fees for caring for the baby, up to about 100,000 yen.
3 A donation to the association (not always given) of 300,000 yen after the adoption.

If the birth mother is unable to meet her hospital bills, the adopters may also be expected to pay:

4 The medical expenses of the birth mother.

These medical expenses sometimes include not only prenatal care but also modest readjustment costs for the birth mother after she has left hospital.

The doctors' association is registered as a welfare provider, but does not have legal status as an adoption agency. Before the adoption is legalized, therefore, the family court will not rely upon the documentation from the association with respect to the adoptive parents but will require a home study from a qualified social worker (in addition to the court's own visits to the parental home). This adds another necessary expense:

5 An independent home study.

The family courts generally approve the adoptions of newborn babies arranged by the doctors' association about one year after placement. The administrator interpreted this time gap as allowing for any disabilities to become apparent before the adoptive parents assumed legal responsibility for the child. (The same explanation has been seen in the infant homes where babies are sometimes kept for a year before being offered for adoption.) In the view of the administrator, if there were disabilities, the family court wanted to ascertain that the parents were still prepared to adopt before granting the adoption. In one case a baby placed by the agency turned out to be blind in one eye and had a heart problem. When the administrator learned this he advised the couple to return the baby as it would be difficult to cope with and would be best placed in an institution. However, to his surprise the couple kept the child.

The choices of an adoptive couple

A foreign wife and her Japanese husband had made unsuccessful efforts to adopt through a number of agencies. They were finally put in touch with the association by an independent social worker who specialized in facilitating private adoptions.

We called the social worker on Thursday and after a long talk with him he advised us to call the association. We did and they asked us to come and meet them on Saturday. There was a typhoon on Friday, but we took a domestic flight anyway on Saturday morning and arrived feeling awful. We went to the hospital where the association is based and met the administrator and he chatted to us for a while. He then went to the chairman, who was waiting in the coffee shop, and must have reported to him that we seemed fine. Then we had an interview with the chairman. He asked us a few questions, said 'Please be happy' and left. Then the administrator came back in with a breakdown of the fees, which seemed pretty reasonable.

After this we went home and waited. About every three days the administrator would call and chat to us and ask us questions about the type of child we would like, such as whether we wanted a boy or a girl. He called us about four different children we might want to adopt, and it was not until the fourth time that we said yes.

The first time we were offered a child was about a month after our meeting. He called up to say that there was a girl available. The mother was in her forties and divorced and wanted to give up the child. We said 'We'll think about it', but he advised us: 'No. I don't think it's right. The mother has come to us because she doesn't want the child in the public care system, but there is a chance that she may want the child back'. So we said no.

Soon afterwards he called again. 'A young man and young woman are expecting a child. They intend to get married, but the man has become involved with gangsters and has got into debt, so they can't marry at the moment and want the child to be adopted. What do you think?'

This time the administrator did not put forward his own opinion. Instead he worked through the possibilities with us, good and bad. We asked him: could the father ask for, say, 6 million yen in return for surrendering parental rights? The administrator said that he could. In the end, we decided no.

He called a third time about a baby weighing two kilograms, born to a thirteen-year old-mother. He advised us to say 'no' to this child because its low weight and the young age of the mother carried a risk of low intelligence. We followed his advice and turned the baby down.

We had just booked a last minute holiday when the administrator called again. A single young woman in her later teens had had a baby girl. The mother claimed that she did not know the father. Quite possibly she said this because he was foreign. For some reason the association had stopped taking on children when it knew that they were half [biracial]. Three days later he called again. There had been a mistake, the child was a boy. He would need to stay in hospital for at least ten days. We went on holiday anyway, then came back and met the child, in hospital in [a northern prefecture] when he was ten days old.

The doctor and nurses were kind, and although we never saw the birth mother we communicated with the grandmother. She was so embarrassed that she paid some of the fees that we were expecting to be charged to us. We stayed with Taro for two and a half days in the hospital before taking him home.

A month after we began looking after Taro we started to try and gain foster parents status. We contacted the CGC, but have found them most uncooperative, they acted like we were bothering them. It was hard to get through on the phone and when we managed to get them to come round and interview us, we got into an argument.

The courts, however, have been very helpful. We met a court-hearing officer three months after we started looking after Taro, and she helped in assembling all the documentation that we would need to present to the court. Three months after that the court first met to consider our application. It has contacted the [southern] prefecture of the birth family to notify the mother and grandmother of the application to adopt and to ask them to sign formal documents that will release Taro to us. We knew that this would be necessary. The administrator had warned us that the agreement signed by the birth mother in the hospital had no legal force. And this is the stage that we are at now.

This account is of interest because of the way in which the parents are given considerable choice in matching, albeit without seeing the children. Before considering this matching process, however, two other points of interest can be noted. First, the assessment of parents in a way that is apparently at once minimal and highly selective is unusual to the association. Second, the fees required of the parents are not fixed, but vary from case to case depending on the bills incurred for the particular child that they seek to adopt. In this case, the bills were actually quite low, because of the contribution of the grandmother, but potentially quite high, as the child required a long stay in hospital, and the birth mother gave birth outside her own prefecture, making it easier for her to conceal the birth, but incurring the full medical costs.

Selecting children

The matching system of the doctors' association provides considerable choice to adoptive parents. The administrator discusses a series of possible placements over the phone as babies, some yet unborn, become available. This matching technique bears some similarity to the initial matching system used by child guidance centres although there are also two notable differences. First, the CGCs do not try and match adoptive parents with unborn children. Second, the couple applying to the doctors' association obtain information about available children through the administrator but do not get to *see* any of these children (who may or may not be still in the womb) before making a decision. This approach parts company with the CGCs, where the typical pattern is for a social worker to suggest a possible child to prospective adoptive parents and then quickly if not immediately take them to see that child before they have come to a decision. For the CGCs there is an underlying realization that when adoptive parents see a child, this in itself is a powerful argument in that child's favour. The doctors' association takes the opposite approach in that it favours a decision based upon a rational calculation, before the adoptive parents have been affected by the emotional impact of seeing the child.

Some of the ways in which children are ruled in and ruled out are seen in the experience of the couple who adopted the fourth child that was offered to them: a child was only selected when the birth mother was seen as being definite in her decision to relinquish the child, where the costs were not extortionate, and where the baby was predicted to be healthy. The first baby to be offered to the adoptive parents had a birth mother who, in the view of the administrator, was uncertain as to whether to have the child adopted; all that she was sure of was that she did not want the child in public care. By advising the prospective adoptive parents to turn down the child the administrator was, in effect, rejecting the birth mother's request for assistance from the association. Unless the mother successfully approached another private agency or decided to keep the child, she would have to approach the CGC. The child would then almost certainly be placed in an infant home. If the birth mother has genuine uncertainties then placement in an institution via a CGC seems a safe option not only for any eventual adoptive parents but also for her, even if this decision is not in accordance with her current wishes.

From the perspective of the baby, however, immediate placement may be preferable to being placed in an institution even if the birth mother *does* later change her mind. In these circumstances the baby faces the possible upset of returning from the adoptive couple to the birth mother, but it is quite possible that this is preferable to living in institutional care before being returned to the birth mother. To draw an analogy, if the baby had the choice between being placed in institutional care or into the care of loving foster parents, it is reasonable to argue that its best interests would lie in going into foster care. The assumption that a baby is better off being placed in a family rather than in an institution is partly based on the relative merits, day by day, of each form of placement. Furthermore, it is easier for a child to get into an institution than to get out, although this applies much more to children's homes than it does to infant homes.

Two hypothetical circumstances can be envisaged where birth parents approach a private agency wanting their child adopted because the father's debts to gangsters prevent them from marrying. The agency knows in advance that the birth parents expect a large sum of money in return for surrendering the child. Alternatively, even if the birth parents do not mention money the agency may still be concerned that once a child is placed, the father might be tempted or pressurized to demand money for the child. If would-be adoptive parents are well off, then an agency might approach them knowing that if a monetary demand is made, they will have the wherewithal to pay up. The problem with taking this course is that it risks setting a precedent for gangsters to ensnare more young parents in debt, and then propose a way out. Turning down birth parents in this situation does not foreclose on the opportunity for the child to be adopted, as the birth parents can always turn to a child guidance centre. The dilemma for the agency is that the imperative for the birth parents to make money may conceivably lead them to market the child for some exploitative purpose if they cannot profit from an adoption.

The third child that was rejected by the adoptive couple weighed 2 kilograms and was born to a mother aged thirteen. The advice given by the administrator to adoptive couples sometimes appears to have been tinged with pessimism about the disabilities, low levels of intelligence and difficult behaviour patterns that babies might have inherited from their birth parents. On this occasion the advice by the administrator not to adopt the child on the grounds that he was likely to be of low intelligence cannot reasonably be deduced from the facts that we know; a child of that weight born to a young mother stands a very good chance of being normal.[31] There may have been other factors, such as the gestation period, but the case might also indicate that the efforts by the association to minimize the risk that a child they place will develop health problems sometimes leads to decisions of excessive caution.

Cherry picking

The overall approach to adoption taken by the association can be characterized as cherry picking. Only the children most attractive to parents and who are liable to be unproblematic are taken on by the association, and there is also a considerable weeding out of potential parents. With respect to the children at least, there is a logic to selectivity as a private agency does not have the public financial backing that would help it to provide post-adoption support services, or make long-term efforts to place a child, or reassume responsibility for a child if a placement breaks down (Buck 1964: 193–4). Does it, however, help placement rates to have a highly selective private agency working alongside other agencies that deal with a variety of children? Cherry picking amongst children would be a poor universal principle for adoption agencies to follow, as it would leave many with no chance of being adopted. However, if there is an adoption system, as in Japan, where a range of agencies in the private, social and public spheres provide different routes for children to get adopted, then a highly selective private organization has two advantages. First, by keeping children out of state care, the organization frees up public resources. Second it allows some children to avoid institutional care.

One effect of the doctors' association is to free up resources for state supported child welfare by arranging the adoptions of children who would otherwise be predicted to come into their care. The uncooperative response of the CGC when the adoptive parents in our case study approached it to register as foster parents might be related to this advantage. Foster parents are entitled to claim reasonably generous expenses from the state, but these payments are implicitly seen as being limited to parents who adopt through the state. In this case, the CGC may have seen the parents as straying outside the boundaries of the adoption route they had chosen by attempting to secure both the benefits of a privately arranged adoption and a state supported adoption.

The second advantage of the doctors' association is that like the Motherly Network and the Christian agency it allows some children to be adopted directly without having to first go through the intermediate step of living in an infant home or children's home. A family environment is preferable to an institution, even for a short period. There is also a risk that, for one reason or another, short term institutional care may become long-term care. Avoiding institutions is not always an overall advantage; it is sometimes best for birth parents and potential adopters of the child to have an intermediate period in an institution to give the birth parents time to be sure that they want the child adopted. However, the care taken by the doctors' association to avoid problems suggests that it will only be placing children where it feels that there is no prospect that the birth parents will wish to reclaim the child.

One might argue that a cherry picking approach will do little to actually increase the chances of adoption amongst children in need. The way in which it is highly selective indicates that the children whom it chooses to adopt would almost certainly be adopted anyway if they came into the care of the CGCs. By cherry picking newborn babies, however, the association may also occasionally have the unintended but beneficial effect of placing children who have undiagnosed health problems.

One way in which short-term care of a baby in an infant home can turn into long-term care in a children's home is if health problems are discovered that were not apparent from birth but which manifest as the child grows older. Once these health complications are known the child becomes much more difficult to place. They may also be defined by the CGC as 'better off' in an institution – although this may be rationalizing the reality that it will be hard or impossible to find parents for them. For all its caution, the fact that the doctors' association is dealing with babies means that on some occasions it will place a child who is later found to have health problems, such as the child who was found to be blind in one eye and with a heart problem after it was placed. This child would have been much more difficult to match with parents had it first gone to an infant home where these health difficulties would have been noticed. The doctors' association, despite itself, may have helped at least one child to get adopted who would otherwise have grown up in an institution.

7   International adoption

The worldwide debate and discussion over intercountry adoption can be divided between its outcomes and its process. Those who support intercountry adoption contend that its outcome is to help more children in need to find a family. Those who do not support it have argued that when the knock-on effects are considered it is uncertain that the global numerical impact on the number of children adopted represents a net gain. To some extent, this argument over outcomes has been assuaged by the widely accepted principle that an intercountry adoption should only be made where a domestic placement cannot be found. However, the worldwide debate and discussion over the process of intercountry adoption continues to be divisive. Support for intercountry adoption as helping needy children has been qualified and countered by the charge that private agencies have exploited vulnerable birth mothers and have been profiting excessively by marketing children for adoption abroad who would have been better cared for within their own state. Further, it has been contended that by straddling two countries they have avoided the safeguards and oversight of either. These arguments are reflected in the UN Convention on the Rights of the Child 1989, Article 21:

> States parties that recognize and/or permit the system of adoption shall ensure that the best interests of the child shall be the paramount consideration and they shall: (a) Ensure that the adoption of the child is authorized only by competent authorities … and that… the persons concerned have given their informed consent to the adoption… (b) Recognize that inter-country adoption may be considered as an alternative means of child's care, if the child cannot be placed in a foster or adoptive family or cannot in any suitable manner be cared for in the child's country of origin; (c) Ensure that the child concerned by inter-country adoption enjoys safeguards and standards equivalent to those existing in national adoption; (d) Take all appropriate measures to ensure that, in inter-country adoption, the placement does not result in improper financial gain for those involved in it.

Although the terms of the Article 21 are quite general, their focus is clear. The call for adoption to be regulated by competent authorities and the stress on intercountry adoptions meeting national standards reflects the charge that agencies may avoid the law. The demand that birth parents give informed consent reflects the charge that agencies may inveigle birth mothers into agreeing to an adoption in an illicit or exploitative way. The condemnation of improper financial gain arises out of the aversion to the idea of an adoption market. The stipulation that adopted children should go abroad only when they cannot find homes in their own countries, therefore, reflects all these apprehensions about the adoption process, in addition to the concern that intercountry adoption should result in a net increase in adoption. This principle is also in keeping with the claim that a child is better off growing up in his own culture, and has also been used to criticize intercountry adoption (Hayes 2000).

Japan ratified the Convention on the Rights of the Child in 1994. It has not, however, ratified or signed the 1993 Hague Convention on Protection of Children and Cooperation in respect of Intercountry Adoption. The Hague Convention has been influenced by 'the concerns of those who emphasize the negative rather than the positive potential' of intercountry adoption (Bartholet 1993: 150). It provides a series of explicit, detailed rules to address these concerns and requires that each state designate a 'central authority'. The authority is meant to ensure that all intercountry adoptions in or out of its borders follow the Hague rules.

When asked to comment by the Permanent Bureau at The Hague, the Japanese government limited itself to a mild observation on the differences between the Convention and private international law in Japan. According to Paragraph 2, Article 26 of the Hague Convention, a child adopted from another state enjoys the same rights as a child adopted in a domestic adoption. This creates inconsistencies between the Convention and two articles of Japanese law.

1   Under Article 20 of Japan's private international law provisions (*horei*), the legalization of an adoption is governed by the law (or laws) of the adoptive parents. At first glance this might appear merely to put the Hague Convention's rule in a different form, in fact it does not because if the adoptive parent of a non-Japanese child is a foreign national resident in Japan, then it is the law of the parents home state, not Japanese law, that is applicable. This has implications for the rights of the child, as it means, for example, that rules about the consent of the child to the adoption depend on the laws of the state of the adoptive parent.

2   *Horei* Article 21 of Japan's private international law identifies the legal relationship between adoptive parents and their child. In some circumstances it is the state of which the child is a national that governs this relationship, even if the family is resident in Japan. If the child and at least one parent are nationals of the same state, then it is the laws of that state which govern the legal relationship between parent and child. Only if a foreign child does not share nationality with either parent does Japanese law govern the relationship, assuming that Japan is 'the place of the child's habitual residence' (Government of Japan 2005).

The differences between the Hague Convention and Japanese law, however, run deeper than is suggested by these rather technical anomalies. The role of a central authority that is integral to the Hague Convention is at odds with the *laissez faire* approach to adoption that has been taken by Japan. There is no authoritative professional body that deals with adoption, whether international or domestic, and there has been little in the way of proactive state policies to oversee international adoptions. The courts and immigration service have had an impact on structuring policy, but this has been in terms of piecemeal reactions to the cases that they deal with rather than establishing an overall policy. Agencies in Japan are free to make their own decisions about how to respond to the Convention and their attitudes vary. Some see a regulated international framework of intercountry adoption as an important way of protecting children; others are more sceptical.

In contrast to Japan, all West European States quickly ratified the Hague Convention, an indication of the general European shift towards the control of adoption by public agencies. In the USA the Senate ratified the Convention in 2000 but has still not implemented the agreement (Hollinger 2004: 47). Where Europe has followed a seemingly inexorable transition from adoption being organized by individuals to agencies in civil society and then the state, statist initiatives in the USA have been contested and the movement towards the control of adoption by public agencies and authoritative central organizations has been patchy. Intercountry adoption, in particular is mediated by many independent agencies, and largely through their entrepreneurial efforts the number of children adopted from abroad into the USA has risen to over 20,000 cases a year (Hollinger 2004: 41–2; US Citizenship and Immigration Services 2005).

Placement in the USA

The policy of the USA towards intercountry adoption is of significance to Japan, whose post-war history of adoption shows a long-term US connection. As the Second World War ended, thousands of Japanese children were orphaned and others were in great poverty. The first result of this was the adoption of Japanese children not in the USA but in China: amidst the suicides and murders in the chaotic evacuation of mainland China more than 2,500 children ended up adopted by Chinese parents (Tseng 1990: 330). This, however, was a one-off event while the US occupation established a continuing pattern of placements that began with the adoption of some of the thousands of children who faced severe discrimination after being fathered by US occupation troops (Burkhardt 1983). Civil initiatives by US citizens and others with a US connection were launched to help these children, and adoption was one of the options pursued. The wives of servicemen stationed in Japan, churches and charities, all began making provision for needy children by funding orphanages and calling for adoption programmes. 'Moral adoptions' in which US parents provided financial support and Christmas presents to needy children, particularly atomic bomb orphans, were created by Kiyoshi Tanimoto, a Japanese pastor and Hiroshima survivor, and by Norman Cousins (Yamamoto 1979: 173–4). These moral adoptions developed into arranging actual adoptions into the USA. In the immediate post-war years an adoption from Japan into the USA was cumbersome as the 1924 Oriental Exclusion Act meant that it was only possible through an individual Bill to Congress. However, the US government made the legalities easier with the passage of the Refugee Relief Act of 1953 (Section 5). Under these circumstances intercountry adoption from Japan to the USA expanded quickly with hundreds of children adopted each year in the post-war period.[32]

The rise in intercountry adoption from East Asia generally in the 1950s was not without its critics in the USA. On one side, it was argued that a regulated approach was needed to ensure safeguards to make sure that children were placed appropriately. On the other, it was contended that in the face of the urgent need of mixed background children in Asia a too nice concern with following rules and developing safeguards could hamper overriding humanitarian imperatives: adoption agencies and others concerned with child welfare should be concentrating their efforts on acting as facilitators rather than gatekeepers. From this perspective regulations, seen in the round as including immigration rules, did not so much serve to protect the child as present an obstacle course that needed to be negotiated to attain the priority of uniting a needy child with loving parents as soon as possible. Thus, Pearl Buck, who since 1949 had been making efforts to assist mixed background children, described bending the rules to ensure the adoption a mixed American–Japanese boy of four, born in Japan, and disabled by polio:

> ... we got him into the United States. It was difficult, all but impossible, for he was not the sort of immigrant we permit to enter our land of the free and home of the brave. At first we had to promise that he was a visitor. As a visitor he went into the home of a physician specializing in his particular handicap. As a visitor he underwent treatment and care and was given love. I saw him last when he was seven years old. He had not been able to walk when he came as a visitor, but now he ran to meet me. A light brace on his leg was all he needed now, and his adoptive father said he would need nothing by the time he was fifteen (Buck 1964: 148).

Koko Kondo who stayed with Peal Buck as a child before returning to Japan, shares some of this same pragmatic attitude in the placements she makes as well as the humanist philosophy that underpins it. Since about 1970 she has followed in the footsteps of her father Kiyoshi Tanimoto, the Hiroshima pastor, and arranged the adoption of around a child a year, 37 children in all, mainly to the USA, although occasionally children have been placed domestically. Mrs Kondo supports foreign parents if they decide to pursue the adoption through the Japanese courts or if they apply for an immigrant visa for the child and conclude the adoption in the USA. The Japanese court system is an obvious route for foreign residents but she has also taken this route on two or three occasions to legalize adoptions for couples in the US. The practical problem with this is that in the interim the child either has to live with her, or at a costly private orphanage. The second route is for the child to get an immigrant visa to the USA, after which the parents can immediately start to care for the child, and apply to adopt the child in the court of their home state (Kondo 2005: 234). From her knowledge of the circumstances of the mother, usually a very young single mother, Mrs Kondo writes a letter explaining the hardship facing the child. If embassy officials ask: 'why not go through the family court?' she explains that the immigration route will save time; to go through the courts will take about a year while a visa can sometimes be issued immediately, and does not take longer than two to four months.

Like other agencies that deal with both Japanese and foreign couples, Mrs Kondo has found prospective Japanese parents to be comparatively demanding, and like the Motherly Network, demanding parents are turned down:

> They want young children, they're concerned about their personality, their background, they ask all kinds of questions. They look ahead to becoming old and think: 'she can take care of us'. Parents who make stipulations, I rule out. But in the USA parents ... say they'd like to adopt 'whoever is in need'. A boy or a girl? 'It doesn't matter'. I want someone who can accept a child, *whoever*.

In one case a US placement had fallen through: after the events of September 11, 2001, the parents' application to adopt a child from Japan was refused in the USA because of a local decision in their home state that the child might grow up to become a terrorist. The child had to be placed with another couple on Mrs Kondo's list.

Despite the wealth of twenty-first century Japan, the pattern of adoption into the USA continues with a modest flow of children across the Pacific. These are undertaken in agency-to-agency arrangements and by individual mediators like Mrs Kondo. Occasionally Christian children's homes arrange an intercountry adoption of a child identified by visiting potential parents (Ransford 2005). The Japan Federation of Bar Associations has asked why 'the Japanese government has taken no measures to prevent our children going aboard to live as adopted children' (2003: 226). Similarly Okuda (2003: 103) has described as 'shockingly large' the generally accepted annual figure of around 40 children being adopted into the USA (the actual numbers are somewhat higher – see Appendix 1). However, in comparison to some other states, including Korea, there is little public controversy over the intercountry adoption of Japanese children in the USA.

Adoption and immigration

Almost all states have signed and ratified the UN Convention on the Rights of the Child. However, one can sometimes learn rather more about governmental policies toward children by the reservations and declarations made on signing the treaty than from the text itself. When Egypt and various other Islamic states signed, for example, they stated that they had reservations over all provisions relating to adoption as this was incompatible with the Shariah. When Japan signed the Convention, it added two declarations to the effect that it was not going to be hampered in its immigration and deportation policy by treaty provisions against separating children from their parents (United Nations 2001a, b).

Japan's restrictive immigration policy sits somewhat uneasily with efforts to uphold children's rights. This is most evident in the difficult position of children born in Japan but who are defined as being stateless, but it can also have an impact on adopted children. For an adopted child to obtain a permanent visa, they are meant to be under six, an age limit that is related in principle to Japan's distinction between a special adoption (also only for children under six or sometimes eight) and an ordinary adoption, which is not seen as severing all ties nor as needing to be a permanent arrangement. In practice older children are also able to gain permanent visas, but this is not guaranteed. Even where a child who is already living in Japan has been adopted, if their visa is not in order the immigration authorities may intervene to attempt to disrupt the adoption. In one high profile case a Thai grandmother married to a Japanese man applied to adopt her thirteen-year-old granddaughter after the death of the girl's parents. The family court in Tokyo approved the adoption but the immigration authorities nonetheless tried to deport the child (Matsubara 2004).[33]

Adoption and foreign law

There is one notable exception to the Japanese state's *laissez faire* attitude towards international adoption. If a couple wish to adopt in Japan and either or both of the prospective parents of the child, or the child himself is not Japanese, then in accordance with the provisions of Japan's private international law, the legal requirements of their state(s) of origin must be satisfied in addition to Japanese law (Ministry of Foreign Affairs 1996: 147, 148; 2001: 194). This rule can be seen as no more than prudent planning for future eventualities, but it may also defer implicitly to those who are concerned to defend Japan's ethnic homogeneity by positing a general expectation that resident foreigners will eventually leave. The result is that international or intercountry adoptions, as the terms are legally understood in Japan are by no means exhausted by children entering or leaving the state, as they include any adoption where one of the parties involved is not a Japanese citizen. This broad definition includes a considerable variety of adoptions, each with different legal and procedural implications. The child to be adopted may be Japanese, he may be a foreign child living in Japan (including stateless children), or he may be a foreign child living abroad who is brought to Japan for adoption. The adoptive couple may be Japanese, they may be a mixed marriage with one Japanese and one foreign spouse, or they may be a resident foreign couple. Foreign single women residents may also seek to adopt. Given the rules that even where these adoptions are finalized in Japan, they should conform to the laws of the states of foreign children or their adoptive parents, Japanese judges may find themselves considering laws from all over the world.

International adoptions that are adjudicated in Japan account for about 300–500 cases per year. This does not, however, account for all international adoptions, as where a Japanese-based couple adopts a child abroad they will normally adopt through the court system in the child's state of origin and on their return to Japan will deal only with the immigration authorities. Conversely, when foreign parents adopt a child living in Japan, although they will have dealings with the court, this may only be to arrange for the child to emigrate from Japan so that the child can then be adopted in the parents' home state.

The acceptance of foreign couples resident in Japan as potential adoptive parents varies from one agency to another. Some CGCs welcome them, but others are either off-putting or refuse outright to register them. If a foreign resident lives in a ward with an uncooperative CGC they may look to adopt abroad instead using an international agency. Other foreign residents adopt from abroad because they want a child that shares their skin colour or ethnicity. For example, white parents from the USA living in Japan have arranged to adopt a child from Russia; dark skinned parents have adopted an Ethiopian child. It can also be noted that there is a widespread reluctance amongst agencies in Japan to allow single women to adopt through an ordinary adoption, and this too may lead foreign single women residents with sufficient financial means to adopt a child from abroad through a more sympathetic international agency.

The legal and bureaucratic procedures required to complete an 'international' adoption within Japan can be quite onerous, as the adoption must comply with the laws of at least two, often three and conceivably four states, and the different sets of rules to be juggled do not always fit very easily with each other. The requirement that the laws of all states must be respected, however has been waived by the courts on a case-by-case basis where there has been an irreconcilable conflict of law. Thus in one case, a Japanese wife and her Egyptian husband, who was also a Muslim, wished to adopt a child in Japan. Egyptian law prohibits adoption within Islam. Japanese law stipulates that both parents must adopt when a married couple adopt a child. The courts decided that as the couple were settled in Japan and the husband intended to nationalize, the adoption by both parents could go ahead (Omura 1998).

If the difficulties of adopting within Japan are too great, the parent may have the option of leaving temporarily and adopting the child in their home state. However, to do this they need to be able to travel across international borders with the child, and this too can be problematic. A British family who had a toddler placed with them by their local CGC found themselves in this quandary. For the child to be adopted in Japan, the adoption needed to comply with both UK law and Thai law – the nationality of the mother. Thai law, however, required the participation of the birth parents to complete the adoption, and both parents had disappeared. The only documentation available was a statement by the mother that she had given up the child, and this was insufficient.

Faced with this problem the couple decided that the mother should travel to Britain to adopt the child there before returning to Japan. The child, however, had no travel documents. He did not have a Thai passport and could not obtain one without first going with the adoptive parents to Thailand on a *one-way* exit visa from Japan. The prospect of getting trapped in Thailand by immigration rules was deemed to be too risky. The child could not get a Japanese passport because there was no proof that the father was Japanese. He could not get a stateless person's passport, because he was defined as Thai. He could not get a UK passport because he was not yet adopted. However, the parents managed to obtain entry documents from the British embassy. They also needed permission for the child to leave Japan, which was obtained by taking the child to the office that dealt with overstayers and illegal workers so that he could be officially deported.

Parents who adopt in an international adoption, may also take it upon themselves to regularize the position of the child in different states. An American husband with a Chinese wife, adopting a Japanese child, described the process as endless; more than a year and a half after the child had been placed with them by their local CGC, the legalities were still not completed. The parents were taking the adoption a state at a time. They had adopted in Japan first (this had taken a year and two months from placement) and were now in the process of fulfilling US requirements to gain citizenship for the child.

Where a foreign or mixed couple adopts a child already living in Japan, the placement comes first and the process of legalizing the adoption comes second. Once a child has been placed, it is rare for them to be taken away again. So as long as the parents are settled in Japan indefinitely, they can afford to be phlegmatic about the time required to complete the adoption. (From a financial perspective, there is even some incentive to move at a leisurely speed in legalizing the adoption in the Japanese courts, because so long as the child is defined as in being in foster care the parents are paid to look after him or her.) However, there are different time pressures at work when a child from abroad is adopted in Japan, as many of the requirements have to be completed before rather than after placement. There is also the potential for a period of limbo if a foreign state places a child with a couple before the Japanese immigration authorities are willing to allow the child into Japan.

Adopting from China

The US director of an international agency, one that specializes in the intercountry adoption of children from China by western parents resident in Japan, took us through the steps needed to coordinate the requirements of Japan, of the 'China Centre for Adoption Affairs' in China, and of the state of the adoptive parents, usually the USA. These steps involve the collection and authentication of documents about the parents including a police statement, financial records, medical records, birth certificates and a home study. To facilitate the process and circumvent problems, the director had developed contacts in various embassies and consulates and had a knowledge of which individuals and organizations were and were not cooperative. For example, the process of gaining Japanese immigration clearance for a Chinese child of US parents was speeded up by a triangular journey. The adoptive parents would fly out from Japan to China to have the child placed with them. They would not then fly back directly to Japan but would rather fly first to a certain airport in the USA where officials were willing to grant expedited US citizenship to adopted children. The child's US passport allowed the re-entry of the new family into Japan.

To indicate some of the difficulties that might be encountered, and how the international agency gets around them, we can follow through how it overcomes problems in obtaining a police certificate for potential adoptive parents. Japan's domestic adopters are not required by law to have a police check, and to our knowledge no domestic Japanese agency has taken it upon itself to insist on one. However, a police certificate is required by the Chinese authorities. Parents who wish to adopt from China must, therefore, apply to their local police force in Japan for a certificate, and when they do, some forces refuse to supply one. At this point the agency steps in and complains to the Ministry of Foreign Affairs that the parents need a police certificate but have been refused. The ministry checks the records to satisfy themselves that the Chinese embassy has asked for such a certificate. Having done this, the ministry is willing to provide a certificate, but not in a way that offends the sensibilities and prerogatives of the local police force. The ministry, therefore, sends a sealed envelope to the agency, bearing the inscription 'do not open'. The director takes the unopened envelope back to the ministry and says: 'I need this certificate certified'. The official at the ministry opens the envelope, stamps the certificate and states: 'This certificate did not come from our office'. (In an immediate sense this is true, the certificate was brought back *to* the office.) The official then reseals the envelope and gives it back to the director, who takes it to the Chinese Embassy, who certifies the certificate again and forwards it to the China Centre for Adoption. The certificate contains a single sentence, 'This person has no criminal record in Japan', written in five languages.

International Social Service Japan

A rather different approach is taken by the International Social Service Japan (ISSJ). Founded in 1952 as the 'Japan–America Joint Committee for the Assistance of Orphans' this organization has its roots in the post-war effort to find adoptive homes in the USA, particularly for mixed background children. However, it has subsequently altered its focus and way of operating. It still occasionally places children directly with unrelated adults living abroad, but deals mainly with relative adoptions from South East Asia alongside other work such as international marriage and divorce, and immigration and repatriation cases.

ISSJ is very much aware of the issue of implementing international standards in intercountry adoption. Japanese NGOs including the Federation for the Protection of Children's Human Rights (1997: 57.2) and the Japan Federation of Bar Associations (2003: 233) have called for Japan to ratify the Hague Convention. ISSJ has added its voice to this call (Otsuki 2004). On various occasions the agency has refused to involve itself with direct adoptions from states, including Russia, Vietnam and Cambodia, where it has had uncertainty over whether there has been a proper effort to keep the child and birth parents together. The agency is not proactive in arranging placements; it takes the view that wherever possible children should be brought up by their birth mothers and so does not want to encourage adoption. It also makes efforts to contact the natural fathers and other relatives (International Social Service Japan 2005). As staff member Keiko Terasaki puts it, 'as an agency we are negative about being positive. We do not go out and look for babies or children to match with parents. We just sit and wait'.

Japanese parents only rarely approach ISSJ seeking to adopt a foreign child. The reasons suggested by Ms Terasaki are the familiar ones of the selectiveness of Japanese couples and their inflexible vision of the type of child they are willing to adopt. More often, the agency deals with mixed couples or foreign resident couples who want to adopt children both inside and outside Japan. On being approached by such a couple, the first question asked by the agency is whether they expect to stay in Japan for at least three years, as the adoption process can be lengthy. The agency also requires the couple to have been married for at least three years. Potential adopters who fulfil these initial criteria are invited to fill in an application, attend an orientation session explaining the process, and are offered a home study.

The ISSJ home study requires the couple to provide extensive documentation. In addition to birth and marriage certificates they must provide a police certificate, a psychological report, a physical examination report and medical confirmation that they are healthy. The agency then interviews the couple separately and together. The results are considered at a meeting of caseworkers who decide if the couple are suitable adopters. Approved couples are informed that their name has been placed on the waiting list. When a child becomes available, the agency considers which are the most fitting parents from the entire waiting list.

Children are referred to ISSJ from a variety of sources. Sometimes the agency is contacted by the child guidance centre or welfare office. Sometimes an obstetrics clinic will refer an expectant mother to them, and sometimes a mother will simply knock on the door at the agency offices. The children who come from any of these sources may be Japanese as well as foreign. However, children referred by the CGC always have some characteristics which, like being foreign, make them hard to place. CGCs that refer such children to ISSJ do so in the realization that foreign couples resident in Japan are open to parenting a wider range of children than are likely to be considered by a Japanese couple. The child may be a Japanese citizen but have a racially mixed background. The child may be classified as having a 'difficult' social background, with natural parents who are mentally ill, in prison or with criminal records, or who have borne the child through incest. The child may also be physically handicapped, although if the disability is mild the agency is optimistic that it can place the child with foreign parents on its list.

ISSJ finds it helpful to have expectant mothers referred to the agency because of the opportunity to gather information in advance. However, they advise mothers not to make a definite decision over whether to have their child adopted until after it is born. Options other than adoption are discussed with the mother, including getting support from grandparents or friends, the possibility of entering a mother and child dormitory, or gaining public financial assistance. The agency does not have a fixed minimum period after the birth before it will consider a mother's decision to adopt to be final, but rather treats each case individually. Mothers who are not firm in their decision to adopt are given more time.

ISSJ will arrange adoption placements within days of birth. If a birth mother is seen as settled in her decision to relinquish the child, she is given a consent form to sign. ISSJ does not imply to the mother that her signature has any legal force, nor that the agency itself has any custody rights over the child. Rather, the agency emphasizes that once a mother has signed the consent form, any change of mind will result in the trauma of separation of the child from its would-be adoptive parents. The baby is then taken from the hospital to be placed with adoptive parents at the agency office. There is never a direct handover, nor any other meeting between the birth mother and adoptive parents, all the adoptions that are arranged through ISSJ are closed, and the agency does not act as a means of indirect contact. However, if children as adults ask the agency to contact the birth mother, it will do so by sending a letter to the mother requesting a meeting, but without specifying the subject to maintain confidentiality.

Ordinary adoption in Japan usually takes place between adults who are already related to the children they adopt (Appendix 1). These domestic adoptions have a parallel in the intercountry adoption by mixed or foreign couples of related children. In the experience of ISSJ many of these adoptions involve a child living in the Philippines. The typical child is related to a Filipino woman who has married either a Japanese husband or an American husband stationed in Japan with the military. The usual pattern is for the couple to adopt the wife's niece or nephew. Sometimes the agency arranges the step-adoption by the husband of a child that the mother left in the Philippines, although it is more normal in step-adoptions for the child to be already in Japan with the mother. A broadly similar pattern is seen in placements of children of Thai nationality. Here the predominant form of adoption is the step-adoption by the Japanese husband of the natural child of his Thai wife.[34]

ISSJ arranges the international adoption of relatives in the Philippines in cooperation with the Philippines Intercountry Adoption Board (ICAB). The agency in Japan conducts a home study of the parents, and forwards this to ICAB in the Philippines. The Board assesses the suitability of the adoption and decides whether to approve the proposed match. Once ICAB has approved the match the child can travel to Japan with his or her parents. ISSJ conducts adjustment visits and after six months forwards a report to ICAB. If ICAB approves the match then the adoption is finalized in the Philippines.

Where a child is involved in a non-relative adoption, they will often be the offspring of a single Thai or Filipino mother working in Japan, sometimes legally and sometimes as an overstayer. In one such case, a Japanese husband and his Thai wife were given a two-month-old boy to care for by a friend, an unmarried Thai woman who had overstayed her visa. They asked to adopt the child, and the birth mother agreed. The agency became involved in formalizing the adoption in Thailand through its Child Adoption Centre and Department of Public Welfare (ISSJ 2002). In another case a birth mother from the Philippines legally resident in Japan, was unable to care for a child. ISSJ asked the Philippines Department of Social Welfare and Development whether there was a Filipino family who could adopt the child. When they were told that none could be found, they put forward a Canadian couple, resident in Japan, to ICAB. After ICAB approved the match, the adoption was legalized in Canada (Otani 2003).

As ISSJ has supported the efforts to establish international rules for intercountry adoption, it is slightly ironic that in one case where children have been regularly brought into Japan with the help of ISSJ child relatives from the Philippines, there is the possibility that not all of these children are truly in *need* of adoption. The Filipino children in question usually belonged to the extended family of the wife in an international marriage to a Japanese husband. In these cases it can be queried whether there is a need for adoption, or whether the practice of adoption is at least partly designed to allow for extended family migration. Relative adoptions from the Philippines may be more analogous to an ordinary adoption in Japan than to a special adoption. The adult parties involved may have taken economic considerations into account with the intent of benefiting the adopted child in terms of increased opportunities, even if the child could be cared for by birth parents. The attitude of ISSJ towards this issue is that one must indeed be cautious, but that every case is investigated by the ICAB in the Philippines, and ISSJ agrees to help only those cases where the Board finds that the child is in genuine need of adoption.

Foreign parents who are matched with a child already living in Japan are undoubtedly adopting a needy child. This has been recognized by some CGCs who welcome foreign couples. Other CGCs however, refuse or are off-putting to foreign residents. The matching of foreign parents with children, therefore, is something of a lottery depending on the attitude of the CGC where the parents live and, if it turns them down, their ability to locate another agency that will accept applications from non-citizens. ISSJ offers the possibility of adopting outside the local CGC, so that hard-to-place children can be matched with foreign parents across Japan. However, the agency has not actively pursued this role, and does not, for example, circulate its list of would-be parents, but rather simply waits to be contacted.

Ms Terasaki expressed a certain ambivalence towards placing children with foreign couples.

> When we place a child [from a CGC], in one way I am satisfied because that child now has a family and will be OK. But in another way I feel a sense of shame. Why are we Japanese not adopting such children? Why do we have to get rid of them to Westerners?

The next chapter considers these questions by investigating the placement of foreign children with western parents resident in Japan.

8 Transethnic adoption

In Tokyo, in Okinawa and in other more cosmopolitan areas of Japan it is not unusual for children in need of adoption to be classified as foreign. There are also mixed-background children who, although they are classified as Japanese, *look* foreign. The general unwillingness of Japanese couples to adopt foreign children makes placement for these children problematic. In response, some CGCs, including ones in and around Tokyo, have sought to make placements with foreign residents and mixed couples. They have also referred mixed and minority children to organizations like ISSJ that make placements with foreign residents and abroad.[35] In this chapter we consider some of the reasons why it is difficult to place mixed or minority children with Japanese couples, look at the experiences of western couples who have adopted mixed background children, and consider the implications of the international debate over transethnic adoption in the Japanese context.

The difficulties of making a placement of a mixed or minority child accentuate the problems of placing *any* unrelated child with a Japanese couple. The difficulties begin at the home study stage. Parents are invited to draw up the criteria of the type of child they would like to adopt, and in response many draw up closely defined stipulations indicating their desire to adopt a child of a good background and with good blood, occasionally extending to a literal concern with specifying blood types. The criteria of 'good' blood and background tend to rule out the adoption of children of a mixed or minority parentage as in both cases it is implicitly assumed that a necessary part of being 'good' is being Japanese.

It would be misleading to describe the particular difficulty of finding homes for mixed and minority children as primarily the result of racism. To draw an analogy, the frequent preference for a girl aged under three amongst potential adoptive couples does not indicate a positive antipathy towards boys or older children. Parents may want a child that looks as much as possible like themselves, or may simply not think about a mixed or minority child when they construct their prior ideal of what the child they adopt should be like. Furthermore, couples often want to retain a degree of secrecy about adopting a child. This also makes mixed background or minority children more difficult to place as, if they are visibly different from their parents, it will frustrate efforts to keep the adoption quiet. However, on some occasions racism is also a factor, indirectly or directly, in decisions by Japanese parents to adopt only Japanese children.

Racist attitudes in Japan, while comparatively mild are also quite common (Debito 2005). Where racist attitudes are held they create aversion to outsiders, including the *buraku* outcast group as well as foreigners, using metaphors of pollution and contamination (Hayashida 1976). Such concepts can all too easily be applied to minority or mixed background children. Derogatory racial stereotypes circulating in society also make adoption of children of mixed and minority background harder. This is particularly true for children with birth parents who are black or dark skinned. Blacks have been stigmatized by many of the same negative stereotypes that have been attributed to them in the West, and darker skin is historically associated with menial outdoor occupations (Wagatsuma 1967). A couple wanting to adopt may not hold these attitudes, but neither may they wish to confront them in their family life by choosing to raise a mixed or minority child.

Given the difficulties of placing mixed or minority children with Japanese couples, some CGCs and private agencies have found that they are more readily accepted by mixed or minority couples in Japan. Most minority couples who apply to adopt in Japan, are, by the very act of putting themselves forward, demonstrating a willingness to adopt transethnically. It is true that in some cases, ethnic matching is possible. A US serviceman and his Filipino wife may, for example, adopt a child with birth parents of the same nationalities. Often, however, the ethnic backgrounds of the child and the parents do not overlap.

Mixed and minority children in need of adoption are commonly born to mothers living either in Tokyo or in Okinawa, but where do their birth and adoptive parents come from? Over the last 100 years, waves of migrants and visitors have established themselves, some permanently and others more precariously, in Japan. The largest group of foreigners are the Korean–Japanese, followed by Chinese. The third largest foreign community are Japanese–Brazilians (Japanese farmers settled in Brazil in the interwar period). The fourth largest group legally present in Japan are Filipinos.[36] Other legally present minorities include Thai and other South Asian women paired with Japanese men through the international marriage industry. The post-war period saw the long term US occupation of Okinawa, where there is a continued military presence. There are also US military bases around Tokyo. The drive to learn English has encouraged the migration of native English speakers on temporary work contracts. Multinational companies have branches in Tokyo with cosmopolitan staff. There are also Embassy staffs from all over the world in the capital. The Tokyo entertainment districts have enabled some visible male minorities, including Ghanaians, to establish a niche for themselves. Foreigners illegally present in Japan include visa 'overstayers' from Korea, China, The Philippines, Thailand and many other states.[37] There are also an unknown number of undocumented migrants from the Philippines and from other South Asian states. Some are men working in the construction industry; others are women in the sex industry.[38]

The birth parents of mixed and minority children in need of adoption and the parents who adopt them are drawn from this patchwork of ethnicities but they are not drawn equally. Minority children relinquished to a child guidance centre or other adoption agency are unlikely to come from settled and self-contained ethnic communities but will rather have a parent or parents who are in a more precarious, marginal or transient position. These children are often of a mixed background, particularly where one of their parents is not a member of a community equally containing members of both sexes, but has rather arrived in Japan as part of a wave of single-sex migration or temporary relocation. Such children include those born to foreign mothers as well as children of single Japanese women who have had a relationship with a foreign boyfriend. In Okinawa, children in need of adoption are likely to have birth parents who are part of the economic and social life around the US military base. As the adoptive parents are likely to be a married couple employed by the US military, an overlapping ethnic background is quite possible. However, in Tokyo, parents who come forward as adopters for minority children are typically married couples who are long-term residents in Japan, employed by large western-based companies. As a result, the adoptive parents and their child often have no shared ethnicity. Neither parent is Japanese, and if the child is of a mixed background, the minority birth parent is often from a non-western state.

When western residents apply to an adoption agency in Japan, it is likely that the adoption will be transethnic regardless of whether the child they adopt is of Japanese, mixed, or foreign background. In states where transethnic adoption has become controversial, applicants would either be rejected or would be assessed as to whether they had the particular skills, level of awareness and attitudes purportedly necessary for raising a child of a different ethnicity (Hayes 1995). There is no such assessment in Japan, where the type of child that a parent is suitable to adopt is taken to be synonymous with the type of child that the parent expresses an interest in adopting. The home study is designed to identify the range of children that the parents would be willing to adopt by using measures including age, personality and sex, as well as ethnic background.

As part of the investigation into their preferences, potential parents are asked if they are interested in adopting a minority or mixed background child. This question has rather different implications for western parents who approach a CGC or other adoption agency than it does for Japanese parents. By applying to adopt a child in Japan, western parents are self-evidently expressing an interest in adopting a child who is unlikely to share their ethnicity. As western couples are already open to the idea of adopting a child of a different ethnicity, it is only a small step to take to say that they are also interested in adopting a child who has a minority background in Japan. In contrast to western parents, Japanese parents, as members of the majority community, may well not have considered the possibility of transethnic adoption. This is not invariably the case; ISSJ has reported an increase in applications from Japanese couples as well as mixed couples (ISSJ 2004). Nonetheless, most Japanese parents enter into adoption with highly specific wants over the type of background the child should have, in a way that is liable to exclude minority and mixed background children.

The following accounts from a white western adoptive father and a white western adoptive mother describe the process of making a transethnic placement from the perspective of an adoptive parent. In both cases, it is notable that the parents identify attitudes towards relations with ethnic minorities and towards skin colour that suggest the difficulties of placing a mixed or minority child with Japanese parents.

An adoptive father

The selection process was no problem. We told the child guidance centre that we did not want to adopt a child with disabilities, but were otherwise fairly open about the type of child we would be prepared to consider, including children of different backgrounds. The home study was a single meeting with a social worker that lasted about an hour. It included some discussion of our relatives, but the social worker's main concerns were finance and house-room. After the home study we attended a half-day training session, which warned us of the difficulties of raising an adopted child. Soon afterwards, social workers visited our home, bringing photos of a boy of almost three.

We said, in a non-committal way, 'We'll take a look'.

They immediately drove us to the orphanage and we watched the boy playing in an adjacent room for about fifteen minutes. Then he was brought in to see us. I thought this was premature, a bit off. But I found him to be quite a nice kid.

The little boy had been in an orphanage since birth, and had received intermittent visits from his mother. She was Japanese with a professional background. We were not told anything of the father's origins, although he appeared to be black. They told us that the mother was not of sound mind, but I think this diagnosis had only been made because she'd slept with a black man.

After this first visit, we went on weekly visits for two months. Then he came home for weekend visits, and played havoc. Then he had week long visit, during which time we found that he had a violent temper. Next month he visited again, fell ill and stayed with us.

We were visited at home by a child guidance centre social worker and the matron of the orphanage, to check how things were going. I tackled them on the subject of the boy's temper, and they 'fessed up: they knew but had not mentioned it.

The legal adoption was straightforward; the child guidance centre had obtained all the necessary documents, including the consent of the birth mother. The judge spoke to us for ten minutes and granted the adoption order.

An adoptive mother

We asked someone with a foreign looking baby. Everyone is friendly here so we just asked and they told us they had adopted. We went to a Catholic children's home first, and they had lots of Filipino children, but the agency wanted us to be very religious, so we went to our child guidance centre and they allocated us a social worker. Two social workers visited our house twice and interviewed us through an interpreter hired by us. They were much more concerned with our background than with whether we would make good parents. They asked about our education, our jobs. They asked detailed financial questions. They said that we had to tell the company we worked for that we were applying to adopt and provide salary details from them, and they required proof we owned property. They also asked about our family, parents, brothers and sisters, although they were embarrassed at asking 'personal' questions like, 'What does your brother do?'

They asked us about the type of baby we wanted to adopt including its age, colour, nationality, sex and character. We said we would prefer a little girl aged up to two years old. When they came to character we took it to mean a deformity or abnormality, and said we did not want a child with a major problem, but that they could discuss it with us. The interpreter said 'No. You have to say exactly what type of child you want'. So we said 'A bright child', as in lively. They took us at our word!

Two months later we attended a training day, and a month after that we had a call about a little boy. His mother had given him up several times and then kept taking him back. I said,

'No, I want a child who is unwanted. Is there anyone else?'

'There's one child, stateless, would she be OK?'

Her details checked in OK. We identified her in photos, but then they told us 'Oh, there's been a mistake. Another social worker has already offered her to someone else'. So we had another interview, as did the other couple, to see who was best for her.

They came back to us and said, 'Do you want to pop in and out to see her at the orphanage?' So we did, and then they asked, 'Are you interested'. We said 'Yes'. They said 'But her skin. It's black. It's so dark it's the colour of chocolate'.

We had one week of getting to know her in the children's home, she was difficult to get through to; she would cry. After a week we took her home for a day, then overnight, and then we kept her. She missed her friends at the children's home and was difficult. She would put her arms out to be hugged, and then she would hit me.

We became legal foster parents, and had three or four weekly visits from the social workers. On one occasion when they came, she whacked me on the head with a bat. The social worker had no idea about children and no sense of humour. He took this seriously, asking how often she did it. But overall there was no problem and the adoption was legalized in two months.

These accounts by adoptive parents reinforce the suggestion that the CGC policy of arranging transethnic adoptions can be characterized as pragmatic. The problem focus is on finding a family for a particular child with a minority background and not on making this task more difficult by imposing matching criteria that may exclude willing parents. The agencies are opportunistic in making use of western parents who approach them. Their assessments of these parents, like other CGC assessments, are based on objective criteria. They are not concerned with information that would assist a cultural 'match', for example they did not ask the parents about their religion. The investigation into what the parents wanted in a child also suggests a collaborative attitude and a willingness to work with them.

Nationalism and humanism

There has been little dispute over transethnic placements in contemporary Japan. Like other potentially controversial issues in adoption, the high degree of agency autonomy helps to defuse debate by allowing different agencies to follow their own policies. However, some of the essentials of the continuing international debate can be found in two distinct justifications for the adoption of non-relatives in the early Tokugawa era, the first encapsulating the case for transethnic adoption, the second presenting a key part of the case against it. According to the seventeenth century samurai Banzan Kumazawa 'If there is no one from the same clan [available for adoption], even someone from a different clan is permissible. Men are all the progeny of heaven and Earth; all belong to the same clan.' A more restrictive justification was put forward by Terumi Atobe in his 1722 treatise on adoption 'Adoption of any person born in Japan with a Japanese endowment of *yin, yang* and the five elements is like grafting a plum tree onto a plum tree. But to adopt a person from a foreign country is like, for example, grafting a persimmon onto a peach. Certainly it would not take' (McMullen 1975: 172, 179).

From Kumazawa's perspective our shared humanity overrides our particular ethnicity in a way that allows people of different backgrounds to enter into the manifold family relationships covered by 'adoption', including the adoption of a child of a different ethnicity. By contrast, Atobe makes a nationalist case for adoption; he argues for a national Japanese identity against feudal clan divisions, but does so by contrasting the Japanese with foreigners. His grafting analogy makes an essentialist division based on ethnicity and his reference to an adoptee not simply being born in Japan but also having 'a Japanese endowment of *yin, yang* and the five elements' is akin to the idea that parents and children should be ethnically matched.

We can visualize the debate in terms of three concentric circles. The smallest circle in the centre is the clan, or extended family. The circle in the middle represents the Japanese nation, and the outer circle contains humanity as a whole. Kumazawa's vision of acceptable adoptions discounts the importance of boundaries between the circles; they are arbitrary divisions, there is no essential difference between a fellow clan member and any other human being. For Atobe, by contrast, the boundary between the nation and the outer circle should not be crossed. Non-Japanese people are seen not so much as fellow human beings as outsiders. According to I. J. McMullen, 'Atobe's argument is at once a narrowing and a reversal of Banzan's. Where Banzan had justified non-agnatic adoption with a general reference to men's common ancestry in heaven and earth, Atobe spoke rather of the separateness and homogeneity of the Japanese people'. It was an argument 'precariously close to the religious belief in the metaphysical preeminence of Japan' (McMullen 1975: 179).

Although the logic of Atobe's nationalist position is one of opposition to all transethnic adoptions, the current policy of making these placements, but only with foreign residents and mixed couples, may contain a discreet element of nationalism. From an integral nationalist perspective, the children and their adoptive parents, although from different backgrounds, share the status of outsiders. Thus, it was suggested to us that CGCs encourage the adoption of mixed background and foreign children by foreign residents, in the expectation that the parents will eventually leave, and take the 'problem' of these children with them. It was also suggested that mixed children would have problems fitting into Japanese society and so might be better off eventually moving abroad, although this explanation focuses on the interests of the individual children rather than integral nationalism. Wherever an adopted child may end up living, from the perspective of the welfare of the child there are strong pragmatic reasons for adoption agencies to look to foreign residents in placing children with a mixed or minority background. The willingness to make transethnic placements when a child cannot be ethnically matched, and the focus on the interests of the child, suggest that the predominant motivation behind the policy follows Kumazawa's universal principle that we all belong to the same clan.

Pragmatism and ideology

Transethnic adoption has been the subject of considerable debate in the Anglo-American world, with humanist arguments in favour of the practice being opposed by claims that there are essential ethnic differences between a child and his adoptive parents, which will cause identity problems (Hayes 1993). The divisions that have arisen as a result are, in a sense, the opposite of those found in Japan. In Great Britain, the USA and in other English-speaking states, there is considerable interest and willingness to engage in transethnic adoption by members of the majority ethnic community, and resistance to the idea has come from social workers and other child care activists. In Japan, the resistance to transethnic adoption is found in the majority community, while at least some CGC workers and other adoption agency staff are willing to arrange transethnic placements. As has been seen, the result is that foreign residents of Japan, including American and British couples, are often matched with children of a mixed or minority background.

An analogous situation pertains in Hong Kong, where children, including ones with special needs or a 'bad' background are placed with resident white couples. Charles O'Brian comments that this policy should be revised and that social workers should try harder to seek out Chinese couples in and outside Hong Kong. He adds:

> Social workers in Hong Kong have a pragmatic attitude toward transracial adoption. They see it primarily as placing a child in need in a permanent family. A lack of training and education on race and culture, however, leaves them ill-prepared to deal with these aspects of their work in any more than a perfunctory manner and calls for more attention (O'Brian 1994: 327).

The difficulty with this line of argument, whether for Hong Kong or Japan, is that the more social workers pay attention to issues of race and culture, the less attention they may pay to the needs of individual children. In seeing the needs of the child as a prime concern, the pragmatist is not necessarily lacking racial or cultural awareness, but is rather prioritising the need that all children have for a loving family. To call this imperative into question on the grounds of race or culture is not the result of neutral expertise gained through education and training, it is an ideological stance that is maintained despite the considerable evidence from outcome studies that transethnic and intercountry adoptions have success rates comparable to same-ethnicity and domestic adoptions (Hayes 2003: 256–7).

Those who arrange transethnic adoptions, and those who would prevent them tend to have rather different mindsets. The use of transethnic adoption as a pragmatic response to children in need is indicative of a specific problem focus on an individual child. Critics of transethnic adoption tend to have a social problem focus on redressing injustice and racism between the powerful and powerless groups that is based on a sharp distinction between majority and minority ethnic communities. This type of analysis can be crudely misleading in its blanket assumptions about discrimination. Nonetheless, discrimination and power disparities do help explain why single Japanese birth mothers of a mixed child and foreign overstayers and undocumented migrants, threatened with deportation, face pressures that might impel them to relinquish their children. What is much more doubtful is whether preventing transethnic adoption would do anything to alleviate the situation. From a pragmatic perspective, adoption placements do not reinforce power disparities in society but rather attempt to help a child in a powerless position find a loving home and avoid institutional care.

9 Comparing institutional care with fostering and adoption

A large four-storey house in a residential suburb is home to 31 children and teenagers aged 2–19. When we visit they are out at school but the mother and daughter who supervise the home show us their photographs on enjoyable looking outings. They also show us pictures of Christmas; a succession of children pose individually for the camera, the younger ones happily displaying toys, the teenagers holding new pairs of shoes. They are not family snaps, but are rather a systematic record, a proof that each child is a recipient of a gift.

The home opened just after the Second World War when its Christian founder began going to the train station and picking up needy children. It has continued as a family concern ever since although the children now come from the city's child guidance centre. Occasionally children still arrive as the result of family dislocation caused by social upheaval, as the home contains one or two refugees. The most common explanation, however, is parental divorce. Accompanying each new child is a memo from the CGC summarizing the reasons for the placement. These official reasons for placement cannot always be relied upon. One girl came with a memo stating that the parents were unable to care for her. Ten years later she told the supervisors she was abused.

This girl is now aged 19, and the staff are helping her to find a job and a home before she reaches legal adulthood on her twentieth birthday. This will be the day on which she leaves the home; it is the day that her funding stops. About 80% of the children who enter the home stay until they leave to live independently. The others generally go back to their parents and if the relationship again breaks down the CGC may then send them to another institution. The young men and women leave to take jobs in supermarkets or department stores. They can return to the home if they wish, but they will have to pay an accommodation fee. Otherwise, they are invited back once a year on Christmas day.

It is rare for a child who enters the home to leave because they are being fostered or adopted. The child guidance centre does not generally initiate such moves for children once they have been placed. After a child has been brought to the home, the only scheduled contact with the CGC is a twice-yearly visit by caseworkers, which includes an open 'group exchange opportunity' between them and the children. Occasionally the home itself will put a child's name forward. One 4-year-old boy had recently left the home for parents who were fostering him with a view to adoption. The victim of abuse, the child had arrived at the home when he was two. His mother cried when she left him there, but she never visited. When no one came to see him, the supervisors decided that he should be adopted and recommended this to the CGC.

'Are there no other children who might be fostered or adopted?' we asked. There was one other possible case. Both her parents were dead: an earthquake, cancer. She had a kind aunt. And she was a very nice person, too. Overall, it was thought that seasonal (summer) foster parents might be best, ones who could take her on holiday, no more than that. Full foster parenting or adoption, we were told, was inappropriate as there was her relationship with her aunt to be considered.

Disadvantages of institutional placement

The home that we visited appeared to be a model of a well-run institution with the children receiving a high standard of care. However, even in the best of circumstances, an institution has a significant disadvantage against fostering and adoption as the children do not have the opportunity to receive the love of parents and develop a close relationship with them. This inescapable problem with institutional care means that there is always at least one good reason to prefer fostering or adoptive placements for children.

There are other disadvantages to institutions that are not impossible to surmount, but which are also likely to be problematic. These disadvantages include the tendency for institutions to place an overemphasis on a controlled, tightly scheduled upbringing with limited opportunities for autonomy, or for privacy (Goodman 2000: 106, 159–60; Japan Federation of Bar Associations 2003: 201). This may make it more difficult for the young people to establish their independence. One CGC administrator described how children growing up in institutions 'do not learn about social or family life, or to cooperate with others as part of a family. They are not good at problem solving, and tend to be passive'. Nonetheless, at an age when a typical young person in Japan will still be living at home and receiving support from his or her parents, a young person or young adult who has grown up in an institution has to make an abrupt transition from the children's home to complete self-reliance. The jobs that they manage to find on leaving institutional care are typically rather poorly paid and insecure; some end up in the *yakuza* (Goodman 2000: 133–4, 200 n.28). The age that a child leaves a children's home depends on funding, which is related to how long they continue in compulsory education. Those who leave school at 15 are funded to live in an institution for a further year (JFBA 2003: 207). Rates of progress into senior high school are comparatively low. In 1993 54% of children in institutions progressed to senior high school as against 95% of young people overall (Goodman 2000: 124).

There is recognition of these problems by the state, which has promoted reforms to try to alleviate the difficulties with institutional care. The traditional children's home is somewhat larger than the one we visited, averaging 51 children in 2002 (Naikakufu 2003). However, since 2000 small 'group homes' for six residents designed 'to encourage social independence of children by building favourable relationships with local communities and caring for children in a homely environment' have also been established (Ministry of Foreign Affairs 2001: 173.3). These group homes are run by CGC staff. 'Family homes' for groups of four to six unrelated children are provided under the aegis of the foster care system. They provide an intermediate environment, part way between home and institution. There are also about 20 local initiatives where homes have been created to help teenagers become self-reliant. These homes are not registered as institutions, but the carers have been able to fund their activities through the subsidies available for foster parents.

The risk of abuse

Another danger of institutional care is the risk of child abuse. Not all children's homes are model homes. There have been instances of children being deprived of food, beaten, raped and occasionally murdered and tortured. This is not specific to Japan, the pattern is world-wide, following the same depressing dynamic of power over children leading to tyranny. Such things can happen in foster and adoptive care too; wherever a child is placed, the external constraints that can be imposed on the behaviour of carers are limited as abuse can all too easily be kept hidden. It may be, however, that the internal restraints that prevent someone from committing abuse are more powerful in a family environment than they are in an institution.

There is evidence of an increasing willingness to report abuse in the domestic home (Ministry of Foreign Affairs 2001: 214). However, the Japanese state has historically been weak in its attempts to tackle abuse in children's homes. On paper it appears that checks and balances are in place to help protect children against institutional abuse, with the governor of each prefecture under an obligation to ensure that all the homes in his area are inspected every six months. The reality can be of an ostrich-like attitude by those who are meant to step in, as shown in one notorious case that did eventually come to light.

In August 1995 an anonymous call to the Chiba CGC alleged that the supervisor of Onchoen children's home, a man named Hiroshi Ohama, was abusing the children there. The child guidance centre investigated and confirmed that abuse, such as placing a child in a tumble dryer and cutting a boy's penis, was indeed taking place. It responded by giving *guidance*. Staff who had been trying to protect the children then resigned and 13 children made a mass escape to the CGC, which handed them back to Ohama. The abuse continued and other evidence of the poor standard of care emerged including the fact that none of the teenagers housed in Onchoen was going on to attend senior high school. The children sent letters to the governor of the prefecture, who ignored them. All but two of the new staff recruited to the home resigned after one of them saw Ohama smash a child's face against a wall. In 1999 a TV show was made about the regime and in December of that year a voluntary group asked the prosecutor to initiate court proceedings. This was done, and in January 2000 the court found that 17 cases of abuse against Ohama were proven, and that the prefecture should have sacked him in 1996. The court, however, did not have the authority to punish Ohama although in July 2001 justice, of a sort, caught up with him when another court sentenced him for cutting a boy's little finger with a pair of garden shears in 1994. He was jailed for eight months.[39]

There have been a number of other cases of institutional abuse that have come to public attention (Goodman 2000: 118–22; JFBA 2003: 169–72). Adult reporting of abuse in children's homes, however, is inhibited by fears of accusations rebounding. In one case a woman volunteer at an institution had worries over abuse, lack of proper health care and lack of proper education of three children at the home. She offered to foster or adopt the children, the institution refused and relations broke down. She made informal complaints, but never made a formal report for fear that it could result in false accusations being made against members of her own family and destroy any hopes she had of adopting a child. When abuse is reported, children's homes, religious organizations that run children's homes, CGCs and the government all have a tendency to be unresponsive or secretive. Thus, Goodman points out, 'it is hard to know exactly the extent to which abuse takes place... since the first reaction of the authorities ...seems to be to stop the news leaking out'. But he also cites the results of a 1998 survey of 448 children over ten and in care in which 289 (65%) said that they were beaten, 98 of them 'often' and a further 191 'occasionally' (Goodman 2000: 122).

The preponderance of institutional care

The lack of love, the difficulties with establishing independence, and the risk of abuse in an institutional placement are all good reasons not to rely too much on children's homes. Nonetheless, these homes play a central role in Japanese child-care. When a child enters into the care of a child guidance centre, they may be fostered, placed in a children's home, or cared for within the buildings of CGCs that combine office space with temporary accommodation. Children who are not reunited with their parents might go on to be adopted, but they might also remain in foster care or the care of an institution until adulthood. Although there is an active programme of adoption in Japan and although fostering is financially well supported, only a small proportion of children who cannot be cared for by their parents will end up adopted or fostered. When the number of children (excluding special needs children) in institutional care is compared with the number in foster care, the foster care rate is about 7–8% (Yonekura 1998: 59; Appendix 1).

Four broad explanations have been offered for the heavy reliance on institutions amongst childcare professionals and others with an interest in the issue. These are lack of suitable adoptive/foster parents; lack of consent by birth parents for fostering or adoption, the incentives for CGC caseworkers to make placements in children's homes, and the incentives for organizers of children's homes to keep them there. These four arguments can be summarized as follows:

1   In some prefectures there is only a small pool of potential adoptive parents and foster carers. In others the number of potential parents might appear high

on paper, but the figures are misleading. Institutions, therefore, are necessary to fill the considerable gap between the number of children in need of care and the number of substitute parents available.

2 (a) Birth parents are more willing to have their child placed in an institution than they are for the child to be fostered or adopted. Institutional care may then be the most appropriate option for children as it allows them to maintain a link with birth parents. To this it sometimes added (b) that birth parents find it more difficult to obstruct an institutional placement by a CGC and (c) that institutional care is needed when birth parents are missing.

3 (a) From the perspective of a caseworker there may be perceived advantages to the child in institutional placements over foster placements. (b) Placing for children in institutional care and then leaving them there can seem the easy option to an overstretched CGC.

4 Institutional care predominates over adoption and fostering because the owners of private children's homes, who are paid per child by the state, have a vested interest in looking after as many children as possible for as long as possible.

In the remainder of this chapter we consider how much weight should be given to these different explanations for the preponderance of institutional care over foster care and adoption.

The pool of potential parents

The pool of potential parents varies from one area to another. In some prefectures there are more potential foster and adoptive parents than there are children. In others, few parents come forward and the CGC has to rely on cooperating with other prefectures in the area to make foster or adoptive placements. But even where there is an apparent superfluity of parents on the books, placement may be difficult. This is partly because there is a mismatch between the kind of children that parents want to adopt and the children available, and partly because some registered foster parents are no longer active in fostering.

It has been seen that while there is no shortage of potential adoptive parents *per se*, the preferences of nearly all of these parents are similar; they want a sweet baby girl of good background, and they are resistant to expanding their options. Thus, where children are advertised, a child who fulfils this ideal categorization is intensely sought after, while a child who does not, say an older boy, may elicit no response at all. This lends plausibility to the argument that one of the reasons that more children in care are not adopted is that it is very difficult to find them parents. Foster parents may have similar attitudes but appear to be somewhat more open to caring for a range of children. The quantitative evidence with respect to age suggests that foster parents, like adoptive parents, gravitate towards younger children, although at least some parents who are willing to start fostering children after their chances of adoption have tailed off (Appendix 1: Table 16). Boys and girls are cared for by foster parents in roughly equal numbers

(Kôseirôdôshô 2004). The overall number of children in foster care, however, has gone down considerably.

In the aftermath of the Second World War there was a pressing need for child-care including not only orphans in Japan, but also children of families made homeless, children born outside marriage and orphaned children fleeing from Japan's former colonies. In response, thousands of individuals and families took it upon themselves to look after children as informal foster carers. Farmers in search of cheap labour also entered into 'fostering' (Takei 2000: 95–7). In 1948 these informal, individual initiatives were recognized by the state and foster carers began to receive funding. Funding levels have become increasingly gener-ous and extensive. Nonetheless, after a period of rapid expansion, foster care has gone into decline. At its peak in the mid to late 1950s, well over 9000 children were in foster homes, by the end of the twentieth century this had fallen to a little over 2000.[40]

The National Foster Parent Association (NFPA) suggests a number of explana-tions for this decline. First it argues that there is less need for foster care. This contention is unconvincing, given the large numbers of children in institutions. More plausible is the suggestion that there have been changes in attitude in society, resulting from the rise of the nuclear family, which have made fostering less attractive. The NFPA also follows the Ministry of Foreign Affairs in pointing out that there is a public perception that only people who are unusually benevo-lent could consider becoming foster carers (NFPA 2000: 6, 7, 12; Ministry of Foreign Affairs 1996: 141).

The arguments that people are less likely to volunteer to foster because of a stronger sense of the nuclear family and, implicitly, because people are less benevolent, has been associated by Shoji with the lack of a Christian tradition of social care (Shoji 2003: 68). In this respect, it is notable that Christians have played a disproportionate role in all kinds of childcare initiatives, although it is not the only religion to have become involved; children are sometimes fostered at Buddhist temples (Takei 2000: 82, 125). Shoji also contends that the retention of the *ie* system and the significance attached to blood relations has inhibited the development of foster care (2003: 68). However, the positive decline of foster care since the 1950s, when concepts of the *ie* and of blood were stronger than they are now, suggests that the opposite may be the case. The *ie* established connec-tions outside the nuclear family, including relatives, servants and unrelated adults in a subservient economic position. If there is a strong sense of extended family, with a family unit blurring at the edges amongst cousins, second cousins and oth-ers this perhaps makes the decision to become a foster carer a shorter, less radi-cal step than it is for a modern, tight-knit nuclear family. The pre-genetic idea of blood as a shared inheritance of a broad family unit can also be contrasted with the modern more inward-looking stress on the uniqueness of each individual's genes that may reinforce the boundaries of the nuclear family. In any event, a fos-ter child is not recorded as having a formal family tie on the *koseki*, and this allows foster parents to sidestep concerns about the supposedly adverse effects that the inclusion of an unrelated child in their family line might have. Furthermore, the public perception of foster care as something benevolent suggests that open foster care does not have a negative impact on the status of the family in which the child is fostered. This can be contrasted with adoption where social attitudes about the importance of a child's blood and background continue to place adoptive parents under pressure to be secretive.

The Japanese government has made several attempts to tackle the long term decline in foster parents. It has progressively increased the subsidies available to foster parents and expanded the training and advice offered to them, including making advice services available at children's homes (NFPA 2000: 7; Ministry of Foreign Affairs 2001: 173.2). In 1988 a revised plan for foster parenting came into effect that made it easier to qualify as a foster parent by reducing areas of investigation for applicants to those that were strictly necessary. There was no investigation, for example, of the local schools of applicants. Lists of desirable factors for foster parents were pruned down, for example, the preference for a foster mother who could breastfeed an infant was cut out, and the range of families that could be approved was increased to include one-parent families (NFPA 2000: 12). In 1999 foster parenting was allowed where both parents were in full time work (Ministry of Foreign Affairs 2001: 173.2). In 2002 a further series of measures to encourage foster care were implemented. Respite care for foster carers was introduced and four additional categories of foster parent were created. These included short-term foster parents; foster parents who would focus on raising levels of education in the children; relative foster parents, such as an uncle and aunt, who became eligible for financial support, and specialist foster parents dedicated to helping abused children (Shoji 2003: 70, 99). There are now few restrictions on foster parents. In Osaka city, for example, the main restrictions are (a) home size, with adverts asking for applicants with at least three rooms, and (b) age, with a bar of 60 (Osaka Cyûô Jidôsôdansho, no date). Applicants are unlikely to be turned down, although CGCs are wary of people who say, or are suspected of thinking, that they would like to find someone to look after them in their old age. The net effect of these policies may have had a modest impact on increasing the number of children in foster care from a low point of 2,122 in 1999 to 2,811 in 2003 (Naikakufu 2005).

Attitudes of birth parents

Some birth parents are willing to have their child placed in an institution but are less willing for them to be fostered and particularly unwilling for them to be adopted. Birth parents may wish to maintain contact with the child, or have the option of maintaining contact. If the child is placed in an institution, visiting is relatively easy; the parents know where their children are and can arrive unannounced or at short notice. Some institutions do limit parental visits; the home we visited restricted them to twice a month. Nonetheless, visiting children is more straightforward than when they are in a foster home, where special arrangements need to be made by the CGC and the address of the foster parents kept concealed. Birth parents may also want to keep a child as part of their recorded family lineage even where they do not visit them. This makes them resistant to adoption, and also, indirectly, to fostering because it is associated with, or might lead to, adoption (Ministry of Foreign Affairs 1996: 141). The traditionalistic emphasis on family lineage, therefore, can discourage birth parents from severing formal ties with children even if they have no contact with them.

Assumptions about parental wishes may be made on their behalf by childcare workers. Birth parents may not be asked if they want their child fostered or adopted; unless they request such a placement it is often simply assumed that they do not. One CGC administrator in a large urban area defended this practice by explaining that if a caseworker explicitly raised the subject of fostering or adoption, the birth parents would react by withdrawing their child from an institution, even if the parents were still in circumstances that made it inappropriate for them to care for the child. In this CGC, as in many others, the rights of birth parents were upheld in all but the most extreme cases of child abuse. Once or twice a year the CGC would apply to the courts for forcible removal of a child from his or her birth parents. Even here there is an implicit deference to the birth parents in that the CGC applies to have the child placed in institutional care rather than to be fostered or freed for adoption. However, CGCs have gradually become more willing to take cases to court to argue for forcibly removing a child to an institution. There were 142 such applications in 2000 as against 14 in 1989 (JFBA 2003: 222).

The law on the rights of parents and the forcible removal of children appears clear. According to articles 27–28 of the Child Welfare Law, if a child's guardian does serious harm to their welfare, then the prefectural government (acting through the CGC) can place a child with foster parents, or in an institution. However, if a child is to be removed, whether this is to an institution or into foster care, the prefectural CGC must first go to the courts:

> Prefectural governments must obtain permission from a Family Court to place a child in the custody of foster parents or a protective trustee or to send him/her to Child Welfare Facilities against the will of the natural parents (Ministry of Foreign Affairs 1996: 125).

In fact, the forcible removal of children to institutions is a grey area, as some CGCs are willing to act without going to court to remove children on their own authority. The forcible removals by CGC caseworkers can reportedly lead to extra-legal stand offs, including one case in which 'the whole family turned up to camp [outside the CGC offices] with axes, and said "give us our child back"'. However, CGCs who remove children to their own facilities or to an institution are only rarely willing to foster a child without court permission (Appendix 1: Table 17).

Missing birth parents, that is, parents who make arrangements for the care of their child and then leave for unknown whereabouts, present CGCs with a placement dilemma: they do not know anything of the wishes or intentions of the parents as they are unable to contact them. The placement of children with missing birth parents is dealt with differently from one CGC to another. In some areas, the 'missing' status of the parents results in the child being placed in an institution indefinitely. Without parental permission, neither adoption nor fostering is seen as appropriate because it is viewed as a violation of parental rights. The open-ended institutional placement is made despite the lack of any contact between parent and child, in the hope that the parents will reappear. An alternative policy operated by some CGCs is to set a time limit on parents who go missing. In one prefecture the CGC looks for parents for six months, and then applies to the courts to have the child freed for fostering with a view to adoption. The courts then conduct their own search. A somewhat similar approach was taken in the prefecture in Mrs Tanaka's case (Ch. 2), although here the child had been placed before the court made its search. In another prefecture the procedure is that after one or two years in institutional care, the relatives of the children are contacted, told that the CGC is planning to start to look for foster or adoptive parents, and asked for their views. However, if the missing parents are found or reappear, they sometimes veto the placement plans.

Attitudes of caseworkers

There are two ways of interpreting the placement of children in institutions as opposed to fostering or adoption. The first is to emphasize the positive: that it helps to leave open the possibility of reconciliation between children and parents and allows for frequent contact in the interim. The second is to stress the negative and to suggest that it leaves many children without a family life throughout their childhood. Depending on the circumstances either situation may be true, but the negative outcome is more common. It has been seen that in the children's home we visited the majority of children did not return to their parents. This reflects the wider picture that reconciliation with parents is not the most likely outcome (Appendix 1: Table 15). In the words of one CGC administrator, 'once a child enters an institution, they tend to stay there'.

From a CGC perspective, the finality of an institutional placement for a child can be seen not as a negative but rather as a resolution of their case. Shoji cites a caseworker enumerating several disadvantages of foster placements. A child in a foster placement may require successive individual visits; these are time-consuming and, if things go wrong and the children end up psychologically hurt, the social worker may not want to repeat the experience. They do not need to visit institutions in the same way, for once a child is placed there they are in the hands of 'professionals'. Furthermore, the caseworker argues, the child is more vulnerable to abuse in the privacy of a foster home than in an institution. Finally, some parents try and 'privatize' the child. They become too attached to the child and try and keep social workers out of their lives and dominate decision making over them (Shoji 2003: 71–2).

These arguments may help to explain why CGCs do not do more to make foster placements, even if some of the reasoning on which they are based is questionable. It is doubtful that the relative risk of abuse in foster care is higher than in a children's home. Children's homes are run by professionals only in the sense that any business can be called a profession. They are often family concerns where a person's family status rather than any formal qualifications determines their role. As for 'privatizing' a child, it is natural for foster parents who come to love a child – one of the great advantages of a foster placement – to want a greater degree of decision-making authority over that child than when he was first placed. The passage of time, however, does not give foster parents custody rights. In one case, a foster couple had a three-year-old child placed with them. Five years later, he was having problems being bullied at school, including by teachers, so the parents removed him temporarily for home tuition. The CGC did not approve of the home tuition plan and diagnosed the child as having ADHD. They claimed that this required institutional care and forcibly removed the boy to a children's home where he remained until he died in a tragic accident aged 17 (Sakamoto 2003).

Institutional and organizational imperatives

Many modern institutions date to the aftermath of the Second World War (Oppler 1976: 184; Goodman 2000: 45, 52). The initial impetus to create an institution may have been similar to the impetus to create a foster family; in both cases individuals and families were doing what they could to help children in desperate circumstances. However, institutional care and foster care have subsequently diverged. Foster care relies on being in a state of continual renewal as new families come forward to offer a child a home. By contrast, institutional care has become institutionalized and self-perpetuating. It is notable in this respect that where foster care has declined institutions have remained fairly full. It is true that places in public care homes, show a declining trajectory in numbers that is similar to the decline in foster placements from 7,672 children in 1955 to 2,994 in 2002. Numbers in private children's homes, however, have remained more or less constant. In 1955 they stood at 25,272, in 2002 they stood at 25,167 (Goodman 2000: 51; Naikakufu 2003). Overall numbers of children in institutions have subsequently increased to 30,416 in 2003 (Appendix 1: Table 15). This may be partly due to the increasing numbers of children taken into care because of abuse and neglect.

The high numbers of children in institutional homes raises the question of whether, in some indirect way, institutions may have diverted the flow of children away from foster care and adoption. The owners of private homes are paid by the national and local government for every child that they look after, at a rate that is about four times the money provided to foster carers. There are obvious financial pressures for institutions to try to keep the children placed in their care under these payment arrangements. At the same time, child guidance centres may work under heavy caseloads, for example, they may have one social worker per 100,000 of the population. As a result, in what may be a rather unlucky dovetailing of interests for the children, the CGCs look to the institutions to reduce their workload, and the institutions oblige in a way that safeguards their financial position.

The implications of this possible relationship between institutions and CGCs have been drawn out by a childcare activist who contends that children's homes, running as profit-making businesses, have an incentive to look after as many children as possible for as long as they are paid to do so. The child guidance centres, which retain formal responsibility for the child, have much else to do and tend to limit their contact with the child placed in an institution to annual visits. Many CGCs fail to fulfil even this modest degree of oversight and rely instead upon a report on the child prepared by the institution. The institution, in pursuit of its financial interests, rarely recommends fostering or adoption in its reports. The exceptions are children who cause so many problems that they are reckoned to be more trouble than they are worth. Unproblematic children are never put forward. The only way of getting out of a children's home is to be a troublemaker.

This argument is controversial, however. The contention that from a social worker perspective institutional placements represent an unproblematic and time-saving decision was confirmed by the CGC administrators we spoke to. They described having few staff and heavy caseloads that limited their ability to pursue fostering and adoption arrangements for children. Even where there were large numbers of foster and adoptive parents waiting for children, placement in institutions was sometimes preferred in order to avoid potential problems with birth parents. After a child had been placed in an institution, CGC administrators confirmed that he or she might not be visited by caseworkers. Sometimes, periodic reports on the child would be prepared by the institution. On other occasions the caseworker would visit the institution and talk to the staff. This was defended on the grounds that the job of a caseworker was to liase with birth parents rather than talk to the children.

Goodman has suggested that 'one of the main reasons why fostering and adoption is not more popular lies in the reluctance of many of the [children's] homes to suggest or encourage it as a viable alternative for the children in their care' (1996: 123). Where institutions are reluctant to have children fostered, CGCs are simply unwilling to override them. One administrator described how, if they suggested fostering for a child, an institution would counter with the suggestion of weekend fostering. Weekend fostering allows institutions to retain their fees for looking after the child. Whether the child went on to full fostering was described as a matter for 'negotiation' between the institution and the CGC.

The two cases of children recommended for foster care at the home we visited have differing implications for the decision-making roles of the CGC and institutions. The first case concerned the boy who, following the institution's recommendation, was being fostered with a view to adoption. This suggests that institutions can sometimes play a helpful role in advising the CGC on the children in their care. However, the case of the girl who was considered suitable for fostering, but only for holidays, suggests that institutions should not be relied upon as authoritative decision makers. The child guidance centre's delegation of decision making to the institution was problematic because it required the supervisors to judge in their own cause. Given their description of the girl's circumstances, an impartial decision maker might well conclude that she was suitable for full fostering, including fostering with a view to adoption. There was obviously no prospect of reconciliation with her deceased parents and several factors would count in her favour to make finding new parents a realistic prospect. She was a girl; she had a pleasant personality; as an orphan her availability for adoption was unproblematic. Furthermore, her parents had died for what might be described as perfectly respectable reasons, suggesting that she was of a good background. (It can be remembered that when Loving Hands advertised a girl whose parents had died in a car crash it generated huge interest amongst potential parents.) The objection to full fostering and adoption that was made by the supervisors appeared to be based on the wish not to disrupt the relationship between the girl and her aunt. However, neither fostering nor adoption precludes continued contact. In this case, contact with the aunt if the child was fostered might well be straightforward, as there were none of the problems that in other circumstances might require the whereabouts of foster parents to be kept secret, and in ordinary adoptions it is possible to have continued contact between the children and their birth families.

Time

Time is a fourth factor to be added to the problems of finding foster/adoptive parents, getting the agreement of birth parents, and getting out of an institution. The younger the child, the more attractive they are, as a category, to new parents. The passage of time makes it progressively harder for a child to be adopted (Appendix 1: Table 4). Although the effect is not quite so marked, time also decreases a child's chance of finding foster carers.

   If we consider the obstacles to placement over time, a shifting three-stage picture emerges as to why children are not adopted or fostered. If a small child enters into the care of the CGC, then the first obstacle likely to be encountered is birth parent attitudes, or presumed attitudes, that oppose a foster or adoptive placement. When this is combined with the temptation of caseworkers to take the line of least resistance, the result is an institutional placement. The second problem is the delegation of decision making to the home, which dampens prospects of being reassigned for fostering or adoption. As years pass, the third obstacle to finding new parents gets ever higher as there is a shortage of parents willing to care for an older child.

1   If the child enters into care when still young, then there are reasonably large numbers of potential foster parents and adoptive parents likely to be interested in looking after him or her. Even if the CGC dealing with the case only has a small pool of foster and adoptive parents, it is able to go to other CGCs, although local pride and bad relations between CGCs sometimes hinder cooperation. Assuming, however, that the prefecture is typical in having a sizeable pool of parents with a marked preference for younger children, then if a child is not fostered or adopted on entering care, the initial obstacle probably lies mainly with opposition by the birth parents and with the weight given to the wishes and feelings of the birth parents by the CGC or family court. If birth parents refuse consent for adoption or for fostering, their wishes will almost certainly be respected. Some birth parents may not be

asked about fostering or adoption for fear of antagonising them. If the birth parents go missing, then some CGCs are unwilling to assume authority for a foster or adoptive placement. Caseworkers may also have some partiality for an institutional placement to reduce their workloads, and justify this preference with a number of tendentious assumptions about the comparative benefits of institutional care.

2   Once a child has been placed in an institution, then the problem arises that the CGC may tend to view the placement as a problem solved, delegating responsibility to the children's home not just for looking after the child but also for deciding on its future placement options. Institutions are unlikely to recommend adoption or fostering, even if the prospects of reconciliation with birth parents are small.

3   By the time it becomes obvious that there is no likelihood of reconciliation with birth parents, it would have become much more difficult to find substitute parents. It is very hard to place a child over the age of six in an adoptive family, and foster carers are also less willing to foster a child, as they grow older. The large pool of potential parents available to the child when they first entered into care, has shrunk away.

In the next chapter we ask what can be done to help children who have fallen into this trap find a family, if they are finally freed for adoption.

10 Decision making in matching

When prospective parents apply to adoption agencies, they may imagine an 'ideal' child. As children fall short of this preconceived ideal, it becomes increasingly difficult for an agency to place them. This chapter considers the logic of two opposing approaches to minimizing this problem. One approach is to try and ensure that the agency has as much control as possible over matching and prospective parents have as little choice as possible. If potential parents have little control and few choices in the matching process, then they can be more easily persuaded to accept a less than 'ideal' child. This approach has been taken in the UK. The second and opposite approach, found in some agencies in Japan, is to put as much decision-making power as possible in the hands of prospective parents. Giving potential parents the power to choose includes letting them meet children without making a commitment to them. This allows prospective parents to move away from thinking of children in an abstract hierarchy of being more or less 'ideal'. Instead, would-be parents have the opportunity to relate to children in need of adoption as individuals. A child who is viewed as part of a more or less ideal category is defined by limited characteristics (e.g. age, state of health) that are interchangeable with other children. By contrast, if children are viewed as individuals then they cannot be categorized because the qualities, character and potential of each child combine to make each one unique and separate from every other child.

The 'ideal' child

A difficulty that faces all child guidance centres and other agencies that deal with a range of children is that almost all couples who approach an agency about the possibility of adoption have more or less the same ideal child in mind: a sweet healthy little Japanese girl of good background. This leads to strong competition for such children, while other children are much harder to find homes for. The unusually high degree of selectivity of potential adoptive parents in Japan is emphasized by the way that children who would otherwise have been hard to place have been parented by foreign residents. However, although the ideal child is delineated particularly sharply in the minds of prospective Japanese parents, a similar ideal is shared by parents everywhere, at least to some degree. Thus, even the foreign residents in Japan were mainly interested in adopting a child who was young and healthy. This considerably increases the range of potential children, to include, for example, a boy of mixed ethnic background, but is still a selective ideal.

The problem posed by the concept of the 'ideal' child, can be restated as follows. Children requiring adoption are equally in need. Unfortunately this does not mean that they are all equally adoptable. To sympathize with these children's plight in a general way is one thing, to adopt one of them is quite another. Detached observers may regard all children in need as equally deserving of adoption, but engaged participants who have decided to try and become adopters soon begin to imagine the type of child they wish to adopt.

Without personal contact with available children, potential parents are liable to base their preferences on the general characteristics of this imaginary desirable child. In the mind of the would-be parent is a scale of preferences that runs from an optimal child, to one who would be acceptable, to ones who are ruled out. These preference orders tend to be similar amongst different sets of parents; for example, younger children are generally preferred over older ones. The point at which particular parents separate an ideal child from the rest varies as the 'ideal' classification may be tightly or loosely applied, with some parents overtly preferring attributes in a child about which other parents profess not to care. However, it is unusual for some parents to positively prefer categories that others wish to avoid. This assumption is admittedly somewhat crude as there will sometimes be different preferences with regard to sex, ethnicity and even temperament, and it may be possible to take advantage of this to increase the numbers of children matched in advance with parents – as Japan has done by including foreign parents in the adoptive pool. Foreign or mixed parents may positively prefer a child with a minority or mixed background and may also be more attracted to a 'lively' child; prospective parents in Tokyo, are sometimes shown a video in which a Latin American family adopts a very energetic child who particularly appealed to them but not to more staid Japanese parents. However, where parents have not actually met prospective children their shared ideals tend to far outweigh the differences. When one surveys the preferences of adopters from states outside Japan, it is often the similarities rather than the differences that stand out. In Morocco, for example, 'the ideals of beauty are actively sought in adopted children' and there is also a preference for girls over boys (Bargach 2002: 97). By and large, the type of child that parents view as ideal is based on universally similar criteria.

The similar concept of an ideal child in the minds of potential parents causes a mismatch as almost all of them wish to adopt a comparatively small number of children who are categorized as desirable while a large group of children have few potential parents willing to adopt them. These latter children are every bit as deserving and their needs just as great as the favoured group, but they are stigmatized by one or more general characteristics that makes them fall short of the 'ideal'. To envisage the result, imagine the superimposition of two diagonal graph lines to form a cross. One rising graph line compares the number of children in need of adoption against their age (or some other characteristic that helps define a child's desirability). As the age of children in need of adoption increases, so do their numbers. The second falling graph line charts the decrease between a large number of parents who are willing to consider babies to a small number who are willing to consider older children. The result is that although the overall number of prospective parents may equal or exceed the number of available children, not all children can be placed. Amongst prospective parents there are many who would be willing to adopt a few younger children, however, only a few parents are willing to adopt many older children.

This is roughly the situation in Japan, where parents wishing to adopt almost invariably start out hoping for a baby and where few are willing to adopt a child older than about three. The age distribution of children in infant homes and children's homes suggests that for younger children, the number in need of adoption rises somewhat with age. In 2003, a total of 975 children under one were in either a children's home or an infant home, this number rises to 1,982 children aged six.[41] However, even if the number of children in need of adoption remains constant or falls as they get older, there will still be a problem so long as there are more older children than there are parents willing to adopt them.

We can define three categories of children in the minds of parents. First, 'ideal' children; second, children who are less than ideal, but whom parents might accept if offered for placement; and third, children they will not accept if offered for placement. Just as some parents define an ideal child more loosely than others, so some parents are more willing than others to countenance adopting a child who departs from their ideal to one degree or another. This gives children in the intermediate category uncertain adoption prospects, depending on whether potential parents attempt to maximize their prior preferences as opposed to merely satisfying (or 'satisficing') them.

From the perspective of an agency attempting to place as many children as possible, potential parents who have a broad definition of an ideal child or who are willing to consider children who depart from their ideal are very helpful in increasing their adoption rate. Conversely, demanding parents who insist on an ideal or near-ideal child, narrowly defined, will not increase the rate but merely add to the work of selecting who should be matched with the small number of children in this category.

Bargaining

The interaction between potential parents and agencies can be interpreted as a bargaining process: each party is brought together by shared interests, but both have to somehow overcome their conflicting interests before a child can be successfully placed. We analyze this process neither to endorse it, nor to suggest that it presents anything like a full picture of the relationship between prospective parents and an adoption agency. We do, however, think that an analysis of placements in terms of bargaining makes it possible to better understand how matching decisions are made when a child is unknown to prospective parents.

Potential parents wish to adopt a child who conforms as closely as possible to an abstract concept of an ideal child shared with many other parents. Adoption agencies that attempt to pursue an optimum policy for children in need will try to ensure that as many as possible of the children on their books are placed, including children quite different from the concept of an 'ideal' child held by most potential adoptive parents. The objectives of the parents and of the agency are, therefore, similar to the extent that both have an interest in the parents adopting a child or children, but differ over which category of child. The parents want a child from the 'ideal' category. However, if the agency simply accepts this preference, the parents become part of a large pool of prospective adopters hoping to be allocated one of a small pool of desirable children while other less desirable children are left unadopted. In order to ensure that as many children as possible are adopted, the agency wants to place not the most desirable child with potential parents, but rather the *least* desirable category of child that they are willing to accept. If, for example, potential parents who are willing to adopt an older special needs child are instead matched with a much coveted healthy baby, the overall result may well be that one less child will be adopted. The baby could have been placed with any number of parents including ones who insist on an infant or nothing, an older child with special needs is much less likely to be accepted for placement by other parents.

To help them to place as wide a range of children as possible, the agency is interested in finding out from potential parents their lowest acceptable category of child. The parents, however, are not necessarily interested in conveying this information. Prospective parents have a dilemma in their discussions with the agency, when questions are posed about what kind of child they might be willing to adopt. The more narrowly that prospective parents specify the categories of children that they are prepared to adopt to the agency, the greater the risk that they will not be able to adopt at all, given the competition for the most popular categories of children. To maximize their chances of adopting a child, they want to identify the broadest possible range of children that they would be prepared to consider for adoption. However, to the extent that the prospective parents admit being prepared to adopt a child from a less desirable category, they risk losing the chance of adopting a child from a more desirable category. Prospective parents, therefore, must balance competing priorities not only in considering for themselves the range of children they would be willing to adopt, but also in divulging this information to the agency.

Bargaining between parents and an agency is informed by how much each side knows about the strategy of the other, how long they are willing to continue interacting and what other options are available to them. For example, parents who adopt a baby in China know that the policy of the state agency is that parents who turn down the first child offered to them will be offered a second, but no more. In this case there is a risky case for the parents to reject the first child and no point in them rejecting the second child in the hope of being offered one that more closely approaches their prior 'ideal'. The parents can continue to search for an 'ideal' child by approaching another agency, but by this stage, they will have made a considerable investment of time and money into adopting from China. An example from Japan, where it is comparatively easy to move between agencies in seeking a domestic adoption, illustrates the opposite case. Mrs Suzuki had travelled some way to attend the Loving Hands meeting described in Chapter 3. She lived in a rural prefecture where she and her husband had been offered a two-year-old boy in need of adoption. Mrs Suzuki had brought the boy home, only once, on trial. The child was not sweet, his face, she said, was 'not right' and he was 'not like a child'. Mrs Suzuki guessed that it was because no one had ever looked after him, but other family members simply did not like him. She explained that she had come to the agency in Osaka, with its huge urban population, to choose a 'better' child. It is just possible that had Mrs Suzuki found it much more difficult to look outside her prefecture, she might have prevailed upon her husband, ignored her wider family and adopted the boy she had been offered.

The bargaining that takes place between an agency and prospective parents can, without too much distortion, be analyzed using game theory by being placed in the framework of a simple two-person game between a couple on one side and an agency on the other.[42] In this game, the agency has a small number of 'ideal' children in need of adoption and a large number of less than 'ideal' children who are equally in need. It is approached by a couple holding a conventional view of the kind of child who would maximize their placement preferences, but who would also be satisfied with adopting a child who falls short of this ideal. The prospective parents make the first move in the game. Using the terminology of game theory, they can choose to 'cooperate' by honestly indicating the full range of children that they would be willing to adopt, or 'defect' by claiming that they will only agree to a placement if the child is ideal. Let us imagine that the couple defect, by telling the agency in the home study that the only type of child that they are willing to adopt is a healthy pretty baby girl of good background. What is the agency to do in response? It can cooperate by placing such a baby with the couple at the first opportunity, or it too can defect. The most radical form of defection is to reject the parents and end the negotiation – this would be the strategy of the Motherly Network. However, an adoption agency that is willing to continue to engage in the adoption 'game' with these parents has another defection strategy: silence – the agency simply does not contact the parents. The adoption agency may also defect, or attempt to defect, by offering a child that is not 'ideal', but who they believe will barely satisfy the parents' unstated minimal expectations.

If the agency 'defects' by not contacting the couple about a child, it relies upon tacit communication to get the message across. It is hard to interpret silence; one Japanese couple we spoke to believed that an agency had ignored their application because the husband had a minor physical disability. However, if a couple suspect that the problem is that they have asked only for an ideal child, they have to decide whether to 'cooperate' by admitting – and perhaps also coming to the realization – that they would be satisfied with adopting from a broader range of children than they originally specified.

If the couple come back to the agency to say that they are interested in adopting a wider range of children than they had earlier indicated, then the agency's policy of defection by silence might be seen as being vindicated. The agency is now in a better bargaining position if it chooses to engage with the couple, although it still cannot be certain as to how far the couple might be prepared to compromise their vision of an ideal child.

A game of prisoner's dilemma[43]

To explore this type of bargaining further we can define the difference preference orders of the agency and the parents by narrowing the possible outcomes to four. Using game theory notation, these outcomes are labelled T, R, P and S.[44]

Outcome T for the parents
Outcome S for the agency
The defecting parents say they want an 'ideal' child or nothing; the cooperative agency responds by placing an 'ideal' child with them.

Outcome R for both parents and agency
The cooperative parents indicate the range of children they would be satisfied with adopting, and the cooperative agency responds by offering a child who is not 'ideal', but who is ranked above the minimal expectations of the parents. The parents accept the child.

Outcome P for both parents and agency
No child is placed. The agency may offer no child at all, or it may offer a barely satisfactory child. If a child is offered, the parents hold out for a 'better' child.

Outcome S for the parents
Outcome T for the agency
The cooperative parents indicate the range of children they would be willing to consider adopting. The defecting agency responds by offering a child who barely meets the parents' minimal expectations. The parents accept the child.

Game 1   The parents approach the agency with an ostensible 'all-or-nothing' attitude defined by a T > P > R > S priority order. In other words, the parents want an 'ideal' child and assert that if they are not offered such a child they are not willing to adopt through the agency. The agency responds with silence. The outcome is P, mutual defection.

Game 2   The parents recontact the agency to say that they are in fact willing to adopt from a range of children that departs from their ideal. The agency suspects that the parents are playing 'chicken' and that their true preference order is T > R > S > P, meaning that they would be willing to take a child at the lower limit of their acceptable range rather than no child at all.[45] In the hope of finding a home for a hard-to-place child, the agency offers one who the prospective parents do indeed categorize as just adoptable. The parents turn down the placement in the hope of a 'better' child. The outcome is P.

Game 3   The agency offers to place a second child with the parents, one who the parents define as some way above their minimal expectations. The parents accept this child, so that the final outcome, R, is one of mutual cooperation.

The underlying strategy of both parents and agency has been T > R > P > S, the preference order known as prisoner's dilemma. In an iterated game, with each side having the chance to learn the strategy of the other, they have reached a compromise solution.

Comparison of the UK and Japan

Some potential adoptive parents in the UK have described how they have been treated by local authority adoption agencies in a cavalier way. This treatment appears indefensible. It has come in for considerable criticism from prospective adopters and the government has instituted a series of reforms in an attempt to end such practices. However, if the poor treatment of prospective parents is seen not as the public sector at its worst, but rather as part of a bargaining strategy to get more parents to consider hard-to-place children, then whether by accident or design it gains a certain logic. Consider five of the charges that have been raised against some UK adoption agencies:

1   *Initial snubs* Parents making initial contact with an adoption agency may find that they are ignored, or turned down informally without being offered a home study (Performance and Innovation Unit 2000: 3.77).

    Discouraging or rejecting parents at an initial stage has a degree of rationality if it is directed at those who are trying to enter the process to maximize their preference for a small range of ideal or near-ideal children. Treating these parents in an off-hand and negative way can operate as an opening gambit to get them to expand their range of acceptable children before allowing them to enter the assessment process.

2   *Humiliating interviews* Home studies wear parents down by a relentless probing into their private life, inducing a sense of disempowerment and helplessness (Laming 1996: 27–9).

    Disempowered parents can be more easily made to admit how far they would be prepared to go in adopting less desirable categories of children. Any efforts by the parents to insist on only being willing to adopt a more desirable category of child can be challenged and tested by extensive interviews.

3   *Secrecy and Misleading Information* Once parents have been approved as adopters, they may be given little information about children they may be asked to consider adopting, and no information about other children available or other potential parents. Alternatively, agencies may sometimes give the impression that most of the children they have available are older and have more severe problems than is in fact the case.

    Without accurate information on the total picture of potential parents and children, it is hard for parents to judge whether or not the particular child they are offered is the 'best' they could reasonably expect. Limiting information about the child on offer may also have advantages for encouraging placement where it allows negative facts about the child to be concealed.

4   *Delay* Every stage of the process from initial application to placement involves delays (Department of Health 2000: 1.15. 2.15; Performance and Innovation Unit 2000: 3.70, 3.92).

When parents are finally offered a child, they are more likely to accept, as delays suggest that a second chance may not arrive quickly, if at all. Parents subjected to delays may also feel pressed to accept a child by their own ageing, particularly as older parents are generally viewed less favourably as adopters.

5   *Arbitrary discrimination against certain parents* Some categories of parents are viewed less favourably than others. Where they are not excluded altogether, the more stigmatized categories of parents may only be considered for certain less-desirable categories of children (Laming 1996: 7–8; Department of Health 2000: 2.16).

There is no logic for the total exclusion of adults, who, under different circumstances, might reasonably have been expected to make loving parents to a natural child, particularly as – with common sense exceptions – there is scant evidence that outcomes are less favourable for any category of parent or for any particular parent–child combination. Nonetheless, a more or less arbitrary hierarchy has some rationale. By categorizing parents in a preference order, those who are placed at the low end may be encouraged to admit that they are prepared to adopt less desirable categories of children as a *quid pro quo* for being considered for adoption at all. With a superfluity of potential parents for desirable children, it can be argued that to reject some categories of parents, such as older parents, if they will not consider hard-to-place children will not lessen adoption rates.

It is possible, therefore, that intrusive, bureaucratic and apparently gratuitous aspects of the selection and matching process that have been subject to so many complaints and reform efforts by the UK government may not be entirely due to inefficiency, ideology and excessive power but also have a logic as a means of maximizing the number of children placed. Agencies can use their control over information, over the selection of potential parents and over placement to increase their bargaining power and so offer children in hard-to-place categories a chance of being adopted. They may do this by using a variety of strategies and pressurizing techniques designed to identify how far parents will go in adopting less desirable categories of child. The UK convention of social workers and adoption panels giving approval to parents only for certain categories of child, in terms of age, sex and sibling group numbers also acts as a way of spreading parents out amongst non-'ideal' children.

Semi-autonomous and private Japanese adoption agencies, including Loving Hands, the Motherly Network and the Christian Agency, follow policies that could be interpreted as part of a similar bargaining strategy with parents. Prospective parents we spoke to described their initial interviews with Loving Hands as off-putting, and the agency also operates an age hierarchy among parents with older parents being offered older children. The Christian Agency has a descending ladder of Christian parents (Japanese, resident, foreign) and attempts to find homes for hard-to-place children with the foreign Christians at the bottom of the hierarchy. The Motherly Network responds to a couple's requests for a specific type of child by rejecting their application altogether; in game theoretic terms it pursues tit for tat defection to encourage other couples to be more cooperative. There is less evidence, however, of bargaining strategies based on rational logic being pursued in Japan's child guidance centres in their negotiations with parents. CGCs are invariably responsive to initial enquiries, and the home study is comparatively painless, focusing on a limited number of objective criteria. Questions are not particularly probing and the social worker may even feel embarrassed over asking about personal details such as a relative's occupation. Although there are delays in the system caused by the cycle of periodic meetings in which applicants have to be approved, these add months – not years – to the process. Most CGC agencies appear to see their role as working with potential parents, and not in any sense against them.

For parents in Japan, therefore, the selection process is faster, more objective and less intrusive that in the UK. In many respects, this might seem commendable. However, bearing in mind the objective of placing as many children in need as possible, the effect of the comparatively efficient, objective and courteous treatment of prospective parents by the CGCs is more difficult to assess. It has the advantage of not doing anything to dissuade potential parents from applying to be adopters, but neither does it dissuade applicants from pursuing an 'ideal' child. On the contrary, prospective parents may be positively encouraged to flesh out their vision of the child ideally suited to them. When the social workers discuss the characteristics of the child in the home study, their enquiries are not directed at the level of problems and disabilities that the parents might be willing to accept, but rather at the attributes of the child that the applicants positively want. The focus is on the kind of children the parents would like, not the kind they would be prepared to take if they had to. At least some CGCs are willing to allow prospective parents to turn down successive placement offers without prejudicing their future chances of being offered another child. This extends as far as occasions where parents who have taken a child on trial and then turned them down are quickly offered another. Although some CGCs favour applicants from their own prefecture, given the range of agencies available, parents also have a somewhat greater opportunity to switch agencies than in the UK.[46]

There are two ways of interpreting the treatment of prospective parents in Japan. The first is to say that it is a reflection of a broader customer service culture, with its effects on adoption rates left unexamined. There is, however, an alternative way of interpreting the approach of the Japanese CGCs. Their apparently compliant attitude towards prospective parents can be seen as a realization that coercive bargaining is not the only way to expand the preferences of parents beyond a narrow ideal. The agencies can be seen as doing the best they can to place as many children as possible, not by pursuing bargaining strategy based on a rational logic, but rather by taking an altogether different kind of approach, one that might be termed seductive.

The seduction of potential parents

If one attempts a rational analysis of the thinking of potential parents it seems logical to assume that they approach adoption with fixed interests about the type of child they want, interests which they will attempt to realize in a way that might be described as rather cold and calculating. Negotiation in these circumstances is possible only by striking a balance between appealing to the applicants' preconceived interest in a certain type of child and threatening to thwart them if they do not cooperate. By contrast, seduction does not rely on coercion. It assumes that prospective parents can change their minds about the type of children they will adopt if they can be persuaded to think about these children as individuals rather than categories. By engaging the feelings and emotions of prospective parents about individual children, a seductive strategy relies on making use of developing feelings of love rather than the adroit use of power.

Child guidance centre methods of getting parents to consider less than 'ideal' children can be interpreted as being based on this seductive logic. The expectations and rational calculations of the parents can change when confronted with a child that does not conform to them. This change takes place as the parents' feelings become engaged with the child they are visiting and the abstract and idealized image of a hypothetical child fades in the face of the reality of the child's unique character as an individual. Their shared experiences with the child can also establish a bond. When CGCs arrange a meeting, they often tell parents that a child is available, give *few details* about them, and take the parents to visit the child almost straight away. This approach is suggestive of a seductive strategy. The CGC withholds any negative information that may dissuade parents from agreeing to see a child in the first place, so that by the time any such information comes out, the parents may already be in love with the child.

This method of placing children raises two questions. The first is whether such a course should be taken given the risk that a child who enters into a series of visits with potential parents may, perhaps quite late in the process, be rejected by them. The second is of whether the parents have in some sense been tricked and their feelings exploited by the agency, particularly if it provides little information about the child prior to their meeting with them. In response to the objection that some children will, inevitably, sometimes be rejected by potential parents, this should not rule out the policy of offering parents the chance to meet a child without commitment. Just as the knowledge that some adoptions will inevitably disrupt does not provide a sufficient argument against adoption, so trial placements can be defended on the grounds that they offer a child the chance of becoming part of a family which they would not otherwise have. For hard-to-place children this is a rare opportunity, one that is worth the risk of rejection. It is also possible that if parents are not censured by the agency for backing out at an early stage, some unsuccessful adoptions may be avoided.

Is the agency justified in withholding information about a child from potential parents before they have met and become emotionally involved with the child? We would argue that although the agency should provide information about the legal position of the child, providing that the parents are meeting with the child without making a prior obligation to adopt, the agency need not disclose information about the child's individual personality. To demand complete prior disclosure by the agency implicitly assumes prospective parents must have their personae as self-interested rational maximizers carefully protected from their better feelings. An agency's failure to disclose its assessment of a child's personality should not be seen in a negative sense of somehow tricking the potential parents but rather in a positive sense of not prejudging the child to them. The parents have the opportunity to assess the child for themselves during the visiting programme. If their feelings are engaged with the child before adverse facts later emerge, and if they then decide nonetheless to keep the child, they have not been fooled; it is their own decision made in a way that reflects the compassionate and loving side to their nature. It is ethical for an agency to try and use these benign feelings to promote an adoption.

Consider the case of the child with a violent temper (Ch. 7). The couple who adopted him were not told of this character trait, and they found out about it only when caring for the child in the introductory period. Had the social workers, at the outset, said 'this child has a violent temper' to potential parents, then they would have effectively placed the child in an exceptionally hard-to-place category, which may have resulted in him remaining in institutional care with no parents willing to consider him. Leaving the parents to discover the child's temper for themselves was acceptable as the choice of whether or not to adopt remained with the parents after they had found this out. In the meantime the parents had the opportunity to learn of all the other qualities of the child, good and bad, to relate to the child as an individual, and start to love him.

Although not part of a deliberate agency strategy, an analogous transition based on changing feelings for an individual child can happen in fostering. Parents who offer to foster a child will know that these children are likely to be somewhat older or otherwise less 'ideal' than children placed for adoption, they may also take into account the financial support for fostering and the positive social image of foster care. These factors notwithstanding, after placement some foster parents who had initially offered only to foster a child go on to adopt the child. The role of individual contact between a parent and child in stimulating adoption and fostering is also seen where potential parents gain access to children's homes as volunteers, become attached to a particular child and initiate suggestions to foster or adopt this child.

Chance too can play a role in bringing potential parents together with children. Special needs children are only rarely adopted in Japan, and adoption agencies rarely even to try to find them adoptive homes. In one case, however, a child with Down's syndrome was adopted by parents who took the initiative after a chance meeting. The boy had been placed in an institutional home, but had become ill and had to stay in hospital on two occasions. The daughter of the eventual adoptive couple was a nurse who was charged with returning the child to the institution, and through her the couple first met him. The couple went to visit the child at the institution after his second stay in hospital, and when he saw them, the child came up to them, at which point they realized they wanted to care for him. The couple went on to foster and eventually adopt the child (Takei 2000: 194–6).

Parental initiatives are not positively encouraged in Japan. There is, for example, no equivalent of the 'adoption parties' between parents and children that have been organized in the USA (Paulson 2001). However the broadly *laissez faire* environment in Japan leaves open the possibility of parents making their own matches; the main obstacles that they face are liable to be the opposition of birth parents to an adoptive or foster placement, or the reluctance of the institution to relinquish the child. Were adoption to be more controlled by a central authority the possibilities for parental initiatives might decrease. Parents who, in one way or another meet children without the intercession of an agency and then foster or adopt them, hark back to a system of private arrangements, and to factors such as serendipity and impulse, factors which may not enter the purview of those who favour a planned and professionally regulated system.

Parental autonomy vs agency control

The UK approach towards matching places considerable decision-making power with the adoption agency and very little with the adoptive parents. This approach can be described either as realistic or as too pessimistic. It assumes that conflict between agencies anxious to help hard-to-place children and parents anxious to adopt an 'ideal' child is inevitable. Giving agencies a high degree of control, however, may help to perpetuate the abstract categorization of children as more or less 'ideal'. Part of a system of control is to give parents little or no access to a child before they have committed to that child. This makes it more difficult for the parent to view the child as an individual not a category. Japanese CGCs have tried to forge a more collaborative approach between agencies and adoptive parents with the use of trial placements. This approach has the potential to overcome the problem of the 'ideal' child by allowing parents to relate to children as individuals.

Which system better serves the overall interests of children in need is an open question. Although the population of Japan is more than twice that of England, far fewer children in need are adopted (Appendix 1: Table 5). This might lead to the conclusion that the Japanese system of adoption is less efficient. However, Japanese parents have a much narrower definition of the ideal child than foreign residents, including couples from the UK. This is evidenced by the way that children who cannot be placed with Japanese couples may find homes with these foreign residents. UK adoptive parents with experiences in both countries also spoke of how the Japanese system was relatively welcoming. It could be, therefore, that under the difficult circumstances of potential parents having a tightly focused vision of an ideal child, the seductive logic of Japanese placement works comparatively well. The system is not off-putting to enter and trial placements may extend the range of children that can be placed.

11 Problems of power and prospects for reform

In the modern history of child adoption in Japan, private arrangements between families have been supplemented by arrangements mediated in civil society, such as the international adoptions in the years following the Second World War, and then by adoptions arranged through the state child guidance centres, including most special adoptions. Taking the end of the war as a starting point, the proportion of children adopted through the family, civil society or state has changed as first voluntary and independent adoption organizations became involved and then the state increased its role. The actual proportion of children adopted through each sector cannot be calculated, but for illustrative purposes it can be assumed, very roughly, that arrangements made through families, civil society and the state now account for an equal share of the adoption of babies and younger children when ordinary, special and international adoptions are combined. This development over the last 60 years is notionally shown in Figure 11.1, a phase diagram.[47] The changing proportion of children adopted by different routes follows the dotted line that starts with family adoptions and curves to a central point between family, civil society and state.

From the point that has been reached one can identify at least four possible pressures for future change. The first and most likely shift is the pressure to reduce the proportion of adoptions being conducted by independent agencies that are not officially registered, by either controlling them more closely or forcing them out of business altogether (Figure 11.1: arrow 1). Some of the adoption policies that have been followed under a largely *laissez faire* system have caused concern within the Japanese state, particularly with respect to the financial practices of unregistered agencies. A report has been commissioned and new guidance promised ('Yôshiengumi' 2005). If Japan follows the path of Britain and other European states this step could be indicative of a movement towards the development of a centrally planned adoption system adhering to common professional standards that leaves little room for any truly independent agencies, registered or not, nor for adoptions arranged privately (Figure 11.1: arrow 2).

It is conceivable, although much less likely, that a contrary movement could take place. If the neo-liberal agenda that has been informing other aspects of Japanese welfare reform was extended to adoption, then the state child guidance centres might retreat from their role in arranging adoptions and leave more

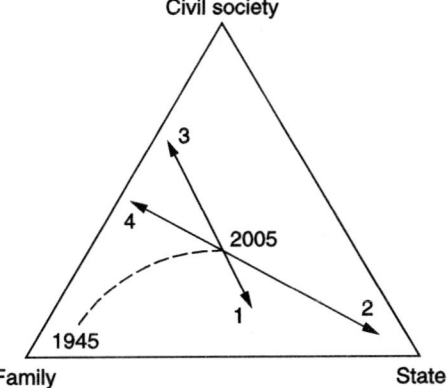

Figure 11.1 Adoptions through family, society and state

room for the independent agencies (Figure 11.1: arrow 3). If such a policy was accompanied by a renewed emphasis on the virtues of ordinary adoption arranged between families, then the proportion of these adoptions might also rise as the state pulls back (Figure 11.1: arrow 4).

Free market reform

Let us turn first to the unlikely case of a neo-liberal policy shift towards adoption, combined with an argument for more latitude towards ordinary adoptions (Figure 11.1: arrows 3 and 4). The free market case for adoption reform has been proposed by Landes and Posner (1978) in support of independent agencies in the USA. The same line of reasoning can be applied to Japan as follows:

> Japan's comprehensive system of state run, taxpayer funded adoption has crowded out the more efficient and responsive independent adoption sector. To help more children in need of adoption, maximum scope should be given for individual initiative and energy in society. The state, therefore, should retreat from its role as an adoption provider, and should not regulate adoptions arranged privately between families or by independent agencies, except to enforce contracts.

How should this argument be assessed? First, it is true that there is only limited scope for a financially viable independent agency to conduct domestic adoptions. Although independent agencies and private adoption arrangements are permitted in Japan, the commercial possibilities are limited because most babies and children available for adoption are placed at no cost. The CGCs do not charge prospective parents for their adoption services. Adoptive parents have to pay one or two trivial fees in completing court procedures and registering the adoption, but these are more than offset by the substantial foster care payments given to parents between the time of placement and adoption. Second, it is much more contentious to suggest that a free adoption service may have disadvantaged the children involved, as it is questionable whether a state withdrawal from this role would result in the placement of a greater proportion of children in need. To increase this proportion, one needs to find ways of reversing the tendency of prospective parents to imagine children in more or less desirable categories and to compete only for the most sought-after babies and toddlers. In this respect, the economic pressure of 'customer demand' for placements of the most desirable categories of child makes it difficult for the independent sector to help hard-to-place children. Third, the argument that relinquishing all control of adoption to the independent sector would make adoption more attractive to potential parents because of the greater efficiency and responsiveness of private adoption organizations is difficult to sustain in Japan, where the CGCs are already efficient and responsive. Furthermore, a free market adoption system implicitly depends on a system of contracts and if pursued to its extreme would end in arrangements akin to commercial surrogacy. This would compound the problem of how to uphold the rights of birth mothers when they deal with independent agencies and might tend only to increase the determination of prospective parents to settle for nothing less than a child categorized as 'ideal'. Fourth, with respect to the idea that ordinary adoptions are over-regulated, it is true that when the courts vet applications for ordinary adoption a significant proportion are turned down (Appendix 1: Table 9). However, these do not represent refusals to approve the adoption of children in need, but rather they safeguard the welfare of children who are not in need of adoption.

Reform through increased regulation

The more likely path of adoption reform in Japan is that it will gain its sense of direction from those who, to one degree or another, favour a centrally planned and more tightly regulated approach as best protecting the rights and interests of the most vulnerable members of society (Figure 11.1: arrows 1 and 2). Those who favour this perspective are concerned about the activities of unregistered independent adoption agencies, in part because of a suspicion that the profit motive is excessive. It can be added that there is a case for closer scrutiny of unregistered independent adoption agencies as 'contracts' with birth mothers seem to be associated particularly with these organizations. Prescriptions on increasing the protective role of the state, however, are not without problems, as a stricter regulatory regime cannot easily be separated from the state's less benign policing functions. The most vulnerable category of birth mothers and their children in Japan, who sometimes turn to the independent sector for help, are undocumented migrants. They are at risk or being deported, not protected, by the state. The more regulatory control that there is over the independent sector, the more difficult their position may become.

The aim of greater regulation and central control also has a close affinity with the more ambitious aim of developing adoption mediation as a profession with a shared ethos, with high standards laid down in authoritative rules and guidelines, and with an expert knowledge on which these rules are based. Simply by doing things differently, placements by independent agencies and adoption agreements made between families present a challenge to a profession's expertise and authority. An across the board effort to impose uniform standards in adoption, however, risks losing some of the advantages of the current lightly regulated approach towards the selection of parents and matching them with children. The opportunity for parents to enter adoption in different ways and with different agencies prevents agencies from entering into an unduly coercive relationship with them and this probably encourages more parents to put themselves forward. The freedom of those with an interest in adoption to develop their own policies makes use of the energy and initiative that might be stifled in a more rigorously planned system.

Current parental selection procedures by agencies tend not to be particularly onerous, for example, there is rarely a criminal record check made on applicants. If there is a move towards greater regulation of adoption in Japan, there may be an attempt to impose more rigorous selection procedures with extensive investigations designed to weed out unsuitable parents. Rigorous selection can be justified on the grounds that it reduces the risk that a couple trusted with a child will turn out to be abusive or otherwise unsuitable. However, if the knock-on effects of rigorous selection of parents are factored in, such a policy may, in fact, increase the level of risk to children in need. Any form of parental selection that requires applicants to undergo a wide ranging and far reaching assessment will deter some couples from applying to adopt, even if many of them would make perfectly good parents. Intrusive assessments have the potential to be particularly off-putting in Japan, as they would go against the cultural tendency to retain a large private sense of self and expose only a small part of one's feelings and beliefs to others (Barnlund 1975: 32–6). If extensive assessment reduces the number of parents willing to put themselves forward, then fewer, not more children will be placed. Leaving aside all the positive benefits of adoption, those who are not placed may either remain with abusive or neglectful birth parents or in institutions where the risk of abuse cannot be regarded as insignificant.

Matching between parents and children in Japan is done in a number of ways, with the parents themselves often having a degree of input. Greater regulation might also result in the imposition of standard matching criteria. However, there is very little evidence-based knowledge of what works and what does not in matching. When it comes to the question of how a particular couple will get on with a particular child who is not known or related to the parent, the only sure rule that the agency can turn to in making a successful placement is the law of averages. This law tells them that most adoptions succeed, however parents and children have been matched. Adoptions succeed in different countries with different selection and matching policies, they succeed in placements made by independent and public agencies, they succeed when children are placed domestically and internationally and with parents of the same and different ethnic backgrounds, with old parents and with young parents (Rowe 1991: 8). The pre-placement factors that make the success or failure of any particular parent–child combination more likely are largely unknown; the associations that have been found in outcome studies tend to be weak and there is only limited replication of findings (Thoburn 1990: 83–4). There are one or two common sense exceptions where the outcome is obviously predicated in the characteristic of the adult or child. Exceptionally punitive parents, almost by definition, make worse carers. Similarly, if a child is hard to place because of marked behavioural problems this makes a successful outcome less certain. There is also strong – but not conclusive – evidence that the older the child, the less likely it is that a placement will be successful.[48] However, increased risks do not justify denying the opportunity of adoption to a hard-to-place child if willing parents can be found.

We suspect that the things that will make for a successful match between parent and child before they have even met are not only unknown but unknowable. It depends on free choices and future circumstances that cannot be predicted, and it depends on love and other feelings that have not yet been called into existence. Where adoption has become established as a profession, love can be downplayed in favour of more objective and scientific sounding terms like 'attachment' and 'bonding', words that can be used interchangeably for human beings, inanimate objects and chemical reactions. Japanese adoption mediators have been less 'scientific' in this respect. The idea that love is important often features prominently in the way they describe an adoption. Nor is this emphasis merely rhetorical. The staff at Loving Hands are searching for signs of love when watching parents take up a child's photograph; the birth mother giving up a child is seen as performing an act of love in the Motherly Network, one for which adoptive parents owe their 'gratitude for unseen things'. There may be a naivety in the efforts of Japanese adoption agencies to incorporate love into the way they understand adoption, but acknowledging love may still help to ensure that decisions of vital importance to a family are made in a humane way.

If it is impossible to predict success or failure of an adoption in advance, then any attempt to impose standard regulations on matching is pointless. However, there is room for a more extensive professional role in providing post-adoption support when things start to go wrong. There have been some moves in this direction, beginning in September 2002 when the Ministry of Health, Labour and Welfare introduced new guidelines on foster care, including regular visits to foster parents (Kôseirôdôsho 2002). In November of that year, a tragic case in which a three-year-old girl was killed by the mother who was fostering her with a view to adoption reinforced the arguments for post-placement support. In her defence at the trial, the mother claimed that the family had received no help from the CGC even though the child was very difficult – two previous foster placements had broken down (Utsunomiya 2004).

Power imbalances

Power can be understood in two ways: it can be an indication of potential capacities: the power to do something, or it can be the ability to control the behaviour of another person, that is, power over someone (Macpherson 1973: 40–57). These two forms of power are in a state of tension, as an excess of controlling, coercive power on one side does not allow those on the other side sufficient capacity power to make choices, act on their wishes and feelings, exercise their rights and create their own destiny. In the web of relationships between children, agencies and institutions, between birth parents and the courts and between birth parents and agencies, there are a number of places where Japan's adoption system has allowed a questionable balance of power to develop.

The child's voice

Japanese law requires a CGC to consult a child over their intentions when it intervenes to protect the child's welfare (Ministry of Foreign Affairs 2001: 177). With respect to adoption and fostering, CGCs do make some effort to examine the wishes of the child after an intervention. In assessing foster placements they may, for example, ask the child: 'Do you like that person?' CGCs may also indirectly assess the feelings of the child towards their new parents by observing their behaviour. The question of how far a child should be consulted over the need for an adoption and with which parents is rarely significant; almost all children who are in need of adoptions and who are also in fact adopted, are too young to be consulted over their fate – most are only babies or toddlers. However, when one considers the position of older children, ones who might well be in need of adoption but who stand little or no chance of actually being adopted, the question of the power, or lack of it, of these children to express their wishes assumes much greater significance.

The scandal of the Onchoen children's home demonstrated how child victims of institutional abuse have had great difficulty in getting the CGCs or other state authorities to step in and protect them. These children lacked the capacity-power to voice complaints or to gain a fair hearing; the closing of ranks by those in authority allowed the coercive power of the abusers to remain unchecked. The lack of a voice for older children in institutions may also adversely affect their prospects of adoption, or if this is not realistic, of fostering. Social workers employed by the CGC only occasionally visit children in institutions, and when they do the sessions may take the form of an open group meeting where it is difficult to speak out. If older children had more opportunities to comment on their care options, they might be in a better position to persuade social workers to try and find them a foster or adoptive placement.

Care options and children's homes

Institutional care in Japan is sometimes viewed as a permanent solution to the care of children who cannot live with their parents. It might be asked whether there should be more effort to make it a temporary stopgap. Under the current system if a child placed in institutional care is not immediately eligible for fostering or adoption, the CGCs may neglect to keep these options under continuing review and rely instead upon institutional reports on the progress of the child and for recommendations for foster or adoptive care. The result is that unless the child returns to his birth parents, or unless the children's home itself takes the initiative and suggests a foster or adoptive placement, the child is likely to remain in institutional care throughout the rest of his or her childhood. To delegate authority to institutional carers in this way does not recognize the conflict of interest between decision making for the welfare of the child and decision making aimed at securing revenue and perpetuating the role of the institution.

The family courts and parental rights

Formal guardianship of a child placed for adoption typically remains with the birth parents until the adoption is legally finalized and is not, for example, reassigned to an authorized agency at the time that a birth mother requests an adoption. When these guardianship rights are combined with different views of what constitutes abuse and neglect by parents, with the courts tending to take a narrow view of the matter, the result can be an overemphasis on gaining the consent of birth parents to an adoption (Iwasaki, Mieko 1999: 36–7). The family court acts as a check upon plans to foster or adopt a child when this is opposed by the birth parents. Applications by the GCG for parents to remove children from their natural parents are scrutinized carefully by the courts and are not agreed to lightly. The ethos of the family court is to seek conciliation where possible, and it has been suggested that in the mind of a family court judge, denying birth parents custody feels like imposing a death sentence (Nishimura and Ootaguchi 2003: 28–9).

The family courts can be criticized for their tendency to be over reluctant to overturn the rights of birth parents who have gone missing, or who do not visit a child in an institution, or who have been abusive or neglectful. When parents have gone missing, the period of absence is often about three years before the court will agree to an adoption. Three years in the life of a child is a long time in terms of their physical and mental development, far more than three years in the life of an adult, and as the child grows older, so it becomes harder to find an adoptive placement for them. The court's reluctance to overturn parental rights can be defended for minimizing the use of coercive power. However, in circumstances where the child is the victim of despotic parents this argument loses its force. Court willingness to accept evidence of abuse may be too limited to obvious signs of physical injury, with other ways of establishing the truth, including forensic interview methods, left unexplored (JFBA 2003: 255). Alternatively, if non-abusive parents are not observing other essential duties to their children, then upholding their rights in court becomes an abstract sterile process. If, for example, the child is in an institution and particularly if he is not being visited, then the 'right' of the parent to the child has become divorced from the effort by the parent to exercise their capacities in creating a family and maintaining a loving relationship with the child. Upholding the rights of parents in these circumstances creates a vacuum – the absence of a home life – for the child, and the child's chance to develop in a family environment is denied to him or her.

The rights of birth mothers

In contrast to cases where the rights of birth parents may be given too much weight when their care for their children is lacking, the rights of birth mothers may not be sufficiently respected when they have their child adopted through a private agency. The birth mother (or grandparents) maintains formal guardianship rights under Japanese law, which does not recognize the validity of adoption contracts, but agencies and lawyers appear to have developed an alternative 'contractual' mode of operating nonetheless. Whereas a parent can be absent for years and still retain rights over the child, a birth mother is given an agreement that can appear to be an irrevocable 'contract' within days of the birth, sometimes while she is still in hospital and faced with fees for her care. To make an apparently final commitment within days of birth is too soon and is potentially coercive. A contractual relationship is inappropriate for birth mothers at a point when their feelings may be in flux and when they are most vulnerable and powerless.

CGCs seek to obtain the signed agreement of a birth mother for adoption, at various stages from the time that they are approached by the mother (or her parents) and asked about the adoption system until the time that the foster parents go to court to get approval for adoption (Iwasaki and Sakurai 1999: 9). They do not, however, present 'contracts' to the mother soon after birth. Newborn babies are almost never offered for adoption by the CGCs, or by Loving Hands, and this helps to minimize problems with mothers changing their minds. An interim period of institutional care allows the birth mother time to reclaim the baby, without the guilt or trauma of taking the baby from its adoptive family. The Motherly Network occupies an intermediate position between adoptions arranged through doctors and the adoptions arranged by CGCs or by Loving Hands. It places a child soon after birth but also provides for a period of three months for the birth mother to reflect on giving up her baby. It attempts to gain the advantages of an early adoption while recognizing that a birth mother may feel torn between her prenatal decision to have a child adopted and her feelings after the birth.

Birth mothers have less control than they should over maintaining their privacy. Mothers who give up their children are dogged with the record of the birth on their *koseki*. Kikuta rightly suggested that birth mothers should be allowed to omit any record of the birth of the child if they wish. Furthermore, a system that ensured anonymity of adoption records on both sides might also encourage more adoptive parents to come forward. One might argue that the current system should be maintained by extending the concern about sibling intermarriage (exceedingly unlikely in a nation of 127 million) to a more general assertion of the right of the child to know of their biological ancestry. There are two responses to this counterargument. The first is that a truly confidential record system could be created, one that was guarded much more carefully than the *koseki* from the attentions of curious outsiders. The second response is that the interests of the child should be judged not *after* the mother has given him or her up for adoption but *before*. In this respect, the anticipated shame of a *koseki* record may weigh heavily in the decisions made by a birth mother, so that the advantage to children of a system that guarantees their 'right' to know their roots, is outweighed by the increased risk that they face not only of illicit adoption, but also of abandonment and even possibly infanticide. If, like Kikuta, one considers the pressures on birth mothers while the child is still in the womb, then the conclusion that ensuring the mother's confidentiality is in the child's interest is further reinforced.

Choices for prospective parents

The relationship between potential parents and adoption agencies tends to be collaborative rather than combative and is largely free of the problems that power imbalances cause between other parties. Potential parents have a choice of routes to adoption. Most adopt through the public CGCs, but others go to the quasi-autonomous Loving Hands, or to a number of private agencies. Potential parents can also make arrangements through a lawyer, or they can approach a children's home. Depending on the route they take, parents have varying degrees of input into how far they can participate in being matched with a child. Kazuko Yokoto of the Motherly Network offers no choice to applicants, and rejects prospective parents who ask for one. Other applicants, however, have choices, shown in Figure 11.2, that can be categorized by distinguishing (a) between children who are offered to prospective parents one at a time, and children who are offered as a group, and (b) between children where the parents make a choice based on information supplied about them, as against children where the parents get to meet them. One can also bear in mind a further distinction (c) between an agency that offers a child or children to a single set of parents at a time and provisionally offering the child/children to several parents at once.

The doctors' association follows a policy that allows parents to make choices based on information on individual children provided in sequence. The association identifies an adoptive couple immediately after birth or before a child has been born and offers information based on what they know of the birth parents

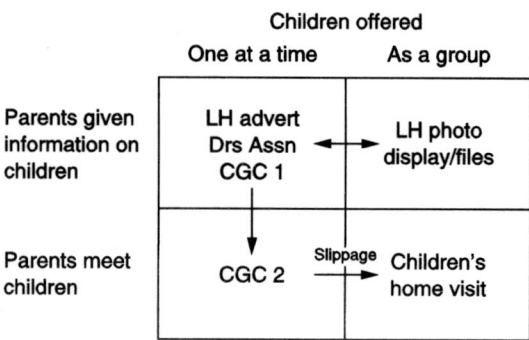

Figure 11.2 Choices offered to potential parents

to one couple and then if they turn the child down, to another. Children who are advertised in the weekly paper by Loving Hands are also offered in sequence, although here the choice offered to all prospective parents is to apply, in competition with other parents, to have the child placed with them.

If the children who are advertised individually by Loving Hands in Osaka are not placed, they may be advertised again and will also be advertised collectively in a photographic display at its training meetings for groups of prospective parents, a public venue that gives a competitive edge to this display. Couples who are registered with the agency may also make appointments to look through the files on available children in the agency office in Osaka.

The policy of allowing parents to meet with children one at a time, and then choosing whether or not to engage in a trial placement is followed by CGCs. The mechanics of this policy begin (1) by supplying information about the child, before (2) quickly taking willing parents to an infant home and introducing the child to them. There is occasional slippage between this method of matching and the parents visiting an institution to get a more general view of children available for adoption there. Parents who arrange to visit children's homes on their own initiative also have the opportunity to compare different children and may approach a CGC about a particular child. Sometimes parents who have visited an institution apply initially just to foster a child they have met, and then later apply to adopt him. Parents may also learn of available children through informal contacts with care workers.

The level of choice is greater where children are presented simultaneously, as it becomes easier to make comparisons between them. Where parents are able to meet a child, choice is also more informed as direct engagement provides a level of experience of a different and higher order to receiving written and pictorial information about a child. It would appear, therefore, that from the perspective of potential parents, a system where they meet several children simultaneously would offer the greatest choice. However, three factors need to be set against this. First, the level of choice tends to decrease as the children in need of adoption get older, and so harder to place. Second, if parents are offered the choice of several children at once this does not guarantee that their choice will be met, as this remains a matter to be negotiated with the agency, and where several children are offered to several prospective parents simultaneously, there may be competition. Third, if parents have met a child, as opposed to merely being given information about them, and selected them in preference to others, if they are subsequently unable to adopt that child the emotional upset is liable to be greater for them and for the child. On more than one occasion we spoke to wistful parents who had met with children in institutional homes, and had tried to adopt them in preference to the children that they actually went on to adopt, but were turned down.

There are pros and cons to all of these arrangements. A matching system that made full use of the judgement and feelings of potential parents would aim to give the greatest breadth and depth to their choices by enabling them to meet several children. However, agencies might decide that they can more effectively place children by offering less choice to parents and so avoid competitions for some children while others go unplaced. Parents will not necessarily feel more comfortable with a process that emphasizes their informed choice of a child, given the strain and possible disappointments that come with it. Preserving a range of approaches to matching gives prospective parents a wider choice of agency methods. Parents put off by the matching system of one agency might feel more comfortable with another and so will be more willing to embark on the process of adoption.

Conflict and collaboration

When special adoption was codified it was only lightly regulated. The law was framed in terms of broad principles; it was not concerned with details. Under this permissive regularity framework, adoption agencies have branched out in different directions. The policies that they have developed have been created autonomously with little management from the state and with no overarching professional body to control and coordinate what is done. Much of this variety has had positive results, a range of approaches not hampered by any one orthodoxy have encouraged prospective parents into the system. However, problems are evident in some of the power disparities in the broader childcare system in which adoption is embedded. There is a case for reforming the power balance to ensure that children have a say; to limit the decision-making power of children's homes over a child's future, and for the institutions of state to be more willing and able to intervene to overturn parental rights in some instances and be more active in protecting the rights of birth mothers in others.

These reforms would have some implications for the extra regulation of independent agencies, and somewhat increase the role of the state. However, if reformist efforts turn into a power struggle between independent and state agencies they are unlikely to increase the rate of adoption of children in need.

The most pressing problem in adoption is how to increase the proportion of children in need of adoption who are actually adopted. However, to tie the effort to increase this proportion too closely to the promotion of any one adoption sector increases the risk that policy reform becomes a zero sum struggle for control. In a power struggle the objective of increasing placements may become lost in the efforts to reduce the proportion of adoptions in 'opposing' sectors. To find family homes for more of these children a broad view must be taken of the situation of all children in care in Japan. The great majority of these children are placed in private children's homes. Most will not return to their parents and are in need of alternative family care. If those involved in placing children in families for fostering or adoption had greater power to access and make plans for these children, then this could have a significant impact on increasing the proportion of these children who go on to be fostered and adopted. This, however, could only occur by diminishing the power over a child's future that is now held by the children's homes.

A shared sense of purpose in trying to place more children currently in the care of children's homes in families might encourage collaboration across independent and public adoption agencies, for example, in making more efforts to share information on hard-to-place children available for adoption. However, a collaborative strategy of reducing the number of children in institutional care could only work in tandem with efforts to increase the number of foster parents and adoptive parents. These efforts could make full use of the whole range of approaches to placement from all sectors, including family initiatives taken when individual parents approach institutions directly to try and arrange foster or adoptive placements. There have been several state initiatives to encourage foster placement, to which can be added the self-evident reform that is always available: pay foster parents more. Raising payments may raise concerns about encouraging foster parents through the profit motive, but the profit motive is already present in private institutional care. A revitalized foster care regime might increase the number of adoptions of foster children, although there is no easy solution to increasing the number of parents who will go beyond concerns over blood and background and apply to adopt an unrelated child. Nonetheless, an adoption system that is reasonably open to enter and which provides a variety of agencies to choose from, will do something to encourage potential parents. A common strategy of reducing the proportion of children in institutional care, by increasing the number of those being fostered or adopted, could provide the basis for greater unity in Japan's adoption system without losing the variety that is a part of its strength.

Conclusion

The child guidance centres, semi-autonomous and private agencies that have pursued special adoption have succeeded in establishing a new form of adoptive placement in Japan. The degree of success has been modest as there are many children in need of adoption who cannot be found homes, but the obstacles have been considerable including the unwillingness of state institutions to abrogate the rights of abusive or neglectful birth parents, and an entrenched system of private institutional care. Despite a long tradition of adoption, one of the greatest difficulties has been the widespread reluctance of Japanese couples to countenance adopting an unrelated child. Where potential parents have been willing to put themselves forward, they have tended to be highly selective over the categories of children that they are willing to adopt. Despite these problems, the agencies have managed to place children by forging largely collaborative relationships with adoptive parents who have been willing, to some degree at least, to go beyond negative attitudes towards the family background and blood of an unknown child. International placements have also been used as a pragmatic and positive way of helping children in need in the face of conservative social attitudes. In particular, the use of foreign residents as adopters has increased the numbers of family homes available to children of a mixed or minority background by side-stepping the reluctance of many Japanese parents to adopt them. Through the combined choices and efforts of birth mothers, agencies and prospective parents, hundreds of needy children in Japan find new families in a special adoption each year.

Through our account of the work of different agencies in Japan we have tried to identify policies that best help children in need while also respecting other participants. Our method of analysis may sometimes seem rather cold, particularly when we discuss bargaining tactics and the search of adoptive parents for the 'ideal' child. This type of analysis is justified, we think, in revealing policy dilemmas in trying to place as many children as possible. However, the actions of adoptive parents cannot be reduced to rational self-interest. The child guidance centre policies of successfully finding families for children who, in a Japanese context, are 'hard to place' by allowing for unconditional trial placements belie any notion that adoptive parents make decisions that can be understood on a narrow selfishly rational basis.

Our answers to the problems that have been identified may often be felt to be unsatisfactory. Sometimes we have equivocated and even where we support one policy over another we are often uncertain that it is the better course. However, leaving our own views aside, it is hoped that this outline of the variety of approaches to adoption in Japan will be useful in stimulating the comparative analysis and critical thinking of those who, in whatever capacity, want to promote adoption for children in need. We hope, therefore, that presenting the approaches to adoption being developed in Japan to an English-speaking audience will make some contribution to the debate over adoption reform not just in Japan, but also in other parts of the world.

Appendix 1
Adoption numbers

Japan's official adoption numbers can be assumed to be reliable in the sense that they are unlikely to reflect a political bias. There is little public debate and controversy over adoption, so there is correspondingly little incentive to manipulate the figures to make a point, justify a policy or show that a target has been met. Nonetheless, the numbers are still somewhat problematic. There are inconsistencies between different sources, there are gaps in the record and some figures are aggregated in a way that makes their interpretation difficult. Furthermore, unorthodox or undocumented forms of adoption are not included in the official figures. When figures from other states are compared with those of Japan, the problems are compounded. Unfortunately, awareness of all these problems does not help to solve them, it merely makes the task of understanding the implications of the figures rather inconclusive and tends to spoil the definiteness and objectivity that gives numbers their appeal. Let us, therefore, ease ourselves into the statistics by providing an overview of some of the more salient numbers without troubling with all the provisos and qualifications that come with the details.

In 2004 there were 423 court applications for special adoption. Between 1998 and 2004 there were an average of 440 special adoption applications made to the courts each year.

In 2004 there were 1,500 court applications for ordinary adoption. Between 1996 and 2004 there were an average of 1,452 ordinary adoption applications made to the courts each year.

In 2000 there were 534 court applications for an international adoption. Between 1996 and 2000 there were an average of 437 international adoption applications made to the Japanese courts each year.

In 2004 there were 45 intercountry adoptions of children defined by the USA as 'orphans' from Japan to the USA.

In 2003 there were 2,811 children in foster care.

In 2003 there were 30,416 children in children's homes.

Special adoption

Figures for special adoption between 1998 and 2004 show the number of cases brought before Japan's courts each year to be in the 400s.

Table 1   Special adoption cases 1998–2004

Year	1998	1999	2000	2001	2002	2003	2004
Cases	478	448	431	418	457	433	429
Annulment Applications	–	1	0	0	–	13	6

Sources: Saikôsaibansho 1999–2004b.

Not all of the cases in Table 1 are adoption applications; one case in 1999, 13 cases in 2003 and six cases in 2004 were applications for an annulment. Annulment application figures for 1998 and 2002 are missing, possibly because as in 2000 and 2001 there were no cases to record. Assuming this to be the case, the courts received an average of 440 special adoption applications between 1998 and 2004.

The 1998–2004 figures do not tell us how many applications were successful, However, acceptance numbers can be found in the more detailed numbers that are available for the years between 1988 (the year special adoption began) and 1997. The only loss of detail for these earlier years is a lack of information on how many cases were annulment applications, although given the low figures from 1998 onwards it can be assumed that the numbers are negligible. In Table 2 annual special adoption approval figures between 1988 and 1997 show numbers ranging from a peak of 1205 in 1989 to a low of 361 in 1997. This table also gives figures on applications that were rejected or withdrawn, and indicates how many of the overall application figures were for the conversion of an ordinary adoption to a special adoption. For successful applications, it indicates whether or not an adoption agency was used and distinguishes between child guidance centres and other agencies.

If the application figures in Table 1 and Table 2 are considered together, they show that in 1988 there was an initial surge in special adoption applications, followed by a steep decline until about 1990, a slow decline until about 1998 and then a more or less steady rate until 2004. The initial surge was probably caused in part by a build-up of aspirant parents before 1988 who took the opportunity to adopt in the first few years after special adoption became possible. There were also parents who adopted in an ordinary adoption earlier in the 1980s when no other form of adoption was possible. After 1988, if the child was still under eight, many of these parents applied to convert the adoption to a special adoption. Thus, out of 3,256 adoptions approved between 1988 and 1991, a sizeable 1,246 or 38% were conversions from an ordinary adoption. By comparison, of the 2,647 approvals between 1992 and 1997 only 87 or 3% were conversions.

In the initial years of the surge, the majority of successful applications did not involve an agency. Non-agency adoptions subsequently show a marked decline and from 1990 onwards, the majority of successful applications were mediated by agencies, with the great majority of these being undertaken by child guidance centres. CGC numbers presumably include adoptions arranged through Loving

Table 2 Special adoptions 1988–97

Year	1988	1989	1990	1991	1992	1993	1994	1995	1996	1997
Cases	3,201	1,287	999	852	700	680	722	558	546	543
Settled	1,747	1,904	1,135	918	688	647	599	607	532	458
Approved	**730**	**1,205**	**743**	**578**	**469**	**460**	**452**	**479**	**426**	**361**
(conversion)	364	597	201	84	35	21	15	9	4	3
Agency:										
CGC	238	354	356	331	289	300	321	322	290	244
Other	16	28	36	30	29	43	47	59	60	53
None	476	823	351	217	151	117	84	98	76	64
Rejected	155	139	87	58	37	36	29	32	17	16
(conversion)	97	89	47	30	16	16	17	14	3	6
Withdrawn	861	560	304	282	182	150	118	96	89	81
(conversion)	424	319	142	102	57	45	40	25	23	30
Unsettled Cases	1454	837	701	635	647	680	803	754	768	853

Source: Adapted from Nakayama and Kaneko 1999.

Hands and may also include occasions where CGCs turn to other agencies. The number of adoptions arranged by the CGCs runs roughly parallel to the number of acceptances. There is some suggestion of a modest upwards trend in place-ments by independent agencies.

Of the 9,235 special adoption cases settled between 1988 and 1997 a signifi-cant number were not approved. Two thousand seven hundred and twenty-three (29%) of applications were withdrawn and 606 (7%) were rejected. Applications for conversion from an ordinary adoption accounted for 1207 (44%) of with-drawn and 335 (55%) of rejected cases. In these cases judges may have opposed a special adoption on the grounds that it would sever all ties with the birth parents.

The destination of children in settled cases between 1989, a year after special adoption began, and 1997 has been defined in five categories: (1) adults who were already adoptive parents in an ordinary adoption, (2) adults who were foster parents to the child, (3) birth parent(s) or the spouse of a birth parent, (4) rela-tives, (5) others. There is no cross-tabulation between these destinations and whether the application was accepted, withdrawn or rejected, nor is there a cross-tabulation with whether the application was for a conversion. However, by com-paring the two sets of figures it is possible to draw some broad inferences about how the outcome of the case affected the destination.

Table 3 shows that there were 1,990 accepted, rejected or withdrawn conversion applications settled between 1989 and 1997. In the same period 1,960 children went to parents who had already adopted them in an ordinary adoption. It appears, therefore, that with the exception of 30 cases, a child would tend to stay with his or her parents in an ordinary adoption even if they withdrew or were rejected in their application to convert it to a special adoption. The 4,204 cases in which the

Table 3 Court decisions and child destinations 1989–97

Decision	No. (%)	Destination (adult's status pre-decision)	No. (%)
All conversions (approve + reject + withdrawn)	1,990 (27)	Adoptive parents	1,960 (26)
Non-conversion decisions		Foster parents	3,353 (45)
(a) Approve	4,204 (56)	Birth parent or spouse	786 (10)
(b) Reject	213 (3)	Relatives	449 (6)
(c) Withdrawn	1,079 (14)	Other	940 (13)
Total (total omits two cases from 1990 included in the destination figures)	7,486 (100)	Total	7,488 (100)

Source: Adapted from Nakayama and Kaneko 1999.

adoption application was accepted can be assumed to include all of the 3,353 cases which ended with the child in the care of his or her foster parents (who would have then become adoptive parents in a special adoption). The 786 cases where a child was placed in their birth family can be assumed to come from a combination of the 213 rejected applications and the 1,079 withdrawn cases. There is insufficient information to speculate on how the children in the remaining cases were divided between relatives and others.

The ages of children in settled cases 1988–97 (including cases where the application was withdrawn or rejected) are shown in Table 4. These figures are presumed to refer to the age of the child at the time of settlement, particularly as they include a significant number of children of eight and above.

The initial years show a surge of older children, which indicates the large number of applications for conversions from ordinary adoptions. There is then a steep decline in applications to adopt older children, with babies under a year old

Table 4 Age of children in settled cases

Age	0	1	2	3	4	5	6	7	8+	Total
1988	91	125	182	233	246	369	243	202	56	1,747
1989	195	161	212	233	225	358	264	239	13	1,904
1990	178	121	149	135	114	193	122	109	14	1,135
1991	162	120	117	115	80	151	89	76	8	918
1992	132	108	100	99	67	77	61	37	7	688
1993	132	109	99	67	68	89	42	35	6	647
1994	115	103	109	88	41	66	50	23	4	599
1995	143	115	86	87	49	52	44	22	9	607
1996	140	89	93	76	41	38	25	28	2	532
1997	105	82	82	57	42	54	21	13	2	458

Source: Adapted from Nakayama and Kaneko 1999.

Table 5 Comparison of Japan and England

Age	Japan (1997) No. (%)	England (2003–04) No. (%)
Under 1	105 (23)	210 (6)
1–4	263 (57)	2,200 (63)
5–9	90 (20)	1,100 (31)
Total	458 (100)	3,510 (100)

Sources: Nakayama and Kaneko 1999; Department for Education and Skills 2005.

being the most popular category every year from 1991 onwards. The figures confirm that there is a marked preference amongst parents for children aged three or less. In 1997, for example, 326 (71%) of children were under four in settled cases. However, the numbers do not continue down uniformly for older children, as in every year except 1996 more children are aged five than four. A minor rush of parents to adopt a child already in their care before the apparent deadline for a special adoption as the child approaches their sixth birthday might explain this, although for children being fostered the actual deadline is not for two more years.

The 458 special adoptions in 1997 allow for a very rough comparison to be made between the numbers and ages of children adopted in Japan with those for adoptions in England. The English figures in Table 5 are for the number and ages of adopted children under the age of ten for the year ending 31 March 2004.

These figures, drawn from different years, provide only a very imperfect comparison of the adoption of children in need; they exclude all ordinary adoptions in Japan and they exclude the adoption of older children in England. Nonetheless, the comparison gives a broad indication that children in need are adopted in much higher numbers in England than in Japan. When considering how many children are given up at birth or soon after birth in Japan as compared to England, it can be noted that although the number of adoptions for children under twelve months in England is twice the number in Japan, at 6% it represents only a small proportion of English adoptions of children under 10. By contrast a much higher proportion, 23%, of special adoptions in Japan were of babies under twelve months old. It can also be noted that CGCs often keep children in an infant home for about a year before placing them for adoption, so a more pertinent figure from 1997 is that 187 or 41% of children in special adoptions were adopted under the age of two.

The detailed, internally consistent figures for special adoption that have been referred to thus far are found in official and semi-official sources and appear to be comfortingly reliable. However, working off the same number of cases each year, the Ministry of Foreign Affairs provided the UN with acceptance figures, shown in Table 6, which show a consistently higher number of court approvals each year between 1991 and 1995 (there is no mention of cases withdrawn or

Table 6 Alternative approval figures 1988–95

Year	1988	1989	1990	1991	1992	1993	1994	1995
Applications accepted	1,814	1,933	1,178	619	509	520	491	521

Sources: 1988–90 from Goodman 2000; 1991–5 from Ministry of Foreign Affairs 1996.

Table 7 Reasons for adoption

Reason	No. (%)
Economic reasons (these include single mothers, children of affairs, children where the male partner provides no support)	30 (41)
Left in the care of another adult (e.g. friends, parents missing)	8 (11)
Left in children's home (parents missing)	7 (10)
Parents have no intention to bring up children	6 (8)
Children from rape	6 (8)
Abandoned (e.g. on street)	5 (7)
No visits by the parents (the location of the parents is known and they are persuaded to relinquish a child in care)	5 (7)
Mother with psychological problems	5 (7)
Death of parents	1 (1)
Total	73 (100)

Source: Author interview notes.

rejected). Goodman provides the same figures and also gives figures for 1988 to 1990 that show higher approval numbers.

Some indication of the range of reasons why children are made available for special adoption can be found in a breakdown drawn up by Osaka City CGC. Between 1997 and 1999 the CGC classified nine reasons for why 73 children had been made available for adoption. These categories are listed in order of size in Table 7.

It can be noted that abuse was not included as a category for adoption.

A broadly similar picture was found in a survey of Japanese CGCs conducted by the Society for Study of Adoption and Foster Placement of Children. Reasons for adoption, in order of frequency were categorized as: (1) the child was born outside wedlock, (2) the birth mother or parent(s) were young and not ready for parenthood, (3) there was no assistance from the birth father, (4) the child was born to 'parents unknown' including abandoned children and missing parents, (5) the parents 'cannot love the child' (Ohtani 1999: 25–9).

Ordinary adoption

Court applications for ordinary adoptions have seen only minor fluctuations in numbers between 1996 and 2004, around an average of 1,452 adoptions per year. Table 8 presents the annual figures.

Table 8 Ordinary adoption court applications 1996–2004

	1996	1997	1998	1999	2000	2001	2002	2003	2004
Cases	1,508	1,393	1,451	1,412	1,483	1,386	1,438	1,500	1,500

Source: Adapted from Saikôsaibansho 2004a.

Table 9 Ordinary adoptions 1988–96

	1988	1989	1990	1991	1992	1993	1994	1995	1996
Cases	2,457	2,150	2,114	2,006	1,761	1,839	1,646	1,603	1,508
Approved 1	1,726	1,491	1,397	1,386	1,185	1,146	*	*	*
Approved 2	2,421	2,151	2,037	1,529	1,310	1,258	1,205	1,111	971

Sources: Case figures are from Nakayama and Kaneko 1999. Approval 1 figures are from Terado 1995. Approval 2 figures for the years 1991–95 are from Ministry of Foreign Affairs 1996, and between 1988–90 and in 1996 from Goodman 2000.

Note: According to Goodman, Approval 2 figures for 1988–90 refer to minors under 20, and for 1991 onwards to minors under 18.

In contrast to the steady rate of applications between 1996 and 2004, application numbers between 1988 and 1996 show a pattern of decline. Earlier figures also give the numbers of accepted applications. Once again there are two sets of such figures depending on the source, both shown in Table 9, with the Ministry of Foreign Affairs favouring the figures showing higher approval numbers.

Most ordinary adoptions occur within the extended family. Using the first set of acceptance figures, out of the 1,146 adoptions approved by the courts in 1993 only 435 or 38% of adopting families were unrelated to the child. By contrast 93% of special adoptions were to unrelated adults (Terado 1995: 140–1). The actual number of ordinary adoptions between family members will exceed the approval figures to some degree, as court authorization is not required in a domestic adoption by grandparents or stepparents.

The total number of ordinary and special adoptions registered by the *koseki* offices for 1993, both adult and children, was 81,762 (Terado 1995: 138). Although the number of child adoptions arranged within families and not requiring court authorization is unknown, this figure still serves to suggest the great preponderance of adult adoptions over child adoptions.

International adoption

The application and approval figures for both special and ordinary adoptions contain within their numbers a subset of adoptions defined as international adoptions. These adoptions are where either the child or at least one of the adoptive parents is foreign. On average there have been 467 international adoption applications between 1996 and 2000.

Table 10 International adoption applications 1996–2000

	1996	1997	1998	1999	2000
Cases	412	426	479	472	534
Ordinary	382	403	450	446	500
Special	30	23	29	26	34

Source: Adapted from Ministry of Foreign Affairs 2001.

The figures shown in Table 10 mean that between 1996 and 2000 the courts recorded 94% of international cases as 'ordinary' rather than 'special' adoption applications. However, this does not allow one to infer that the overwhelming proportion of these adoptions were akin to a typical ordinary adoption (e.g. the adoption of a foreign child by an aunt and uncle in Japan) and that very few were like a special adoption (e.g. the adoption by foreign residents of an unrelated Japanese child). On the contrary, if one takes the key feature of a special adoption as being the adoption of a child in need, then it is likely that most international adoptions are similar to special adoptions. International adoption has its own legal status in the requirement that it is consistent with the law of the states of all foreigners involved. Treating the adoption as an ordinary adoption, where the rules are fewer, makes it somewhat easier to square foreign law with Japan's domestic law.

Earlier figures shown in Table 11 present the same pattern of a broadly steady rate of international adoption cases, mostly recorded within the ordinary adoption numbers. On this occasion the approval figures given by the Ministry of Foreign Affairs are consistent with other sources.

The international adoption figures refer only to cases where the adoption was concluded in Japan. They do not include cases where the adoption was legalized abroad unless the parents apply to have the child adopted again once they have returned to Japan. Similarly, they do not include cases where the child migrated from Japan for the purpose of adoption in a foreign state, unless they were first

Table 11 International adoption 1988–95

	1988	1989	1990	1991	1992	1993	1994	1995
Cases	*	*	*	512	437	484	451	452
Approved	448	385	361	381	359	337	339	299
Ordinary	445	370	346	366	329	312	*	*
Special	3	15	15	15	30	25	*	*

Sources: 1991–95 application and acceptance figures are from Ministry of Foreign Affairs 1996; special and ordinary adoption approval figures 1988–93 are from Terado 1995.

Note: Ebisawa gives similar approval and special adoption figures for 1989–93 but has a figure of 447 approvals in 1988 (1995: 146). Ebisawa adds that of the 381 approved cases in 1991, a foreign parent was involved in 82 cases and a foreign child in 299. It is unlikely, however, that there was no overlap between foreign parents and foreign children and more probable that foreign parents were only counted where the child was of Japanese nationality.

adopted within Japan. Finally, they do not include information on whether the children remained in Japan or were taken abroad.

Adoption to the USA

To a limited extent it is possible to augment the figures on international adoption by considering US immigration visas issued to children from Japan. Between 1948 and 1962, 2,987 'orphan' children were adopted into the USA, an average of 199 per year. One thousand one hundred and thirty-five were adopted in the ten years between 1963 and 1972, an average of 113 per year (Altstein and Simon 1991: 14–15). More recent figures based on the same 'orphan' visa categories, suggest that the average number of adoptions per year to the USA has now dropped to about 40. If these children have already been adopted in Japan by US parents, they are issued with an IR-3 visa. Children obtaining this category of visa will, therefore, have been recorded as an international adoption within Japan (unless they were adopted in a third country). However, if the children have been placed with a US couple, but not yet adopted, they are issued with an IR-4 visa, which enables the family to travel to the USA to legalize the adoption. These children, therefore, are in addition to the international adoption cases recorded in the Japanese courts.

Between the fiscal years 1996 and 2004, there are two official sets of figures for orphan visas providing slightly different numbers, as shown in Table 12.

When either annual total of orphan visas is compared with State Department figures going back to 1989 (Table 13) there appears to have been a decline in the

Table 12 US orphan visas 1996–2004

	1996	1997	1998	1999	2000	2001	2002	2003	2004
IR-3	9	31	15	18	9 or 11	6	8	6	*
IR-4	24	24	31	24	31 or 25	33	32	30	*
Total 1	33	55	46	42	40				
Total 2	36	45	39	37	36	39	40	36	45

Sources: IR-3, IR-4 and Total 1 figures 1996–2000 are from US Department of State 2001. IR-3 and IR-4 figures 2002 and Total 2 figures 1999–2002 are from US Department of State 2004. Total 2 figures 1992–2004 are from US Department of State 2005b. IR-3 and IR-4 figures 2000, 2001 and 2003 are from US Department of State 2005c.

Table 13 US orphan visas 1989–95

	1989	1990	1991	1992	1993	1994	1995
IR-3 + IR-4 total	74	57	87	68	64	49	63

Source: Adapted from US Department of State 2005a.

Table 14 US IR-2 visas 2000–03

	2000	2001	2002	2003
IR-2 visa	89	67	87	116
Orphan visas	36	39	40	36
Total	125	106	127	152

Source: Adapted from US Department of State 2005c.

numbers of children adopted into the USA from Japan, with the earlier numbers uniformly higher than the later figures.

The picture of adoption of children in Japan by US parents changes if the IR-2 visa category is also taken into account. This visa is available for children who have been in the custody of a US parent or couple for at least two years and been legally adopted during that time. In the fiscal year 1994, the US embassy in Japan reported that it had issued 98 visas for adopted children in the IR-2 category alongside 48 orphan visas made up of 13 IR-3s and 35 IR-4s (US Embassy Japan). The total number of adopted children given immigrant visas to the USA in 1994, therefore, was 146, three times more than the 48 (or 49) orphan visas issued that year. More recent figures, given in Table 14, show that IR-2 visas continue to outweigh the orphan visas issued each year.

A leaflet written for members of US armed forces emphasizes that in contrast to IR-3 and IR-4 visas, the child on an IR-2 visa can be relinquished for adoption by the birth parents for any reason. However, it also emphasizes that the child must be in the custody of the adoptive parents for two years with the cautionary story of how: 'a child, unable to obtain an immigrant visa, had to be returned to the natural parents after living with the adopting family (an older sister and her Navy husband) in Japan for only a year' (*International Adoption* 2005: 7). It is not known what proportion of IR-2 visas are issued to parents who adopt a child in need, albeit one who may not be classified as an 'orphan' and what proportion are stepparent adoptions by a US citizen married to a non-citizen, adoptions within an extended family, or other forms of adoption.

Foster care and institutional care

A survey of children in public care in February 2003 shows the heavy reliance upon institutions and indicates the small likelihood that a child placed in an institution will be adopted or fostered. The survey results, shown in Table 15, give the numbers of children currently in children's homes (excluding infant homes and other special categories of home) and foster care and then categorize the planned future for each child.

Of the 32,870 children in either foster care or children's homes, 92% have been placed in children's homes. If the plans for these children are reasonably accurate, then about 35% of them will be returned to their parents or placed with relatives.

Table 15 Plans for children in public care in 2003

	Children's home	Foster care
Number (%)	30,416 (100)	2,454 (100)
Plans		
Return to parents	9,976 (33)	342 (14)
Place with relatives	479 (2)	19 (1)
Stay put until self-reliant	17,199 (57)	1,207 (49)
Adoption	*	697 (28)
Fostering or adoption	420 (1)	*
Other	2,342 (8)	189 (8)

Source: Adapted from Kôseirôdôshô 2004.

Only about 1% of the children in homes have been earmarked for fostering or adoption; the plan for the majority is to remain in the home until adulthood. For the 8% of children in foster care, the prospects of being returned to their birth parents or placed with relatives are lower, at about 15%, but the prospects of adoption are much greater at about 28%. From other government figures it appears that sometime later in 2003 the number of children in foster care increased to 2,811 (Naikakufu 2005).

There are other forms of institutional care aside from children's homes, although only children in infant homes stand a significant chance of being fostered or adopted. In 2003 there were 3,023 children in infant homes; adoption or fostering was planned for 295 or 10% of these children. The survey identifies 1,657 children in reformatories; adoption or fostering was planned for 11 or 0.7% of these children. There were also 768 children with mental health problems in special homes; adoption or fostering was planned for two or 0.3% of these children.

The ages at which children entered into foster care, infant homes and children's homes are shown in Table 16. For both foster care and children's homes, the modal age is two years. A small part of the explanation for this in children's homes can be attributed to children transferring from infant homes when they are two. Foster parents overlap with adoptive parents and like adoptive parents, most prefer to have younger children placed with them. Two thousand and seventy-seven or 85% of the children in foster care in 2003 were placed with foster parents when they were aged eight or less, and amongst these children there is a further skewed preference towards the 1,389 children placed when aged three or less.

In addition to children in children's homes and infant homes, there are also homes for several categories of special needs children. The numbers of these children are included in a comprehensive snapshot of children in public care in Osaka Prefecture in 1999, which found 889 children with a variety of special needs in institutional care alongside 1,642 children in children's homes, 140 babies and young children in infant homes, 136 young people in institutions to support self reliance and 44 children in foster care (Osakafu kodomo kateisentâ

Table 16 Age of entry into care for children in care in 2003

Age	Foster care	Infant home	Children's Home
Under 1	272	2,442	74
1	315	522	1,024
2	525	49	6,577
3	277	4	3,968
4	196	2	2,640
5	183	1	2,421
6	136		2,452
7	107		1,840
8	66		1,691
9–11	144		4,027
12–14	122		2,971
15–17	103		671
18 plus	4		9
Total	2,454	3,023	30,416

Source: Adapted from Kôseirôdôsho 2004.

Table 17 Abused children placed in institutions or foster care 1999–2001

	1999	2000	2001	Total (%)
Reports of child abuse	11,631	17,725	23,310	52,666 (100)
Child placed in institution	2,081	2,527	2,857	7,465 (14)
Child placed in foster care	48	91	149	288 (0.5)

Source: Adapted from Seisyonenno 2002a.

1999: 100–1). The Ministry of Foreign Affairs gave overall capacity numbers for special needs institutions in 1999 as 33,739. These included 15,659 places for mentally disabled children, 8,887 places for severely handicapped children 6,972 places for physically disabled children, 1,883 places for children with sight, hearing or speech difficulties and 338 places for autistic children (2001: 217).

Table 17 shows a rising number of reports of child abuse to child guidance centres between 1999 and 2001. On most occasions the abuse was tackled by counselling or other methods. However, in about 14% of cases the child was placed in an institution. Occasionally, in about 0.5% of cases, the child was placed in foster care.

Abuse reports to the CGCs have continued to rise. In 2002 the figure was about 23,770, in 2003 it was 26,573 ('Reports' 2004). On 1 February 2003, a total of 320 or 11% of children in infant homes, 350 or 14% of children in foster care, and 6,935 or 23% of children in children's homes were classified as being in care as a result of abuse or neglect (Kôseirôdôsho 2004).

Appendix 2
Adoption, surrogacy and abortion

When agencies pursue a rational bargaining strategy with parents, they assume that the parents have an abstract concept of more or less desirable categories of children. When agencies pursue a more seductive strategy, they rely upon the concrete feelings that parents may gain for a particular child. The distinction between an unknown invisible child and a known visible child, has implications for the birth mother as well as for adoptive parents. It has implications too for surrogacy and abortion.

Surrogacy has become an issue in Japan after one or two well-publicized cases of Japanese couples who returned from the USA with children born to a surrogate mother. At present, parents who enter into surrogate arrangements abroad can only fully regularize the child's relationship to them and establish the child's Japanese nationality through adoption. There is a debate over whether Japan should make surrogacy illegal, or whether it should be allowed on a voluntary basis. However, there appears to be little appetite for following the USA in recognizing the validity of commercial surrogacy arrangements with their associated contracts. One argument against such arrangements is that the feelings of the surrogate mother can change. A contract is entered into by a surrogate mother while the child she will bear is an abstract unknown entity. Once the baby is born, however, then the feelings of the mother for the child she can see, feel and touch, may suddenly deepen, making it unreasonable to hold her to a contract.

A similar change of heart can affect birth mothers, who may decide while they are pregnant to have a child adopted based on a calculation of the difficulties of raising the child, but then develop powerful feelings for a baby once born and wish to keep it despite the adverse circumstances that they face. In the case of a woman facing an unwanted pregnancy, the opportunity to see the child in an ultrasound scan has sometimes been found to turn her against an abortion. Here too, a decision based on a calculation of the difficulties involved in having a child, can be changed by feelings that are generated on seeing the child in the womb.

Those involved with women with unwanted pregnancies, with surrogate mothers, with birth mothers and with adoptive parents can encourage and facilitate a change from abstract logic to concrete feelings, stay neutral, or attempt to try and block such a change. Trial placements are a facilitating mechanism for adoptive parents. Adoption contracts and surrogacy contracts are a blocking mechanism for birth mothers. With respect to abortion, there is a debate over whether to encourage or block women with unwanted pregnancies from seeing ultrasound images. A British study of why young women chose to abort reported that two respondents 'opted against terminating a pregnancy after having first decided to do so' as a result of being 'encouraged by staff to view the scan images at the consultation stage'. The authors comment that 'where a pregnancy is screened in order to date it, the woman should not be encouraged to view the image unless she says she wants to' (Lee 2004: 35). Conversely, pro-life groups in the USA offer free ultrasounds as a way of facilitating the transition from abstract logic to concrete feelings.

Notes

1 After the 1988 reform an adopter with birth children can only nominate one adopted child as an inheritor. An adopter who does not have any birth children can nominate no more than two adopted children as inheritors (Nakagawa 1989).
2 Three of Tanizaki's siblings were also fostered or adopted (Tanizaki 1991: 89).
3 Although ordinary adoption is not limited to married couples, when a couple are married they are both meant to adopt. However, it is possible to deceive one's spouse by registering an agreement on his or her behalf at the family registration office. Paulson charts the legal consequences when judges reach different decisions on whether such an adoption is valid (1984: 227–47).
4 Paulson reports a variation on this procedure in circumstances where an unmarried mother wishes to keep her child but avoid the stigma of illegitimacy. The mother makes an arrangement with a married couple, who claim that the child is theirs by birth. The real birth mother then 'adopts' the child from them (1984: 138–9).
5 In 1955 there were 1,170,143 abortions; in 1985, there were 550,127, in 1995 there were 343,024. After this 40-year decline the abortion rate appears to have flattened out; in 2001 there were 341,588 abortions (Seisyonenno 2002b).
6 Goodman dates the discovery of child abuse from the late 1980s (2000: 166–74). The Ministry of Foreign Affairs states that reports of child abuse increased throughout the 1990s (2001: 214).
7 Figures for Denmark during the post-war development of the welfare state illustrate this transition. In 1948, 30% of children born to unmarried mothers were given up for adoption. By 1958 the figure had gone down to 14% and by 1974 to 4%. (*Statistik om adoption i Danmark* 2003).
8 2003 figures for children born outside marriage in other western states include Sweden 56%, France 44%, and the USA 34% (Shôshika shakai hakusho 2004).
9 Welfare benefits to single parents are summarized in Ministry of Foreign Affairs 2001: 45.
10 In 1980 there were 142,000 divorces. By 2002 the annual divorce numbers had more than doubled to 290,000. In 2004 the numbers decreased to 271,000 (Naikakufu 2005: 56).
11 In her comparative study on adoption professionals in Japan and the US, Kirino found that none of the 116 Japanese respondents had a master's degree, while 11 of her 18 US respondents had a master's degree (1999: 115).
12 The age of the bride in marriage has risen from 24.2 in 1970 to 27.6 in 2003. This has been closely followed by the rising average age of the mother at the birth of her first child from 25.6 in 1970 to 28.6 in 2003 (Ministry of Internal Affairs and Communications 2005: Ch. 2, Table 2.5, Table 2.6).
13 In other circumstances, the phrase 'We don't know where this horse's bones come from' is applied to a doubtful fiancé. Goodman discusses the phrase with respect to adoption (1996: 123).

14 The argument that sympathy is a natural attribute is made by Rousseau (1973). Popper contended that the relief of suffering is a universal moral imperative (1966: 235 n.6).

15 A *tatami* mat provides a bed for one male adult. It is roughly 90 cm x 180 cm in size, although dimensions vary from one part of Japan to another. In high-rise apartment blocks, the *tatami* mat sizes are slightly smaller so that the flat appears bigger.

16 Indirect figures for parental preferences are given in a 1997 survey of CGCs. This found that of parents who applied to foster children with a view to adoption, 68% preferred a girl, 19% preferred a boy, and 23% did not mind which sex was placed (Iwasaki and Sakurai 1999: 5).

17 People asking to see a *koseki* on the grounds that they are family members need to provide a family signature stamp, but these stamps are available at any corner shop.

18 The problem parents face in trying to ensure that a summary record, rather than a full record of the adoption, is made quite common and it appears that it is not only the supreme court which has uncertainties about the matter. According to Mieko Iwasaki, when the special adoption system was introduced the supreme court sent an official notice to family courts stating that judgement documents were acceptable in summary form, but this information has been largely forgotten (1999: 36–8). When the matter was raised at a committee meeting of the House of Councillors, a court official asserted that the family courts did issue summary judgements. When it was countered that this was hardly done systematically, a second official shifted ground to say that full judgements were necessary (Sangiin 1999).

19 Japanese women who marry foreigners are likely to face opposition from their parents, although most become reconciled after marriage (Habu 2000a: 201–3).

20 A 1997 questionnaire was sent to all 175 CGCs and gained responses from 111 or 63% of them (Iwasaki and Sakurai 1999). Only 4 or 4% of the respondent CGCs were willing to take the initiative to go to court to remove the custody right from birth parents so that the children could be adopted by foster parents (Kikuchi 1999: 48).

21 This case concluded with both the birth mother and the foster parents seeking damages in the local court. The birth mother asked for damages for being denied access to the child, but her case was dismissed as an 'abuse of rights'. The CGC admitted that they were at fault with respect to the foster parents and came to a settlement with them. For discussion of the Yamagata foster parents case see Nishimura and Ootaguchi 2003.

22 In 1997 there were 21 cases in which the custody rights of parents were revoked by the courts (Nishimura and Ootaguchi 2003: 29). Goodman refers to figures that show only three children were placed in children's homes on court orders that year (2000: 6).

23 Between 9 November 1997 and 6 December 1998, 54 children were advertised by the agency. Their average age at the time the photograph was taken was 23 months. The youngest child was only 1 month old, the oldest was 7 years and 10 months. This child was an exception as the next oldest child was 4 years 11 months old. The children were sometimes some months older than their photographic ages.

24 The *boshi techô* is the medical record of a mother and child from pregnancy until the child goes to school. It carries the birth mother's name.

25 The agency has published several books that encourage early telling. See Kateiyôgo, 1998: 60–3; Kateiyôgo, 1999; Yonezawa, 1993: 175–92; Kateiyôgo, 2001: 107–36.

26 An alternative explanation is that expectant mothers, knowing in advance the sex of their babies, are more likely to be able to make a private adoption arrangement if the unborn child is a girl.

27 The home study is based on a template with 15 sections: (1) identification information and the social history of the adoptive father and mother, (2) details of their marriage, (3) details of any children of the marriage, (4 and 5) details of the adopted child and their progress – these sections are not applicable as the home study is provided prior to matching, (6) purpose and plan of the adoption, (7) the social and cultural environment of the family, (8) the current living situation of the family, (9) the financial status

of the parents, (10) references, (11) any criminal convictions, (12) the health of the parents, (13) overall assessment, (14) recommendation, (15) appended information.

28 Not all states of the US specify minimum time periods between the time of birth and the time that a birth mother can give her consent to adoption. Amongst those that do, the most common choice is 72 hours. Alaska and Hawaii allow pre-birth agreements, although these must be confirmed after birth. Rhode Island specifies the longest waiting period of 15 days (National Adoption Information Clearing House 2004: 2).

29 In the survey of the Obstetrician Association in Osaka, 292 (64%) of respondents reported 527 cases over the course of a year when women who were more than 22 weeks pregnant with an unwanted pregnancy had approached them. Extrapolating from these figures to non-respondents, Iwasaki estimates that about 1,300 women a year in Osaka approach doctors beyond the time limit. Iwasaki also states that in some instances women under the age of 20 have a baby because they do not wish to tell their parents that they are pregnant and parental permission is required for an abortion (2000, 2–5).

30 There have been at least two instances where parents have become pregnant after the association has placed a child for adoption with them. On both occasions the parents kept the child.

31 Personal communication with Dr L. Williams, consultant paediatrician.

32 The US government also followed up two temporary periods in which servicemen had been allowed to marry Japanese brides with a reformed immigration law that ended the prohibition on marrying Japanese women, although units within the armed forces continued to be obstructive. See Strong 1978: 20; Kalischer 1952; Burkhardt 1983: 526–7.

33 After widespread publicity and a petition campaign, the child's visa was extended for a year in December 2004.

34 In 2002 the agency reported that it was dealing with 40 cases of step-adoptions. Twenty-six of these cases were for the Japanese husband of a Thai wife with a natural child; eight cases were relative adoptions and the remaining six were non-relative adoptions. Five of the non-relative adoption cases involved children born in Japan to Thai birth mothers with expired visas; one case was of a Japanese couple adopting a child from an institution in Thailand (ISSJ 2002).

35 A 1997 survey of CGCs asked: 'For children who are very difficult to adopt, do you seek parents who are foreign residents or who are abroad?' Nine CGCs responded that this was indeed what they did, whereas 101 CGCs said that they did not seek to make such placements (Iwasaki and Sakurai 1999: 12).

36 In 2004 there were 607,419 registered foreign nationals from North and South Korea; 487,570 from China; 286,557 from Brazil, and 199,394 from the Philippines (Nyukokukanrikyoku 2005a).

37 In 2005 it was reported that overstayers included 43,151 people from Korea, 32,683 from China, 30,619 from the Philippines, 12,787 from Thailand and 88,059 from other states (Nyukokukanrikyoku 2005b).

38 It has been estimated that between 100 and 200,000 foreign women, mainly from the Philippines, are in Japan legally and illegally as sex workers (Douglass 2004: 26).

39 A son of the director was also convicted of indecently assaulting and raping a child at the facility. Accounts of the case are given in '*Ganbare*' 2004; Goodman 2000: 120; JFBA 2003: 170, 193.

40 The decline in fostering is complicated by a second factor; not only has the number of children fostered gone down, but so has the proportion of registered foster parents who are actually engaged in fostering children. In the mid-1950s a little over half of registered foster carers were engaged in foster care, by 2001 this had fallen to just below a quarter (Shoji 2003: 30–1). The impression created by this increasing discrepancy between registered foster carers and actual foster carers is that foster care is an underused resource. However, the apparent superfluity of foster carers may be exaggerated by former foster carers who have remained on the register even though they are not seeking further placements.

41 Between the ages of six and fifteen the numbers in children's homes flatten out. They range between 1,999 at seven and 2,197 at fourteen. At sixteen the number drops to 1,544 (Kôseirôdôshô 2004).

42 A simple game takes place between two players. Each player has a nominal choice between (1) being nice or 'cooperating' with the other player, or (2) being nasty or 'defecting' from the other player. An introduction to game theory is found in Axelrod 1984.

43 Prisoner's dilemma is named after a game between two suspects who are arrested for a crime and held in separate cells for interrogation. (To avoid confusion keep in mind that although the prisoners cannot communicate with each other, they are about to enter into a game with each other and *not* with their interrogator.) Each prisoner is asked by the interrogator to implicate the other, with the promise that he will go free if he does. However, both the suspects know that this offer is not the full story. If both prisoners cooperate with each other by staying silent in the face of the interrogator's offer, then they will both be imprisoned on a lesser charge for one year. Each suspect also realizes that if he 'defects' by implicating the other suspect, then he will indeed go free, but *only* if the other prisoner stays silent. In these circumstances the silent suspect will be sent to prison for ten years. If both suspects defect by implicating the other suspect, then both will go to prison for five years.

44 The origin of the letters helps to keep their implications in mind: T is the *temptation* to defect when the other player cooperates; R is the *reward* for mutual cooperation; P is the *punishment* for mutual defection; S is the *sucker's* payoff for a player who cooperates when the other player defects.

45 This preference order is called 'chicken' after the game played by delinquent teenagers in which two players race towards each other in cars. There are three outcomes. (a) One player wins by driving straight ahead while the other 'chickens out' by swerving (outcomes T and S). (b) The players achieve an honourable draw by swerving simultaneously (outcome R). (c) Neither player swerves leading to a head-on collision (outcome P).

46 Switching agencies in the UK is made more difficult by the 'interagency fee'. If a couple approved by a first agency adopts a child from a second agency, then the second agency must pay a fee to the first.

47 A triangular phase diagram compares the proportions of three components. In materials science they might be three elements of a rock, in psephology they might be votes in a three party election. Each apex represents 100% of one component descending to 0% at its opposite baseline. In the centre of the triangle each component accounts for one third of the total.

48 The preponderance of evidence suggests that the older the child the less likely that the outcome will be successful, as disruption increases with age. Tizard summarizes this research for adoptive placements (1994: 52). Sinclair, Wilson and Gibbs present a similar picture for foster placement disruption (2005: 138). However, there are studies which have found that the age of the child at placement has only a weak or no correlation with outcome. This research includes a study conducted by Tizard that found no relationship between age and success of placement, except when success was measured in terms of the child's IQ (1977: 214–7). Kadushin found parental satisfaction with older children to be 'only slightly lower' than for infants (1970: 211). Raynor found no relationship between age and parental satisfaction, child satisfaction or later adult adjustment (1980: 41–2, 55, 69). Triseliotis and Russell found that adoption outcomes were was not related to age at placement (1984: 181) Berridge and Cleaver found only a weak relationship between age and disruption in foster placements (1987: 177).

References

Akaishi, C. (2003) 'Shinguru mazâ no genjyô to kadai' (Current issues single mothers face), *Jyoseirôdôkenkyû* (The Bulletin of the Society for the Study of Working Women), 44: 65–8.

Altstein, H. and Simon, R.J. (1991) 'Introduction', in H. Altstein and R.J. Simon (eds) *Intercountry Adoption: A Multinational Perspective*, New York: Praeger.

Amino, T. (2000) 'Satooyaseido no arikatanituite 2: kôseikagakukenkyû satooyaseido no arikatanikansuru kenkyû' (The ideal form of the foster parents system part 2: reports on a study on the ideal form of foster parent system), *Atarashi Kazoku* (Studies of Adoption and Foster Care), 36: 57–85.

Ashino, Y. (2001) *Reproductive Health/Rights: The Present Situation of Japan and Its Problems*. Available: <http://wom-jp.org/e/JWOMEN/repro.html> (accessed 23 September 2005).

Axelrod, R. (1984) *The Evolution of Cooperation*, New York: Basic Books.

Bargach, J. (2002) *Orphans of Islam: Family, Abandonment and Secret Adoptions in Morocco*, Boston, MA, USA: Rowman and Littlefield.

Barnlund, D.C. (1975) *Public and Private Self in Japan and the United States: Communicative Styles of Two Cultures*, Tokyo: The Simul Press.

Bartholet, E. (1993) *Family Bonds: Adoption and the Politics of Parenting*, Boston, MA, USA: Houghton Mifflin.

Berridge, D. and Cleaver, H. (1987) *Foster Home Breakdown*, Oxford: Basil Blackwell.

'Bills to cut welfare for single mothers pass committee' (2002) *Japan Times*, 9 November.

Bryant, T.L. (1990) 'Sons and lovers: adoption in Japan', *American Journal of Comparative Law*, 38: 299–336.

Buck, P.S. (1964) *Children for Adoption*, New York: Random House.

Burkhardt, W.R. (1983) 'Institutional barriers, marginality, and adaptation among the American-Japanese mixed bloods in Japan', *Journal of Asian Studies*, 42: 519–44.

Debito, A. (2005) 'On racism in Japan: why one may be hopeful for the future', paper presented at the Meiji Gakuin University Symposium, 'International Studies of Our New Era: Immigrants, Refugees, and Women', July. Available: <http://www.debito.org/meijigakuin071705.html> (accessed 23 September 2005).

Department for Education and Skills (2005) *Statistics of Education: Children Looked After in England (Including Adoptions and Care Leavers): 2003–2004*. Available: <http://www.dfes.gov.uk/rsgateway/DB/VOL/v000569/index.shtml> (accessed 22 September 2005).

Department of Health (2000) *Adoption: A New Approach*, London: Department of Health.

Douglass, M. (2004) 'The singularities of international migration of women to Japan', in M. Weiner (ed.) *Race, Ethnicity and Migration in Japan*, London: Routledge Curzon.

Ebisawa, Y. (1995) 'Kokusaiyôshi no mondaiten' (Problems in international adoption), *Jurisuto* (Jurist), 1059:145–50.

Federation for the Protection of Children's Human Rights (1997) *The Convention on the Rights of the Child: 95 Issues to Be Solved in Japan*, database of NGO reports presented to the UN Committee on the Rights of the Child. Available: <www.crin.org/docs/resources/treaties/crc.18/Japan_NGO_Report.pdf> (accessed 22 September 2005).

Fetters, M. (1997) 'Cultural clashes: Japanese patients and US maternity care', *Journal of the International Institute*, 4(2). Available: <http://www.umich.edu/~iinet/journal/vol4no2/medcult.html> (accessed 22 September 2005).

Fujiwara, K. (2003) 'Jidôfuyôteate no kaikaku to syugyôshien no kadai' (Reform of the child support allowance and issues surrounding measures to enable single mothers to work), *Joseirôdôkenkyû* (The Bulletin of the Society for the Study of Working Women), 44: 53–64.

Ganbare! Onchoen no Kodomotachi. Ganbare! Onchoen no Syushinsha (Fighting Spirit! Children of Onchoen. Fighting Spirit! People of Onchoen) (2004). Available: <http://onchoen.yogo-shisetsu.info/index.html> (accessed 24 September 2005).

Gayford, Y. (2004) 'The impact on voluntary sector adoption agencies of quality protects and choice protects legislation', paper presented at the All Party Parliamentary Group on Adoption, House of Commons, 9 November.

Goodman, R. (1996) 'On introducing the UN Convention on the Rights of the Child into Japan', in R. Goodman and I. Neary (eds) *Case Studies on Human Rights in Japan*, Richmond, Surrey, UK: Japan Library.

Goodman, R. (2000) *Children of the Japanese State: The Changing Role of Child Protection Institutions in Contemporary Japan*, Oxford: Oxford University Press.

'Government looking to boost adoption rate' (2005) *Japan Times*, 29 August. Available: <http://www.japantimes.co.jp/cgi-bin/getarticle.pl5?nn20050829a2.htm> (accessed 24 September 2005).

Government of Japan (2005) *Comments by Japan Relating to the Hague Convention of 29 May 1993*. Available: <http://www.hcch.net/upload/adop2005_jp.pdf> (accessed 18 September 2005).

Habu, T. (2000a) 'Japanese women in Britain', unpublished thesis, University of Sunderland.

Habu, T. (2000b) 'The irony of globalisation: the experience of Japanese women in British higher education', *Higher Education*, 39: 43–66.

Hayashida, C.T. (1976) 'Identity, race and the blood ideology of Japan', unpublished thesis, University of Washington.

Hayes, P. (1993) 'Transracial adoption: politics and ideology', *Child Welfare*, 72: 301–10.

Hayes, P. (1995) 'The ideological attack on transracial adoption in the USA and Britain', *International Journal of Law and the Family*, 9: 1–22.

Hayes, P. (2000) 'Deterrents to intercountry adoption in Britain', *Family Relations*, 49: 465–71.

Hayes, P. (2003) 'Giving due consideration to ethnicity in adoption placements – a principled approach', *Child and Family Law Quarterly*, 15: 255–68.

Hendry, J. (1981) *Marriage in Changing Japan*, London: Croom Helm.

Hollinger, J.H. (2004) 'Intercountry adoption: forecasts and forebodings', *Adoption Quarterly*, 8: 41–60.

Hoshii, I. (1987) *The World of Sex, Vol. 3: Responsible Parenthood*, Ashford, Kent, UK: Norbury.

International Adoption for Active Duty Military Personnel (2005). Available: <http://www.adoptionguides.org/pdf%20files/Military%20Adoption%20Information.pdf> (accessed 23 September 2005).

International Social Service Japan (ISSJ) (2002) 'Assistance to international families', *Intercountry*, 20. Available: <http://www.issj.org/english/Intercountry/ic20-2e.htm> (accessed 23 September 2005).

International Social Service Japan (ISSJ) (2004) 'Recent tendency of intercountry adoption and the assistance of ISSJ', *Intercountry*, 27. Available: <http://www.issj.org/english/Intercountry/ic27-1e.htm> (accessed 23 September 2005).

International Social Service Japan (ISSJ) (2005) 'International child and family social services: intercountry adoption'. Available: <http://www.issj.org/english/f_projectmenu. htm> (accessed 23 September 2005).

Iwasaki, Michiko and Sakurai, N. (1999) 'Jidôsôdansho niokeru satooyaitakugyômu: jidôsôdansho heno ankêtochôsa no bunseki' (A survey of the practices of family placements at the child guidance centers, and its analysis), *Atarashi Kazoku* (Studies of Adoption and Foster Care), 35: 2–23.

Iwasaki, Mieko (1996) 'Jyûdai no ninshin: jittutai to seishinhoken' (The pregnancy and mental health of teenagers), *Seishinhokenkenkyu* (Mental Health Research), 42: 19–25.

Iwasaki, Mieko (1999) 'Tokubetuyôshiseido no mondaiten' (Problems with the special adoption system), *Atarashi Kazoku* (Studies of Adoption and Foster Care), 35: 36–8.

Iwasaki, Mieko (2000) 'Cyuzetsu, ninshin, syutsusan nikansuru Oosakafuka no sanfu-jinkai heno ankêtocyosakettuka kara' (Results of a questionnaire about abortions, pregnancies and childbirths to gynaecologists in the Osaka area), *Atarashi Kazoku* (Studies of Adoption and Foster Care), 36: 2–10.

Iwasaki, Mieko (2003) 'Kodomo no shirukenri to kokuchi' (The right of the child to know and the telling), *Atarashi Kazoku* (Studies of Adoption and Foster Care), 43: 1.

Iwase, H. (no date) *Akachan wo Sukuukai* (Agency to Rescue Children). Available: <http://www2.odn.ne.jp/~cae26630/wa004.html> (accessed 18 September 2005).

Japan Federation of Bar Associations (JFBA) (2003) *Alternative Report to the Second Report of the Japanese Government on the Convention on the Rights of the Child.* Available: <http://www.nichibenren.or.jp/en/activities/statements/20030601.html> (accessed 23 September 2005).

Jidôsôdansho (2005) *Jidôsôdansho Uneishishin* (CGC Management Guidelines). Available: <http://www.i-kosodate.net/mhlw/varieties/guide_cnsl/management06-04. html> (accessed 23 September 2005).

Jordan, M. (1999) *Japanese Couples' Aversion to Child Adoption Changes only Slowly*, 29 June. Available: <http://www.fww.org/famnews/0629a.html> (accessed 23 September 2005).

Kaji, N. (1999) Dai 8 kai seishokuhojyo iryôgijyutu nikansuru senmoniinkai gijiroku (Presentation in the Minutes of the 8th Specialist Committee on Medical Technology to Help Reproduction), Kôseisho Jidôkateikyoku Boshihokenka (organized by Children and Families Bureau, Ministry of Health and Welfare), October. Available: <http://www1.mhlw. go.jp/shingi/s9910/txt/s1005-1_18.txt> (accessed 3 February 2005).

Kalischer, P. (1952) 'Madame Butterfly's children', *Collier's*, 20 September: 15–8.

Kateiyôgo Sokushin Kyôkai (1995) *Tokubetu Yôshi Engumi Seiritsu Katei: Ankêto Cyosa Houkoku* (Special Adoption Families: Questionnaire Responses), Osaka: Kateiyôgosokushinkyôkai.

Kateiyôgo sokushin kyôkai (1998) *Chino Tunagari wo Koete: Oyako ni Naru* (Becoming a Family, Transcending Blood Ties), Osaka: Kateiyôgo sokushin kyôkai.

Kateiyôgo sokushin kyôkai (1999) *Otona ni Tatsuta Yôshi kara no Mettusêji* (Messages from Grown-up Adopted Children), Osaka: Kateiyôgo sokushin kyôkai.

Kateiyôgo sokushin kyôkai (2001) *Shinji Attute Oyako Katari Attute Kazoku: Kodomo, Satooya, Kêsuwâkâ* (Trusting Each Other as Parents and Children and Becoming a Family Through Talking: A Record of Children, Foster Parents and Case Workers), Kobe: Epic.

Kateiyôgo sokushin kyôkai (2004) *Osaka Jimusho Jigyôhôkoku* (Service report 2003). Available: <http://www5f.biglobe.ne.jp/~ainote/joho/H17/gaiyo-top.html> (accessed 25 September 2005).

Kateiyôgo sokushin kyôkai (2005) *Satooya ni Natte Yokattuta* (We Are Glad to Become Foster Parents), Kobe: Epic.

Kawakami, S. (2000) *"Moshikasuruto Jibundeha Umanai" Anatahe: Yôshitoiu Sentaku, No. 3, Okurugawa no Ronri: Saitamaken no Fujinkaino Hanashi* (You 'Who Might Not Give Birth': Adoption as a Choice, No. 3, The Mediator's Story: A Gynaecologist in Saitama Prefecture), 21 August. Available: <http://www.cafeglobe.com/news/adoption/ch00821.html> (accessed 1 September 2005).

Kawanishi, Y. (2004) 'Japanese youth: the other half of the crisis', *Asian Affairs*, 35(1): 22–32.

Kikuchi, M. (1999) 'Yôshiengumino attusen to oyano dôi' (Adoptive placements and the consent of birth parents), *Atarashi Kazoku* (Studies of Adoption and Foster Care), 35: 47–8.

Kikuta, N. (1987) 'Tokubetsu yôshi no tsuminokoshita kadai' (An unresolved problem of special adoption), *Jurisuto* (Jurist), 895: 62–4.

Kikuta, N. (1988) *Okâsan, Boku wo Korosanaide: Kikuta Ishi to Akachan Atsusenjiken no Shogen* (Mummy, Please Don't Kill Me: Dr Kikuta and the Case of Baby Adoptions), Tokyo: Akatsuki Shobô.

Kimura, T. (2003) *Satooya Seido to Chiiki Shakai: Miyagi ken Oshikamachi no Kêsu* (The Foster Parent System and the Local Community: the Case of Oshika Village in Miyagi Prefecture), Tokyo: Akashi Shoten.

Kirino, Y. (1998) 'Ishikichôsa wo tôshitemita nihon no kodomonotameno yôshi engumi: sono 1, Tojisha to hitojisha no hikaku' (Japanese arrangements for child welfare in adoption assessed through an attitude survey, No. 1: Adopted parents, natal parents and third parties), *Kwanseigakuin Daigaku Shakai Gakubu Kiyô*, October: 129–41. Available: <http://syass.kwansei.ac.jp/kiyou/81_jp.htm> (accessed 23 September 2005).

Kirino, Y. (1999) 'Ishikichôsa wo tôshitemita nihon no kodomonotameno yôshi engumi: sono 2, Nichibei senmonsyoku no hikaku' (Japanese arrangements for child welfare in adoption assessed through an attitude survey, No. 2: Japan and the USA), *Kwanseigakuin Daigaku Shakai Gakubu Kiyô*, November: 113–25. Available: <http://www-soc.kwansei.ac.jp/kiyou/83/83-ch8.pdf> (accessed 23 September 2005).

Kondo, K. (2005) *Hiroshima: 60nen no Kioku* (Hiroshima: 60 Years of Memories), Tokyo: Riyonsha.

Kôseirôdôsho Koyôkintô Jidôkateikyoku Chô (Director of Equal Employment, Children and Families Bureau, Ministry of Health, Labour and Welfare) (2002) 'Satooyaseido no un'ei ni tsuite' (On the foster parenting system), Kojihatsu No. 0905002. Reprinted in J. Shoji (2003) *Fosuta Kea: Satooya to Satooya Kyoiku* (Foster Care: Foster Parents and Education for Foster Parents), Tokyo: Akashi Shoten.

Kôseirôdôsho Koyôkintô Jidôkateikyoku, Kateifukushika (Family Welfare Division, Equal Employment, Children and Families Bureau, Ministry of Health, Labour and Welfare) (2004) *Jidôyôgoshisetsu Nyushojijôtôcyôsa Kettukano Gaijyo Heisei 15nen 2gatsu 1nichi* (Summary of Survey Results on Children in Institutions etc. on 1st of February 2003). Available: <http://www.mhlw.go.jp/houdou/2004/07/h0722-2.html> (accessed 24 September 2005).

Kôseirôdôshô Koyôkintô Jidôkateikyoku, Kateifukushika (Family Welfare Division, Equal Employment, Children and Families Bureau, Ministry of Health, Labour and Welfare) (2005) 'Hitorioya setaino heisei 14nenno nenkansyûnyû' (Average income for single parent families in 2002), in *Heisei 15nendo Zenkoku Boshisetai Tou Cyosakettuka Houkoku* (Report on National Single Mother Households Survey). Available: <http:// www.mhlw.go.jp/houdou/2005/01/h0119-1b16.html> (accessed 18 September 2005).

Kuono, A. and Johnson, C.F. (1995) 'Child abuse and neglect in Japan: coin-operated-locker babies', *Child Abuse and Neglect*, 19: 25–31.

Kurosu, S. (1998) 'Long way to headship, short way to retirement: adopted sons in a north-eastern village in pre-industrial Japan', *The History of the Family*, 3: 393–410.

Laming, H. (1996) *Adoption* (circular to social service directors), CI (96) 4, 1 February, London: Department of Health. Available: <http://www.dh.gov.uk/PublicationsAnd Statistics/LettersAndCirculars/ChiefInspectorLetters/ChiefInspectorLettersArticle/fs/ en?CONTENT_ID=4003574&chk=wJkbDU> (accessed 23 September 2005).

Landes, E.M. and Posner, R.A. (1978) 'The economics of the baby shortage', *Journal of Legal Studies*, 7: 323–48.

Lebra, T.S. (1989) 'Adoption among the hereditary elite of Japan: status preservation through mobility', *Ethnology*, 28: 185–218.

Lee, E., Clements, S., Ingham, R. and Stone, N. (2004) *A Matter of Choice? Explaining National Variation in Teenage Abortion and Motherhood*, Southampton, UK: University of Southampton.

McMullen, I.J. (1975) 'Non-agnatic adoption: a Confucian controversy in seventeenth- and eighteenth-century Japan', *Harvard Journal of Asiatic Studies*, 35: 133–89.

Macpherson, C.B. (1973) *Democratic Theory: Essays in Retrieval*, Oxford: Clarendon Press.

Mass, J.P. (1989) *Lordship and Inheritance in Early Medieval Japan: A Study of the Kamakura Sôryô System*, Stanford, CA: Stanford University Press.

Matsubara, H. (2004) 'Adopted Thai girl allowed to stay', *Japan Times*, July 7. Available: <http://www.japantimes.co.jp/weekly/news/nn2004/nn20040710a3.htm> (accessed 23 September 2005).

Ministry of Foreign Affairs (1996) *The Initial Report of Japan under Article 44, Paragraph 1 of the Convention on the Rights of the Child, V. Family Environment and Alternative Care.* Available: <http://www.mofa.go.jp/policy/human/child/initialreport/care.html> (accessed 23 September 2005).

Ministry of Foreign Affairs (2001) *The Second Report of Japan under Article 44, Paragraph 1 of the Convention on the Rights of the Child.* Available: <http://www.mofa.go.jp/ policy/human/child/report2/index.html> (accessed 23 September 2005).

Ministry of Internal Affairs and Communications (2005) *Statistical Handbook of Japan*, Tokyo: The Japan Statistical Association. Available: <http://www.stat.go.jp/english/ data/handbook/c02cont.htm> (accessed 23 September 2005).

Mostyn, B. (1993) 'Favourite bedtime stories', in M. and H. Humphrey (eds) *Inter-country Adoption: Practical Experiences*, London: Routledge.

Naikakufu (Cabinet Office) (2003) *Seishônen Hakusho: Heisei 15nenban* (White Paper on Youth: Year 2003 Version). Available: <http://www8.cao.go.jp/youth/whitepaper/ h15zenbun/html/honpen/hp020303.htm> (accessed 24 September 2005).

Naikakufu (Cabinet Office) (2004) *Shôshika Shakai Hakusho Heisei 16nendoban* (White Paper on a Society with a Declining Birthrate: Financial Year 2004 Version), Tokyo: Gyôsei. Available: <http://www8.cao.go.jp/shoushi/whitepaper/w-2004/html-h/html/ g1211040.html> (accessed 23 September 2005).

Naikakufu (Cabinet Office) (2005) *Kokumin Seikatsu Hakusho: Kosodate Sedai no Ishiki to Seikatsu* (White Paper on People's Life: Perception and Lives of the Childrearing Generation). Available: <http://www5.cao.go.jp/seikatsu/whitepaper/h17/01_honpen/html/hm01030011.html> (accessed 21 September 2005).

Nakagawa, T. (1989) 'Yôshi no sôzokuken' (The rights of adopted children), *Hanrei Taimuzu*, 688: 27.

Nakamura, R. (1994) 'Japanese system of adoption tangled in web of cultural taboos', *Japan Times*, 18 September.

Nakayama, N. and Kaneko, M. (1999) 'Tokubetsu yôshi to jitsuoyano kengen: "yôshi-hôkaiseigono tokubetsuyôshiengumino jitsujyo" wo cyûshintoshite' (Special adoption and the rights of the birth parents; particularly after cases of special adoption have come to court), *Hanrei Taimuzu*, 996: 67–73.

National Adoption Information Clearing House (NAIC) (2004) *Consent to Adoption: Summary of State Laws*, Washington, DC: NAIC. Available: <http://naic.acf.hhs.gov/general/legal/statutes/consentall.pdf> (accessed 18 September 2005).

National Foster Parent Association of Japan (NFPA) (2000) *Foster Care in Japan* (updated and corrected version of 1998 edition), Tokyo: National Foster Parent Association.

Neary, I. (2003) 'State and civil society in Japan', *Asian Affairs*, 34: 27–32.

Nihon Sanfujinka Ishikai Okayamashibu (Japan Association of Obstetricians and Gynaecologists, Okayama Branch) (2005) *Tokubetsu Yôshi Attusen Jigyô* (Special Adoption Arrangement Services). Available: <http://www.jaog.or.jp/JAPANESE/MEMBERS/sibu/33okayama/33okayama.htm#youshi> (accessed 10 September 2005).

Nishimura, E. and Ootaguchi, H. (2003) 'Yamagata satooya jikenno gaiyôto sonomondaiten' (Foster parents' lawsuits in Yamagata: a view to better practices of adoption and foster care), *Atarashi Kazoku* (Studies of Adoption and Foster Care), 43: 22–31.

Nishioka, Y. (1991) 'Yôshiga yô'oya yori nenchôto naru yôshi engumino kouryoku' (The legality of adoptions where the child is older than the parent), *Hanrei Taimuzu*, 747: 232–4.

Nyukokukanrikyoku (Immigration Bureau of Japan) (2005a) *Heisei 16nenmatsu Genzaini Okeru Gaikokujin Tôrokushatôkeinitsuite* (The Number of Registered Foreign Nationals at the End of 2004). Available: <http://www.immi-moj.go.jp/toukei/index.html> (accessed 23 September 2005).

Nyukokukanrikyoku (Immigration Bureau of Japan) (2005b) *Honpôniokeru Fuhôzanryusha nitsuite* (On Overstayers in Japan). Available: <http://www.moj.go.jp/ PRESS/050328-1/050328-1.html> (accessed 23 September 2005).

O'Brian, C. (1994) 'Transracial adoption in Hong Kong', *Child Welfare*, 73: 319–30.

Ochiai, E. (1996) *The Japanese Family System in Transition: A Sociological Analysis of Family Change in Postwar Japan*, Tokyo: LCTB International Library Foundation.

Ohtani, M. (1999) 'Jidôsôdansho niokeru satooya itaku gyomu: jidôsôdansho no attusen de yôshi to nattuta kodomono bunseki No. 2, Jidôfukushi no shiten' (Analysis of the children adopted by the hands of child guidance centers – from the viewpoint of social welfare), *Atarashi: Kazoku* (Studies of Adoption and Foster Care), 35: 24–35.

Okuda, Y. (2003) 'The United Nations Convention of the Rights of the Child and Japan's international family law including nationality law', *Zeitschrift für Japanisches Recht*, 15: 87–110. Available: <http://www.law.usyd.edu.au/anjel/documents/ZJapanR/ZJapanR 15 08 Okuda.pdf> (accessed 22 September 2005).

Omura, Y. (1998) 'Isuramukyoto wo yôoyatosuru tokubetsuyôshiengumi no kahi' (The possibility of special adoption with an Islamic adoptive father), *Jurisuto* (Jurist), 1140: 150–2.

Oppler, A.J. (1976) *Legal Reform in Occupied Japan: A Participant Looks Back*, Princeton: Princeton University Press.

Osaka Cyûô Jidôsodansho (Osaka Central Child Guidance Centre) (no date) *"Satooya" San Bosyu: Anatamo Kosodateni Sankashimasenka!* (Looking for Foster Parents: Would You Like to Join in Child Rearing?).

Osakafu kodomo kateisentâ (Centre for Children and Family) (1999) *Osaka Kodomo Katei Hakusho* (Osaka Prefecture Children and Family Service Report), Osaka: Osakafu kodomo kateisentâ.

Otani, R. (2001) 'Future tasks of NGOs with the nationality issues', *Intercountry*, 19. Available: <http://www.issj.org/english/f_icmenu.htm> (accessed 18 September 2005).

Otani, R. (2003) 'Philippine case study: "The best interest of children" and the parental authority', *Intercountry*, 23. Available: <http://www.issj.org/english/f_icmenu.htm> (accessed 18 September 2005).

Otsuki, Y. (2004) 'New Year's greeting', *Intercountry*, 26. Available: <http://www.issj.org/english/Intercountry/ic26-1e.htm> (accessed 18 September 2005).

Paulson, A. (2001) 'Adoption parties: caring or cruel?' *Christian Science Monitor*, 10 September. Available: http://www.csmonitor.com/2001/0910/p1s3-ussc.html (accessed 22 September 2005).

Paulson, J.-L. (1984) *Family Law Reform in Postwar Japan: Succession and Adoption*, Ph.D. thesis, University of Colorado at Boulder, 1983, Ann Arbor: University Microfilms International.

Performance and Innovation Unit (2000) *Prime Minister's Review: Adoption*, London: Cabinet Office.

Peterson, M.A. (1996) *Korean Adoption and Inheritance: Case Studies in the Creation of a Classic Confucian Society*, Ithaca, NY: Cornell East Asia Series.

Popper, K. (1966) *The Open Society and Its Enemies, Vol. 1: The Spell of Plato*, London: Routledge and Kegan Paul.

Ransford, C. (2005) 'Army families host Japanese orphans', *Arnews*, Army News Service, 11 August. Available: <http://www4.army.mil/ocpa/read.php?story_id_key=7719> (accessed 23 September 2005).

Raynor, L. (1980) *The Adopted Child Comes of Age*, London: George Allen and Unwin.

'Reports of child abuse skyrocket; rise tied to greater public awareness' (2004) *Japan Times*, 30 June. Available: <http://www.japantimes.co.jp/cgi-bin/getarticle.pl5?nn2004 0630a5.htm> (accessed 25 September 2005).

Rousseau, J.-J. (1973) *The Social Contract*, trans. G.D.H. Cole, London: J. M. Dent.

Rowe, J. (1991) 'Perspectives on adoption', in E.D. Hibbs (ed.) *Adoption: International Perspectives*, Madison, CT, USA: International University Press.

Saikôsaibansho (Supreme Court) (2004a) 'Kajishinpan, chôteijiken no jikenbetsu, shin-cyakukensû: zenkateisaibansho dai2hyo' (The number of new cases for family court arbitration: Table 2, all family courts), in *Shihôtoukei Nenpô* (Annual Record of Legal Case Statistics). Available: <http://courtdomino2.courts.go.jp/tokei_y.nsf/Tokei YearSearch?OpenForm&Seq=1> (accessed 24 September 2005).

Saikôsaibansho (Supreme Court) (1999–2004b) 'Kajishinpan, chôteijiken no jikenbetsu, shincyakukensû: kateisaibanshobetsu dai9hyo' (The number of new cases for family court arbitration: Table 9, breakdown of each family court), *Shihôtoukei Nenpô* (Annual Record of Legal Case Statistics). Available: <http://courtdomino2.courts.go.jp/tokei_y.nsf> (accessed 25 September 2005).

Sakamoto, T. (2002) 'Jidôsôdansho no rekishiteki tenkai' (Historical development of the CGCs), in K. Machida and T. Sakamoto (eds) *Jidôsôdansho Enjyokatsudôno Jitsusai* (CGC Assistance Activities in Practice), Kyoto: Minerva Shobo.

Sakamoto, Y (2003) *Budô no Ki: 10nin no 'Wagako' to Sugosihta Satooya 18nen no Kiroku* (Vine: A Record of 18 Years as Foster Parents Spending Time with 'Our' Children), Tokyo: Gentosha.

'Sangiin ketsusan'iinkai kaigirokuyori' (From the proceedings of the Audit Committee of the House of Councillors) (1999) *Atarashi Kazoku* (Studies of Adoption and Foster Care), 35: 55–7.

Seishonenno ikuseini kansuru yûshikisha kondankai (Expert Consultation Group on Youth Development) (2002a) 'Heisei 13 nendo jidôsôdansho niokeru jidôgyakutai sôdan shorikensu tô' (How the CGCs dealt with abused children and other cases in financial year 2001), in Seishonenno ikuseini kansuru yûshikisha kondankai dai7kai gijishidai haifushiryô. Available: <http://www8.cao.go.jp/youth/suisin/ikuseikon/kondan021003/07shiryou/07sankou2.pdf> (accessed 23 September 2005).

Seishonenno ikuseini kansuru yûshikisha kondankai (Expert Consultation Group on Youth Development) (2002b) 'Jinkôcyuzetsunitsuite' (on abortion), Seishonenno ikuseini kansuru yûshikisha kondankai dai7kai gijijidai haifushiryô. Available: <http://www8.cao.go.jp/youth/suisin/ikuseikon/kondan021003/07shiryou/07sankou5.pdf> (accessed 23 September 2005).

Shiseido shakai fukushi jigyô zaidan (Shiseido Social Welfare Foundation) (1999) *Dai 26 kai Shiseido Jidô Fukushi Kaigai Kensyû Houkokusho: Kanada Montorioru* (Report No. 26, Shiseido Child Welfare Foundation: A Study Visit to Montreal in Canada), Tokyo: Shiseido shakai fukushi jigyô zaidan.

Shoji, J. (2003) *Fosuta Kea: Satooya to Satooya Kyoiku* (Foster Care: Foster Parents and Education for Foster Parents), Tokyo: Akashi Shoten.

Sinclair, I., Wilson, K. and Gibbs, I. (2005) *Foster Placements: Why They Succeed and Why They Fail*, London: Jessica Kingsley.

'State targets single moms in bid to fight divorce rate' (2002) *Japan Times*, 8 June. Available: <http://www.japantimes.co.jp/cgi-bin/getarticle.pl5?nn20020608a3.htm> (accessed 23 September 2005).

Statistik om Adoption i Danmark (2003). Available: <http://statistik.adoption.dk/> (accessed 23 September 2005).

Strong, N.O. (1978) 'Patterns of societal interaction and psychological accommodation among Japan's konketsuji population', unpublished thesis, University of California, Berkeley.

Sugioka, I. (1993) 'Kyôtoshi no satooya kêsuwâku no jitsusai: watashi no manifesuto' (The real situation of case work in Kyoto: my manifesto), in *Hagukumu*, June.

Sumner, B. and Noguchi, M.S. (2001) 'The day we met Sho-chan', *Japan Times*, 1 June.

Takahashi, M. (2003) 'Care for children and older people in Japan: modernizing the traditional', in A. Anttonen, J. Baldcock and J. Sipilä (eds) *The Young, the Old and the State: Social Care Systems in Five Industrial Nations*, Cheltenham, UK: Edward Elgar.

Takei, Y. (2000) *Tanin ga Kodomo wo Sodaterutoki: Satooya to Kurashita 50nin no Ima* (When Others Bring Up Children: 50 People Who Lived with Foster Parents), Kyoto: Kamogawa Shupan.

Takenoshita, Y. (1997) *Yôshi, Tokubetsuyôshi, Kokusaiyôshi: Kurashino Hôritsu Sôdan 110 ban* (Adoption, Special Adoption and International Adoption: References for Daily Legal Matters), Tokyo: Cyûôkeizaisha.

Tamura, G. (1996) *Oyako no Saiban: Koko30nen* (Parent–Child Court Cases in the Last 30 Years), Tokyo: Cyûou Daigaku Syupanbu.

Tanizaki, J. (1958) *The Makioka Sisters*, trans. E.G. Seidensticker, London: Secker and Warburg.

Tanizaki, J. (1991) *Childhood Years: A Memoir*, trans. P. McCarthy, London: HarperCollins.

Terado, Y. (1995) 'Tokubetsu yôshiseido no tenken' (Examination of the special adoption system), *Jurisuto* (Jurist), 1059: 137–44.

Thoburn, J. (1990) *Success and Failure in Permanent Family Placement*, Aldershot, Hampshire, UK: Avebury.

Tizard, B. (1977) *Adoption: A Second Chance*, London: Open Books.

Tizard, B. (1994) 'Recent developments in adoption: social work policy and research outcomes', *Journal of Child Law*, 6(2): 50–6.

Tomita, Y. (1998) 'Face to face with Tomita Yoko', *City Life News: Tokyo Sky*, 133: 4–5.

Triseliotis, J. and Russell, J. (1984) *Hard to Place: The Outcome of Adoption and Residential Care*, London: Heinemann.

Tseng, W.S., Ebata, K., Miguchi, M., Egawa, M. and McLaughlin, D.U. (1990) 'Transethnic adoption and personality traits: a lesson from Japanese orphans returned from China to Japan', *American Journal of Psychiatry*, 147: 330–5.

United Nations (2001a) *Convention on the Rights of the Child: Consideration of Reports Submitted by States Parties under Article 44 of the Convention, Japan*. Available: <http://www.unhchr.ch/html/menu3/b/k2crc.htm> (accessed 22 September 2005).

United Nations (2001b) *Convention on the Rights of the Child: Declarations and Reservations*. Available: <http://www.unhchr.ch/html/menu3/b/treaty15_asp.htm> (accessed 22 September 2005).

Uno, K.S. (1999) *Passages to Modernity: Motherhood, Childhood, and Social Reform in Early Twentieth Century Japan*, Honolulu: University of Hawai'i Press.

US Citizenship and Immigration Services (2005) *Inter-country Adoptions*. Available: <http://uscis.gov/graphics/services/index2.htm> (accessed 23 September 2005).

US Department of State (2001) *International Adoption: Japan*. Available: <http://travel. state.gov/family/adoption_japan.html> (accessed 23 September 2005).

US Department of State (2004) *Report of the Visa Office 2002*. Available: <http://travel. state.gov/pdf/FY2002_TOC.pdf> (accessed 14 February 2006).

US Department of State (2005a) *Immigrant Visas Issued to Orphans Coming to the US – Top Countries of Origin*. Available: <http://travel.state.gov/family/adoption_resources_ 02.html> (accessed 23 September 2005).

US Department of State (2005b) 'Table XIII: Significant source countries of immigrant orphans (totals of IR-3 and IR-4 immigrant visas issued to orphans), fiscal years 1992–2004'. Available: <http://travel.state.gov/pdf/visa_office_report_table_xiii.pdf> (accessed 22 September 2005).

US Department of State (2005c) 'Table VIII: Immediate relative visas issued, fiscal year 2000'; ditto 2001, 2003. Available: <http://travel.state.gov/pdf/FY2000%20table% 20VIII.pdf> <http://travel.state.gov/pdf/FY2001%20table%20VIII.pdf> <http://travel. state.gov/pdf/FY2003%20table%20VIII.pdf> (all accessed 23 September 2005).

US Embassy Japan (1995) 'International adoption – Japan', draft document, reference: draft/31mar95/jstunis/4252J.

Utsunomiya Jiken wo Kangaerukai (Support Group for Ustunomiya Case) (2004). Available: http://www.foster-family.jp/utsunomiya/index.html (accessed 24 September 2005).

Wagatsuma, H. (1967) 'The social perception of skin color in Japan', *Daedalus*, 96: 407–33.

Yamamoto, M. (1979) 'Seishin yôshi ni tsuite' (On moral adoption), in *Yôshi Hô no Kenkyu I* (Study on Adoption Law No. I), Kyoto: Hôritsu Bunkasha.

Yonekura, A. (1998) *Tokubetu Yôshiseido no Kenkyu* (Study on Special Adoption), Tokyo: Shinsei Shupan.

162   *References*

Yonezawa, H. (1993) *Ainote Sagashite* (Searching for Loving Hands), Kobe: Epic.

'Yôshiengumi attusen mutodokejigyôsha, Kôrôsho, Hatsuno jittutaichosa he' (The Ministry of Health, Labour and Welfare launches its first investigation into the situation of unregistered adoption agencies) (2005) *Yomiuri Shinbun*, 19 June. Available: <http://www. yomiuri.co.jp/iryou/news/kyousei_news/20050620ik06.htm> (accessed 28 August 2005).

Yôshi to Satooya wo Kangaeru Kai (1999) *Yôshi, Satooya Atsusen Mondai no Saikento to Kaikakuteigen* (A Re-examination of Adoption and Fostering Agencies with Proposed Reforms), Tokyo: Chi'iki Shakai Kenkyûsho.

Yuzawa, Y. (2004) *Satooya Seido no Kokkusaihikakku* (International Comparison of Foster Parent Systems), Kyoto: Minerva Shobo.

Zenkoku Satooyakai (National Foster Parents Association; NFPA) (2001) *Satooya Kenkyukai Tekisuto* (Handbook for Foster Parent Training), Tokyo: Zenkoku Satooyakai.

'Zoku akachan attusen no. 1' (Second series, baby placement arrangements no. 1) (2005) *Yomiuri Shinbun*, 17 May.

Index